STAYING IN
THE GAME

STAYING IN THE GAME

The Playbook for Beating
Workplace Sexual Harassment

Adrienne Lawrence

A TarcherPerigee Book

tarcherperigee

An imprint of Penguin Random House LLC
Penguinrandomhouse.com

Most TarcherPerigee books are available at special quantity discounts for bulk
purchase for sales promotions, premiums, fund-raising, and educational needs.
Special books or book excerpts also can be created to fit specific needs. For details,
write: SpecialMarkets@penguinrandomhouse.com.

Library of Congress Cataloging-in-Publication Data

Names: Lawrence, Adrienne, author.
Title: Staying in the game : the playbook for beating workplace sexual harassment /
Adrienne Lawrence.
Description: New York : TarcherPerigee, an imprint of Penguin Random House LLC,
[2020] | Includes index.
Identifiers: LCCN 2019055416 (print) | LCCN 2019055417 (ebook) |
ISBN 9780593084113 (hardcover) | ISBN 9780593084137 (ebook)
Subjects: LCSH: Sexual harassment—Prevention. | Professional employees—
Sexual behavior. | Sex discrimination in employment.
Classification: LCC HF5549.5.S45 L38 2020 (print) | LCC HF5549.5.S45 (ebook) |
DDC 331.4/133—dc23
LC record available at https://lccn.loc.gov/2019055416
LC ebook record available at https://lccn.loc.gov/2019055417

Printed in the United States of America
1   3   5   7   9   10   8   6   4   2

Book design by Katy Riegel

To the fierce, the brave, the bold, the survivor . . .

and to every woman who just wants to do her fucking job

Contents

CHAPTER 15

CONCLUSION

STAYING IN
THE GAME

The Game

What You're Up Against
and Why You Need a Game Plan

HELLO! QUICK QUESTION FOR YOU: You've grinded for years to get your degree (or degrees), and now you're in the professional world, informed and fierce, looking to conquer accordingly. You've read about how to negotiate pay, navigate office politics, and dress for success—but what's your game plan for beating *sexual harassment*?

Sure, you've had annoying experiences at past summer jobs or filler positions. But those jobs were disposable, just part of the tattered path to your dream career. Now you're *finally* here! . . . But unfortunately, so is sexual harassment. You may want to get used to that dirty little term, as it's a reality for any professional—especially working women. If you don't have a game plan in place, sexual harassment could be devastating for you—your career, financial well-being, mental health, and much more.

Do you think sexual harassment won't happen to you? I wish that were true, but running into a harasshole is all but certain. At least 81 percent of women report experiencing workplace sexual harassment at some point in their careers, 77 percent of whom have experienced verbal harassment, more than 50 percent have been touched, and at least 60 percent received unwanted sexual attention or coercion.[1] Approximately five million employees are sexually harassed at work each year, yet the overwhelming majority (99.8 percent) never file formal charges with government agencies.[2]

Being harassed can be extremely upsetting and isolating—even traumatizing, as most women never even report the situation to their employer but ultimately just leave the job. That's junk. We can all agree that no professional goes to college for five years just to do a cost-benefit analysis between giving up ass and staying employed. Yet so many professionals targeted for harassment think they must do just that. Even if you're fortunate enough never to be targeted, simply being a bystander can be hazardous professionally, financially, and psychologically.

No one escapes sexual harassment unscathed. It's everywhere—no matter your profession. Whether you're working in STEM, media, marketing, or education, you need to know how to get a handle on it. Your professional future—your economic independence—hinges on your knowledge of how to navigate this social ill because it's *not* going away anytime soon.

Despite being outlawed since before Keanu Reeves was born back in '64, workplace sexual harassment is still an everyday part of the matrix. Recently, the National Sexual Violence Resource Center called workplace sexual harassment "one of the most widespread and pervasive problems in U.S. society." But it's not an epidemic. Sexual harassment is *endemic*—a natural and enduring aspect of women's work lives.[3] Many academics and researchers have made this observation, and many women continue to live it.

The #MeToo movement, started in 2006 by activist Tarana Burke and ignited in 2017 by Hollywood actors, has been monumental. Bolstered by voices of strong survivors and devoted journalists, #MeToo has brought important issues to the forefront and created opportunities to speak up about sexual misconduct in all aspects of life. But there's still a lot of work to do, particularly in the workplace.

⬆ **HEADS-UP!**

The contribution journalists have made to the #MeToo movement and the reckoning that's followed cannot be understated—and must never be forgotten.

Throughout this playbook, the first time an allegation of misconduct is discussed, the journalist who broke the story and the news outlet will be noted in-text or in parentheses.

Please remember those names, for those individuals are just as worthy of praise as the survivors who bravely spoke out, the plaintiffs who fiercely fought, and the passionate attorneys who stood by their side.

The fact remains that society doesn't protect women in the workforce. The laws can be super limiting, the agencies that monitor workplace sexual harassment have a bunch of nonsense hurdles, and management and human resources departments are either looking out for the company or trying to preserve the status quo. All said, you need to have your own back and be unapologetic about it.

I've had my own back for a while now. From car dealerships to classrooms to law firms to sports newsrooms, I've worked at tons of dude-dominated places, occasionally losing jobs along the way because I was running from ol' boys or pushing back against their club rules. Over the course of my many careers, I've come across horrendous mentors and hit professional land mines, trusted coworkers who turned out to be toxic, and taken jobs and advice that turned out to be terrible. I've filed a lawsuit to make change. I've been lied about in the media and mobbed on social media. I've been unwilling to turn my head and unwilling to give head. I've really done it all. Now, building off those crazy and creepy experiences, and drawing from enlightening empirical studies, interviews with exceptional individuals, and chats with informed academics, I share with you what I've learned along this jarring and life-changing journey. In this playbook, I give you *all* the things I wish I'd known and that you deserve to know. You've worked really hard. No one should take away your dreams because you're *their* "dream girl" . . . or competition, for that matter.

Before you dive into this playbook, there are three things you'll want to know. First, *Staying in the Game* focuses solely on workplace sexual harassment—that is, the harassment involving those with whom you interact professionally, such as coworkers, clients, customers, mentors, and prospective employers. But don't be misled by the term "workplace," as this isn't limited to interactions *at* the office. Workplace sexual harassment can—*and does*—go down anywhere, from DMs to cubicles to conference rooms.

Second, most sexual harassment that we hear of involves cis men harassing cis women, which is why the majority of this playbook is written from that standpoint. (BTW, should "cis" be a new term for you, it refers to people who identify with the same gender they were given at birth.) That's *not* to suggest that cis men, cis women, trans men, trans women, and all others are not harassed or do not harass—as we know that is *not* the case. The guidance in *Staying in the Game* can be applied across genders, gender identities, sexual orientations, races, religions, political beliefs, professions, and all else. We're all in this struggle together. #StayWoke

And third, please know that this playbook isn't a legal manual. In fact, sexual harassment is rarely a legal issue. What can I say? Men wrote the law in their favor and set the bar really high, leaving women in the workplace without much legal recourse. But just because a harasshole's behavior won't get you a day in court doesn't mean it can't ruin your daily life and be difficult to overcome.

🛑 TIME-OUT

Although this isn't a legal manual or basic business book, there are some law- and business-related terms and acronyms commonly used when talking about sexual harassment. They show up throughout this playbook and are good to know.

- **EEOC**—The Equal Employment Opportunity Commission is the federal agency that regulates workplace sexual harassment claims. Most states have their own version of the EEOC.
- **HR**—Human Resources refers to a department or person at a workplace that handles sexual harassment complaints and other personnel needs. Some employers don't have a designated department or person, leaving management with the task.
- **NDA**—A nondisclosure agreement essentially is a contract to keep quiet. Employers often use it when settling sexual harassment claims to prevent you from talking about the harassment.

If you break an NDA, you can be sued for damages, most likely money.

■ **Arbitration**—Arbitration is an alternative to court that typically involves one or three people playing the role of both judge and jury. Arbitration significantly limits employees and is not public.

We talk more about the EEOC, NDAs, and arbitration in chapters 11 and 12 when we cover legal topics.

This quasi-legal stuff can be really complicated and costly, which is why I made this playbook super easy to understand and focused on real issues you face in your professional life. Indeed, I'm not here to give you legal advice or even to tell you what's best for *you*. I'm simply sharing some real talk, proactive tactics, rarely known options, and effective strategies you may want to consider in light of your particular needs and situation. My goal is to empower you with knowledge, uplift you with insight, and maybe make you smile a bit because sexual harassment sucks and a pick-me-up is always appreciated. And just a warning, I do use colorful language at times, keeping it real in hopes of keeping you *happily* employed and somewhat sane.

With all that said, may you enjoy this playbook, become better prepared to beat sexual harassment, and know that no matter what you're facing, you're not alone. I'm in your corner fighting with you.

xoxo,
Adrienne

CHAPTER 1

||||||||||||||||||||||||||||||||||||||||

Knowing the Score

Your Instincts, Uphill Battle, and Inner Bawse

....

Women don't need to find a voice . . . they need to feel empowered to
use it, and people need to be encouraged to listen.
>—*Meghan Markle, uplifter of women and*
>*Duchess Who Dared*

LET'S TRAVEL WAY back in time to the early 1950s, when *I Love Lucy* made
its debut on black-and-white TV, states still approved of segregation, and a
woman's job was to keep her husband happy.

Seventeen-year-old Kiki was a quiet coed at Cornell University in up-
state New York. In that era, most girls her age married their sweethearts
straight out of high school, and the few girls who went to college studied in
pursuit of an MRS degree. College girls like Kiki were expected to find a
man, marry, make a home, multiply, and maybe even finish her degree—if
her husband approved, of course.

The unwed Kiki knew Cornell was ideal for any woman looking to become a wife—there were four men for every one woman on campus. It was
marital mecca. "If you came out without a husband, you were hopeless," Kiki
would later joke. She knew society's expectations of her and understood the
occupational limitations imposed on her. But Kiki wasn't like other girls.
The Brooklyn-born, Jewish barrier breaker wasn't attending Cornell to bag
a boo. She was about her education, her independence, and her promising
professional career ahead.

To say Kiki was a "supreme intellectual gawdess" would be an understatement. The studious pupil consistently set the class curve. Nonetheless, one
day her male chemistry professor offered to give her a practice test before he
administered the real exam. Kiki entertained the offer, only to discover that

her professor had slipped her a copy of the *real* exam—and she knew *exactly* what ol' boy expected in return. She may have been a teen at the time, but Kiki was not having it . . . and she made the time to let him know.

The five-foot-one, reserved Kiki went to her professor's office and unleashed her inner Brooklyn. She demanded, "How dare you?! How dare you do this, clown?!" (I may have added the "clown" part, but you get the gist.) That was the end of that, Kiki said. When she took the real exam, she deliberately made two mistakes as an act of protest.[1]

That intellectual gangsta from Brooklyn went on to become U.S. Supreme Court Justice Ruth Bader Ginsburg—aka Notorious RBG—who friends called "Kiki" back in the day. As you may have guessed, her experience at Cornell was just the beginning of the sexual harassment Justice Ginsburg would go on to face in the working world.

After graduating Columbia Law School in 1959 tied for first in her class, Ginsburg was denied a prestigious clerkship with Supreme Court Justice Felix Frankfurter. He refused to hire her because she was a mother (as if she were better suited to be at home) and he didn't like the fact that she would be exposed to his cursing in chambers (as if a woman's ears were too delicate for such talk). Despite her extraordinary legal acumen, law firms also wouldn't hire Ginsburg because they didn't hire women to do anything other than clerical work back then. Plus, many employers weren't hiring married women and law firms were just starting to hire Jews. When Ginsburg finally got to argue cases in court, judges seemed more taken by her gender than with the persuasiveness of her arguments. The discrimination was real, and she got it from all angles. But instead of giving up or giving in, she fought back, molding legal minds as an Ivy League law professor, founding the *Women's Rights Law Reporter*, and cofounding the American Civil Liberties Union (ACLU) Women's Rights Project, before ultimately earning a spot as the second woman ever appointed to the U.S. Supreme Court.

It's been more than sixty years since Justice Ginsburg was denied professional opportunities on account of her gender, yet women today still face the same type of workplace discrimination and barriers that Ginsburg encountered over the course of her career before joining the high court. Notwithstanding the Civil Rights Act of '64, sexual harassment is still everywhere, in all aspects of women's professional lives. And it's not okay.

No matter the occupation, the industry, the person, the state, or the state of the law, you *are* entitled to work in a safe and harassment-free environment, and you should never have to tolerate anything less to fulfill your professional dreams. With that said, on the advice of the Duchess of Sussex, it's time to use our voices.

Herein lies real talk. Whether you're on the right or the left, from the west or the east, you deserve to know the truth, even when it's difficult to confront. To that end, we first talk about trusting your instincts, and then we discuss the workplace gender-equity journey, so you know what you're up against. After that, I summon your unapologetic inner bawse by giving you the Ten Truths to Beating Sexual Harassment. Please take your seat at the table, Your Highness. It's time.

TRUSTING YOUR INSTINCTS

POP QUIZ: How do you think Justice Ginsburg *knew* her professor was truly looking to exchange exam answers for "action," as opposed to genuinely trying to help her succeed in his chemistry class? Her professor didn't say anything to her about sex. Nor did he ask her to Netflix and chill. Yet Ginsburg *knew*, and she was so confident about his ill motives that she stormed into his office to boldly confront the man—an authority figure with the power to make or break her GPA. She likely knew his angle because she listened to that still, small voice within. She trusted her instincts.

All of us have instincts. Your instinct tells you whether something is right or wrong, and it's pretty on point whether you're in tune with it or not. Instincts don't always involve rationalization but resonate from your gut. It's that nagging feeling that something's off; that it's not quite right, regardless of whether you know *why* you know it.

Unfortunately, society has conditioned women to deny their instincts. We're implicitly, and sometimes explicitly, encouraged to do so in favor of advancing the power dynamics that elevate the desires of men while subjugating women and denying them individual agency. Said another way, society wants women to ignore their instincts because otherwise they'd probably rise up and rule—or at least seize half the American pie.

Overriding your instincts is problematic, as they're an important source of truth that aids in your survival and ability to prosper. By denying that essential source of truth within, we as women are left to question ourselves and doubt our own judgment, leaving us vulnerable to manipulation and control.

Instincts play a powerful role in all aspects of beating sexual harassment. They can help you decipher whether you're being harassed, whether a company is a sexual harassment hotbed, whether it's safe to call out a harasshole, and so on. If you're disconnected from your instincts in any way, disabuse yourself of whatever is holding you back from plugging into that essential source of truth. Ask questions, engage in self-critique, embrace change. Are you afraid of what your inner voice reveals about your work situation—perhaps that you *are* offended or that everything is *not* fine? How often are you hoping you're wrong about someone's motives or overriding your gut feeling with rationalization? Are you afraid to trust your instincts because you question your worth, or prize the judgments and opinions of others more than your own? Were you taught that it's not "polite" or acceptable for *you* to challenge authority, to be independent or assertive? These are the kinds of important questions you should reflect upon so you can fully embrace this playbook. Maybe check out Jen Sincero's *You Are a Badass*. Read *Rage Becomes Her* by Soraya Chemaly. Review *Boundaries* by Drs. Henry Cloud and John Townsend. Take in whatever you need to fully appreciate that your instincts are valid, reliable, and powerful. No matter what anyone else says or thinks, your instincts deserve your trust.

WOMEN'S HISTORY IN THE WORKPLACE

Although you likely grew up watching women thrive in a range of careers outside of the home, the concept of "the independent woman" is still very new in our society. Women have had high heels longer than they've had the unrestricted right to work. In fact, marriage bars—laws that allow companies to refuse to employ married women—were still on the books in the States when Ford released the first Mustang in '64.

Women have fought for years for equal employment opportunities and *still* have yet to attain equal treatment and pay. This is an issue not of politics or party lines but of protecting women's inalienable rights—rights that have been consistently and systemically denied. The following highlights landmarks in women's labor history from the twentieth century onward, showing how discrimination against women is very much a part of the game and giving you a clearer picture of what we're up against when it comes to beating sexual harassment. If you're going to advance women, you'll want to familiarize yourself with the struggle. It's an uphill battle.

1900–1925

1900: It's the turn of the century and women's rights are getting turnt! Women in all U.S. states now have *some* right to keep their own wages and property in their own name. Yay!

1908: The U.S. Supreme Court rules that states can restrict women's work hours to protect their health, implying that women are physically weak and cannot make decisions for themselves.

1917: As men went to serve in World War I, more than nine million women mobilized, many filling manufacturing and agricultural positions on the home front. Apparently, women can't be trusted to vote but are capable of keeping the workforce afloat.

1920: The Nineteenth Amendment grants women the right to vote in federal elections.

1924: The Supreme Court upholds a New York law banning women from working night shifts from 10:00 p.m. to 6:00 a.m. except for women working as entertainers and servers. (Translation: Women must stay at home unless they're willing to entertain men or are necessary to prevent men from entering "pink" professions.)

1926–1950

1932: As the nation struggles through the Great Depression, Congress passes the Federal Economy Act, prohibiting more than one member of a family from working for the government, forcing many women out of the workforce in favor of their man-kin staying employed. (To note: Justice Ginsburg was born the following year.)

1943:   During World War II, Rosie the Riveter is front and center as women are persuaded to rejoin the workforce, with more than four hundred thousand working on behalf of the military. Once again, working women are in high demand now that men are unavailable.

1945:   After WWII, Congress introduces the Women's Pay Act of 1945 to require equal pay for equal work (although it is *not* signed into law until nearly two decades later).

1948:   The year after baseball broke the color barrier with Jackie Robinson joining the Brooklyn Dodgers, the Supreme Court upholds a Michigan law banning women from being bartenders— that is, unless their father or husband owns the bar.

1951–1975

1961:   The Supreme Court rules that state laws excluding women from jury pools are not discriminatory but are an "inoffensive" way to accommodate women's "special responsibilities" as "the center of home and family life."

1963:   The Equal Pay Act finally passes, requiring equal wages for women and men doing equal work (at least in theory). This becomes the *first* federal law prohibiting workplace sex discrimination. Coincidentally, this is the same year Martin Luther King Jr. gives the "I Have a Dream" speech and the first woman enters space (courtesy of the country now known as Russia).

1964:   Congress passes the Civil Rights Act to prohibit discrimination based on characteristics such as sex. This ends marriage bar laws that allowed employers to deny employment to married women, like what Justice Ginsburg experienced early in her career.

1965:   Because progress would be too much to ask, the EEOC approves sex-segregated job advertising (for example, "Help Wanted Male Only"), claiming it served "the convenience of readers." Yeah, sure.

1967:   President Lyndon B. Johnson signs an executive order banning government contractors from discriminating based on sex and requiring affirmative action for women hires. That next year, the EEOC rules it illegal to set age restrictions for flight attendants.

1969: The EEOC invalidates workplace laws meant to "protect" women from themselves, such as those nonsense curfew and industry bans. For frame of reference, this is the year the Manson murders went down and Woodstock popped off.

1971: The Supreme Court finally bans private employers from refusing to hire women with preschool-age children (unless it's a business necessity), and it rules that states can't keep women from practicing law.

1973: The Supreme Court says sex-segregated job advertising is no good. (It also issued a landmark decision to legalize abortion in *Roe v. Wade*.)

1974: The Supreme Court rules that it's illegal to force pregnant women to take maternity leave on the assumption they're incapable of continuing to work. Apparently, women having infants aren't infants; they *can* make decisions for themselves.

1976–2000

1976: The Supreme Court upholds women's right to unemployment benefits during the final three months of pregnancy.

1978: The Pregnancy Discrimination Act bans employment discrimination against pregnant women.

1981: As Sandra Day O'Connor becomes the first woman appointed to the Supreme Court, the court overturns "head and master" laws, which gave the husband unilateral control over property owned jointly with his wife. Imagine your husband selling your home and all of your property without having to consult you first. Yikes!

1984: Thirteen years after ruling that women could be lawyers, the Supreme Court rules that law firms may not refuse to promote women lawyers to partnership positions.

1986: Some twenty-two years after the Civil Rights Act passes, the Supreme Court decides that a hostile or abusive work environment can qualify as sex discrimination. *Meritor Savings Bank v. Vinson* becomes the landmark workplace sexual harassment case! You'll hear more about badass Mechelle Vinson in the next chapter.

1987:   As an extension of affirmative action, the Supreme Court rules
that employers may give women and minorities preference over
men and whites in hiring and promotions.

1989:   The Supreme Court rules in *Price Waterhouse v. Hopkins* that
employers cannot enforce gender stereotypes about how women or
men should act, look, dress or otherwise do them. This ruling,
which we also discuss more in chapter 2, is significant for members
of marginalized groups in the workforce.

1991:   As attorney Anita Hill testifies before Congress about her sexual
harassment allegations against then Supreme Court nominee
Clarence Thomas, the high court deems it illegal for employers to
completely exclude women from certain jobs, such as hazardous
occupations.

1992:   This becomes the "Year of the Woman," with women elected to
federal, state, and local offices in unprecedented numbers that
nonetheless pale in comparison to today. This same year director
Penny Marshall hits a home run with *A League of Their Own.*

1993:   As Ruth Bader Ginsburg becomes the second woman appointed to
the Supreme Court, the high court rules that you don't have to
suffer physical or serious psychological injury to sue for sexual
harassment. Also, the Family and Medical Leave Act is passed,
which gives employees twelve weeks of unpaid leave for a new
child, among other protections.

1994:   The Supreme Court bans jurors from being selected based on
gender, helping quash some of the harmful stereotypes that kept
women from playing meaningful roles in our democracy.

1997:   Famed feminist attorney Gloria Allred gets Hunter Tylo a $4.8
million jury award after she's fired from the show *Melrose Place*
upon becoming pregnant. The case establishes that actors may
continue to work if they become pregnant. (This is the year
Hanson released one of the most successful debut singles of all
time—"MMMBop.")

1998:   The Supreme Court says you can bring a claim for workplace
sexual harassment against a member of the same sex because the

harasser's gender is irrelevant, as is sexual motive. The Court also specified when employers can be held liable for sexual harassment.

2000:   CBS Inc. pays $8 million to settle a sex discrimination and retaliation lawsuit the EEOC brought on behalf of two hundred women, which is about $40,000 per woman *before* legal fees. That's not much considering the value of two hundred ruined careers.

2001–Today-*ish*

2006:   The Supreme Court changes the standard for retaliation in sexual harassment cases to include any adverse employment decision or treatment that would be likely to discourage a "reasonable worker" from making or furthering a discrimination complaint. Don't get too jazzed though. In chapter 12, we dive into how courts have interpreted this standard to favor employers.

2010:   A federal appellate court rules that sexually explicit language and porn can create a hostile work environment, even when it's not targeted at any particular employee.

2013:   Women are no longer banned from combat positions in the military, and the Supreme Court clarifies who a "supervisor" is for purposes of sexual harassment lawsuits.

2017:   Large companies are no longer required to report to the government how much they pay workers by race and gender, hampering accountability for unequal pay. With the *New York Times* report (Megan Twohey and Jodi Kantor) exposing the sexual misconduct of movie producer Harvey Weinstein, the year ends with the igniting of the #MeToo movement. Woot! Woot!

2018:   California becomes the first state to require that women be included on executive boards of publicly traded California companies.

2019:   The Supreme Court agrees to decide whether Title VII of the Civil Rights Act prevents employers from discriminating against members of the LGBTQ+ community, even though the EEOC has been enforcing the law as protecting sexual orientation and gender identity since at least the early 2000s.

The gender-equity journey has been long and treacherous for women in the U.S. workforce, right? Men have dominated the domain for centuries, serving as gatekeepers to the professional world and forcing women to tend the home with few options. When women wanted more, men enacted exclusory laws under the guise of "protecting" women's frailties. Groundbreakers like Justice Ginsburg, Audre Lorde, Gloria Steinem, Dolores Huerta, Betty Friedan, and many other devoted architects of change paved the way for women desiring occupational options outside of the home. Despite those warriors' valiant efforts, many of which continue to resonate today, barriers like sexual harassment remain in place, derailing careers and destroying lives. There's much work to be done.

THE TEN TRUTHS

She may have been a petite teenager from a working-class family part of a historically oppressed religious minority in the early '50s, but none of that noise stopped young Justice Ginsburg from standing up to a privileged, male professor who tried to leverage his power over her into something sexual. Ol' boy likely thought she was a sure bet. But he lost because no matter what game men were playing, Ginsburg *always* knew the score.

Knowing the score is about knowing who you are, what you deserve, and what you need not tolerate. It sets the tone for your professional life and then some. As you dive into this playbook, there are ten core truths you'll need to know and commit to heart. They'll help ensure that you *always* know the score. Recite them aloud, embrace them, and read them often. They are more than your truth. They are *the truth*. With that said, here are the Ten Truths to Beating Sexual Harassment:

1. You're a bawse.
2. Your instincts are trustworthy and correct.
3. Your personal safety and comfort come first.
4. You have the right to pursue any career path that you wish.

5. Your employer is lucky to have you and your valuable skills.
6. You're entitled to work in an environment where you are treated fairly and with respect.
7. You deserve professional relationships that respect your boundaries.
8. You have the right to hold a harasshole accountable for his behavior.
9. You need not ever ignore or endure behavior simply because others do.
10. You never, ever have to tolerate sexual harassment.

Got it? Okay! Now read them again. Take a moment to say these Ten Truths aloud. Let them soak in. When you're ready, consider writing them out and posting them somewhere you can see them each day. Don't hesitate to review the Ten Truths before you start each workday or anytime sexual harassment rears its ugly head. You *are* a bawse. Own every damn bit of it.

REPLAY

* Always trust your instincts. Never try to override them with hope or rationalization. Your instincts protect you and tell you the truth. They are vital to helping you navigate workplace sexual harassment.
* Over the centuries, women have fought for professional opportunities and equality in the workplace. Even in the #MeToo era, there is still a lot of fighting to do, as sexual harassment remains endemic.
* Knowing the score is about knowing yourself, what you deserve, and what you need not tolerate. The Ten Truths to Beating Sexual Harassment are core principles that will help you always know the score.

CHAPTER 2

The Truth We'd Rather Not See

What *Is* Sexual Harassment and *Why* Does It Happen?

We need fantasy to survive because reality is too difficult.
—*Lady Gaga, incredible force,
inspiring survivor, and Academy Award winner*

HE WAS A PROMINENT, experienced reporter for the *Seattle Times*. She was a ballsy, young freelance writer based out of Brooklyn. They were on opposite coasts but both in the media game. So, it didn't come out of left field when he sent her a private message on Twitter one morning in May 2019.

He asked if she'd considered applying for reporting jobs. She thanked him and said no. He suggested she had the requisite skills. She said market conditions kept her from applying. He replied, "Hm, I hear you."

Their conversation was as riveting as a day at the DMV. Nothing seemed off or unprofessional. It was just two journalists talking shop, with the more experienced party providing guidance and encouragement—that is, until his inner harasshole emerged.

Not more than fifteen minutes after their unremarkable exchange, the married Seattle reporter messaged the twenty-nine-year-old New York freelancer, "Anyway you're so beautiful," quickly followed by, "Anyway you are hilarious." About forty minutes later, when she hadn't responded, he whipped out, "There is so much cum on your face."

You're probably thinking what I'm thinking: WTF, right?

The Brooklyn-based writer in this conversation, Talia Jane, likely had the same thought running through her head while deciding how to handle these wildly inappropriate messages from a fellow member of the media. But in the end, Jane knew what she had to do. She had to check a mitch.

"This isn't acceptable or appropriate," Jane responded, before sharing screenshots of his messages on her Twitter feed for all to see. Jane then relayed to her forty-thousand-plus followers what a woke woman would call a universal truth. She tweeted, "[T]he emotional exhaustion that comes with calling out bad behavior from cis men in positions of relative power cannot be talked about enough."[1]

There's a world where sexual harassment isn't a problem, where it's not an everyday occurrence, and where it can't just happen to anyone. Unfortunately, that world is a fantasy. Yet many people choose to live in that fantasy because, as Lady Gaga suggests, reality may be too difficult to face. As a result, many people still misunderstand sexual harassment. You may think that Jane's experience is an anomaly, but much of what we've been told about sexual harassment has been muddled by myth.

This chapter breaks away from the fantasy. Using cases from the court of law and the court of public opinion, I explain why sexual harassment happens, what it really is, and how you can identify it. Fortunately, you don't have to be an academic armed with a law degree to understand what we know to be true about sexual harassment. All you need to do is forget everything you think you know and disabuse yourself of what your friends may have told you and what you've seen online. Be open-minded—and emotionally available to get pissed. It can be disturbing to learn that certain behavior you may have experienced is sexual harassment. But it's better to know now that you don't have to tolerate that colleague who continually offers unsolicited Kegels advice or makes you feel uncomfortable with sexist slights.

All right, prepare yourself. Your mind's about to be blown.

WHY DO PEOPLE SEXUALLY HARASS?

In 1999, researchers conducted a study involving more than one hundred men who were sent one of two emails. Here's the gist: Half of the men received an email from a woman who said she was an economics major aiming to become a financial manager, was part of a group that defended women's rights, and thought women were just as capable as men. The other half of the men received an email from a woman who said she was studying education in hopes of becoming an elementary school teacher so she could have more time for family and children, explaining that she chose not to become a lawyer because the job was more fitting for men with whom she did not want to compete. Each man in the study was given a variety of photos he could use to respond to the email he received, including a host of offensive images. Which woman do you think the men chose to harass with the most dick pics, porn, and other digital garbage?[2] . . . Wait! Before you answer, let's talk about *why* people sexually harass.

Under the leading theory, harassholes harass to preserve the traditional power structure in our society. What does that power structure look like? Historically, there's been a hierarchy that places men in a dominant position over women. Why do harassholes want to keep that power structure? The benefits, of course! The group with the most power gets to call the shots and create a society that caters to them, limiting the opportunities available to those who are less powerful. To that end, harassers protect their place on the totem pole by diminishing the status of those they perceive to be a threat to their own power. In the workplace, a microcosm of our larger society, sexual harassment is just another tool used by tools to keep that traditional power structure in place.

Think about it: A person's position in the workforce impacts her economic power, which bolsters her overall power in society. Historically, women have been excluded from or marginalized within the workforce, giving men the economic power and the accompanying social power to control their own destinies *and those of women*. When a woman elevates her position in the workforce, she becomes more economically independent, making her less likely to rely on a man and more likely to gain her own social power. When men and women have comparable levels of power in the workforce, we have a more egalitarian society! That should sound awesome to everyone, but harassholes aren't down for it. They seek to maintain traditional gender roles that subordinate women and limit women's opportunities— and they'll do so through any means necessary, from policing gender roles by enforcing stereotypes to hypersexualizing women with tasteless remarks. Sexual harassment is not about—*and has never been about*—coitus or the carnal pleasure that is sex. It's about preserving power.

 TIME-OUT

Sexual harassment is a bit of a misnomer, as it gives the impression that there must be a sexualized element to the harassment. That's not the case. As Yale Law Professor Vicki Schultz explains: "[Sexual harassment] takes a wide variety of nonsexual forms, including hostile behavior, physical assault, patronizing treatment, personal ridicule, social ostracism, exclusion or marginalization, denial of information, and work sabotage directed at people because of their sex or gender."[3]

As you take in the playbook, keep in mind that sexual harassment comes in many forms, from sexual to hostile to benevolent. But no matter how it manifests, sexual harassment always derives from the same twisted and insecure push for power.

You may be asking, "If it's just about power, why do some harassers repeatedly hit on me, send me dick pics, or grope me?" Because one of the ways that harassholes can reinforce their dominance is by relegating you to be a means to a sexual end. Said another way, when harassholes come at you sexually, they're communicating that your primary use is to serve their physical gratification. That would make you pretty lowly, right? Exactly.

Gender is not the only traditional power structure in our society. Race also is a major power structure that places whites in a dominant position over people of color, which is why minorities are more likely than whites to be targeted by harassholes—particularly when the person of color is perceived as a threat to those in power. Sexual harassment research focuses nearly exclusively on gender, seldom considering the interplay of race. But as we discuss in the next chapter, sexual harassment also can be a conduit for reinforcing the racial hierarchy.

↥ **HEADS-UP!**

If this is the first you're hearing of race being a power structure, you may want to check out the New York Times bestseller White Fragility: Why It's So Hard for White People to Talk About Racism by Robin DiAngelo and/or national bestseller Why Are All the Black Kids Sitting Together in the Cafeteria?: And Other Conversations About Race by Beverly Daniel Tatum.

You cannot afford to focus solely on gender discrimination, because gender and racial oppression go hand in hand. Where there's one, there's the other. Stay alert!

As you likely already know, women aren't the only ones who can be targets of harassment, as men are harassed too. You may be wondering why men target other men if men are the ones in power. Because undermining another man is a way that harassholes can establish their own dominance and implicitly reinforce the power structure that keeps "masculine" men on top or the racial hierarchy in order.[4] Why do women sexually harass men and other women? Women harass for the power boost they get directly by subjugating another or indirectly by being a good soldier of the status quo.[5] Power is a helluva drug.

Basically, harassers are committed to keeping "others" down, so they can stay on top. In the profound words of researchers Louise F. Fitzgerald and Lilia M. Cortina:

> Sexual harassment—targeted at women because they are women, and at men largely because they are not-men, at lesbians because they are not heterosexual, at women of color because they are not white as well as female— is a particular incarnation of a societal-level pattern of dominance and oppression by the powerful of those seen as Other.[6]

Now taking what you know about sexual harassment, let's look back at that study with the hundred-plus men who were deciding how to respond to the email they received from one of the two women. Which woman do you think received the most uncivil and filthy responses—the empowered econ major with the career ambitions and progressive gender outlook, or the schoolteacher-in-training who believed in traditional gender roles and didn't want to compete with men?

If you guessed the former, you're correct; most men didn't bother the woman who "knew her place."

WHAT IS SEXUAL HARASSMENT?

Sexual harassment is trash. That's not the technical definition, although it's one that resonates with me. As far as you should be concerned, there are two main sources of definitions for the term—one is social, and the other is legal. Because sexual harassment is always a social science issue (that is, dealing with human interaction) but *not* always a legal issue (that is, dealing with the law), your focus should be on the social science definition. Let me explain.

Essentially, the law defines sexual harassment as unwelcome sexual advances, requests for sexual favors, and other offensive conduct of a sexual or nonsexual nature that is gender based. We'll fully dive into the law in chapters 11 and 12, but for now, think about this: If you could sue each time a coworker said you had the best legs in the business (à la Tina Turner), you'd never leave the courthouse, right? That's why the U.S. Supreme Court decided that only *certain* sexual harassment situations should be resolved in court—specifically, situations where the harassment is "sufficiently severe, persistent, or pervasive" or that which hinges professional opportunities on sexual favors. In layman's terms, the courts won't do anything unless the sexual harassment is utterly heinous or the situation is play-for-pay. So really, what's law got to do with it? We all know there's plenty of misconduct that may not cross the legal threshold but can mess up your life, nonetheless. While we can use the facts in legal cases to better understand sexual harassment, we can't pretend experiences that fall short of the legal standard aren't still sexual harassment. For that reason, the law isn't where we look to define sexual harassment *outside* of the courthouse doors. Instead, we look to social science.

Research conducted by those "in the know"—that is, academics who get paid to study society and human relationships—define sexual harassment in a way that focuses on the harasser's behavior *and* the recipient's outlook. Although there are several schools of thought, the prevailing sociological definition basically says sexual harassment is gender-related behavior that the recipient finds offensive, threatening to her well-being, or beyond her resources to shut down.[7] We're talking about behavior that derogates, demeans or humiliates.[8]

It's pretty simple, right? Now let's see what behavior meets this standard.

WHAT BEHAVIOR IS CONSIDERED SEXUAL HARASSMENT?

Perspectives on what behavior constitutes sexual harassment differ based on several factors—although the most significant is gender. Men are more likely to consider behavior harassing when it challenges their beliefs about traditional gender roles, whereas women often find behavior harassing when it reinforces female subordination.[9] Even as our society continues to evolve, however, women consistently have higher standards for behavior than men. (Like you didn't already know that.)

🛑 TIME-OUT

Gender plays a significant role in whether people interpret behavior as sexually harassing. The American Family Survey, for example, asked three thousand people their attitude about sexual harassment based on whether the initiator was male or female. Check out the responses on the next page.[10]

Other factors also may dictate whether behavior is considered harassing, such as industry norms, power differentials, and individual experience. For example, what may be acceptable behavior on the set of an adult film probably would be a no-go in a Facebook conference room. *Probably.* A group of women may enjoy the title "female mafia" in a female-dominated space but find it insulting in an office inundated with dudes. A rape survivor

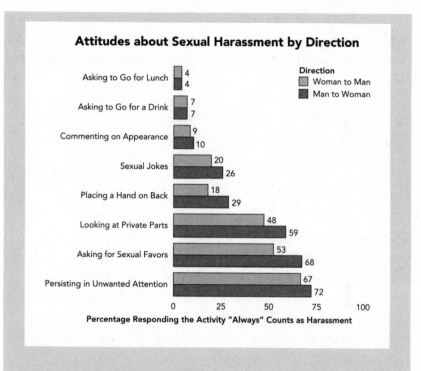

Attitudes about Sexual Harassment by Direction

Direction
- Woman to Man
- Man to Woman

Activity	Woman to Man	Man to Woman
Asking to Go for Lunch	4	4
Asking to Go for a Drink	7	7
Commenting on Appearance	9	10
Sexual Jokes	20	26
Placing a Hand on Back	18	29
Looking at Private Parts	48	59
Asking for Sexual Favors	53	68
Persisting in Unwanted Attention	67	72

Percentage Responding the Activity "Always" Counts as Harassment

may not be as tolerant of random hugs from "overfriendly" co-workers. There are numerous factors that can come into play. Just remember it doesn't matter how *someone else* perceives a behavior. If it makes *you* uncomfortable, it's not okay. You do not have to tolerate it.

Based on our society's current prevailing standards, here are the five types of behaviors considered sexual harassment:[11]

1. Sexist remarks and behavior
2. Bullying because of gender
3. Inappropriate and offensive sexual advances
4. Sexual assaults
5. Coercing sexual activity by bribery and/or threatening punishment

The easiest way to explain these five types of sexual harassment is to put each into one of three categories based on their similar features. These three categories are gender harassment, unwanted sexual attention, and sexual coercion.[12]

Gender Harassment	Unwanted Sexual Attention	Sexual Coercion
Sexist Remarks and Behavior and Gender-Based Bullying	*Inappropriate and Offensive Sexual Advances and Sexual Assaults*	*Coercing Sexual Activity by Bribery or Threatening Punishment*
▪ Disparaging or unprofessional comments related to sex/gender ▪ Sexist teasing, comments, jokes ▪ Intimate questions related to sex ▪ Sexual photos, videos, or written material ▪ Sexually charged topics and conversations	▪ Touching, groping, invading personal space, leaning over ▪ Emails, calls, notes, texts, social media messages of a sexual nature ▪ Sexually suggestive looks or gestures ▪ Forced or unwelcome sexual contact	▪ Offering or threatening to rescind preferential treatment or professional opportunities, contingent on whether you provide sexual favors ▪ Pressuring for sexual favors or dates, stalking (including physical or electronic intrusion into one's personal life)

These three categories of sexual harassment are not based on law, although you will see in chapters 11 and 12 that there is some overlap between these categories and the legal claims; specifically, gender harassment and unwanted sexual attention align with the hostile work environment claim, and sexual coercion is akin to the quid pro quo claim. No need to bother yourself with the legal stuff right now though. Just something to keep in mind!

Category 1: Gender Harassment

The most common and widespread form of sexual harassment is gender harassment, which includes sexist remarks, sexist behavior, and bullying because of gender. Oftentimes, gender harassment involves expressing insulting, degrading, or contemptuous attitudes about women. Common examples are sexual epithets, excluding women from opportunities, gestures intended to offend women, and treating women with hostility—mainly, making them feel like second-class citizens all because they are women. Professional women report experiencing more of this type of incivility and aggression used to alienate them than sexual advances meant to attract them.[13]

Disgraced producer Harvey Weinstein, for example, would regularly yell and curse at his assistant, Zelda Perkins, over the nineteen years she worked for him, wearing her down emotionally with sexist abuse.[14] Likewise, some of the behavior actor Jeffrey Tambor was accused of engaging in would qualify as gender harassment. The now-former *Transparent* star was said to have verbally abused his personal assistant, Van Barnes, who is a trans woman. While on the set of *Arrested Development*, Tambor also was accused of verbally attacking co-star Jessica Walter, who rivaled him in award nominations stemming from her work on the show. In a March 2018 interview with the *New York Times* (Sopan Deb), through tears Walter said this about Tambor's behavior toward her: "In 'almost sixty years of working [in Hollywood], I've never had anybody yell at me like that on a set and it's hard to deal with[.]'"

⚖ BONUS POINT

When it comes to sexual harassment, you may not think much of rude or discourteous behavior—but don't ignore incivility. Even without discriminatory intent, incivility is a precursor to sexual harassment, and it contributes to its occurrence.[15]

In addition to verbal attacks, gender harassment may appear as woman-bashing jokes, insults about competence and women having no place in the workplace, as well as comments about the perceived irrelevance or sexual unattractiveness of older women. It may also take the form of work-family policing where employers treat mothers as less than because they are not at home with their kids.[16] This is what Laurie Chadwick described happened to her at Wellpoint Inc., a Maine insurance company. She had an eleven-year-old son and six-year-old triplets at home, but her caregiving responsibilities never interfered with her work performance, as she was a rising star. Still, upon denying her a promotion, a company representative said she "had a lot on her plate" while caring for children and working. This outlook reeks of a "pervasive sex role stereotype that caring for family members is women's work."[17]

Another form of gender harassment is known as gender policing, where scorn is shown for women who don't fall in line with "traditional notions of femininity." This was the case for Ann Hopkins, a superstar at Price Water-house, a high-profile accounting firm, in the '80s. She often outperformed her male colleagues but was ostracized and repeatedly denied partnership because she was not "woman enough" by their standards. In Hopkins's evaluation, one of the partners had the nerve to say she needed "a course in charm school," and her head supervisor suggested she dress "more femininely, wear make-up, style her hair, and wear jewelry." She was being punished for not conforming to "traditional" gender stereotypes. Being the bad bitch that she was, Hopkins sued for sexual harassment and won in the U.S. Supreme Court in 1989, establishing that sexual harassment need not involve sexual attraction and making way for every woman to be her own woman in the workplace.[18]

Gender harassment can have sexual elements, such as littering the office with porn or suggestive imagery, making crude comments about female sexuality or sexual activity (for example, calling a colleague a "dumb slut"), or referencing women by female body parts (*"Hey, Tits McGee! Is this your client?"*). These forms of harassment are aimed not at getting sexual cooperation but at degrading women. It's hostility without sincere sexual interest.[19]

When men are targeted for gender harassment, they're often called pussies, homophobic slurs, and other degrading terms intended to convey that they're weak or "not man enough."[20] Gender harassment highlights the fact that sexual harassment is about power systems, not sexual desire or romance.

Category 2: Unwanted Sexual Attention

The second category of sexual harassment is unwanted sexual attention, which spans verbal and physical behaviors, namely inappropriate and offensive sexual advances and assaults. Examples include sexually suggestive comments and compliments (*"Don't you look sexy today!"*), attempts to establish sexual or romantic relationships, and unwanted touching (for example, groping, grabbing, holding, sexual assault, attempted or completed rape/sodomy).

Unwanted sexual attention also includes pressuring for dates or for sexual favors but without conditions that could hurt or help your career. This isn't the *"Sleep with me or find another job!"* type of situation. It's more touching the saleswoman's thigh, ogling the manager's breasts, forcing a colleague to perform oral sex, come-ons, and so on.[21]

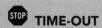 **TIME-OUT**

Sexual assault—that is, physical contact of a sexual nature without your consent—is a crime whether it happens in the workplace or not. When it has professional ties, it also may be a form of sexual harassment.

Despite being the least common form of sexual harassment, workplace sexual assault *does* happen. Don't be afraid to report it. No one should be fondling you, grinding their genitals against you, or forcing you to participate in anything sexual at the workplace or elsewhere. If someone is touching you without your consent, please consider contacting law enforcement. Just because the situation has ties to your work does not mean the employer is the appropriate party for resolving the situation or protecting you. Always put your safety first.

Amazon's now-former programming chief Roy Price, for example, was said to be notorious for unwanted sexual attention. In August 2017 via *The*

Information, journalist Kim Masters broke a story about a night in July 2015 when Price sexually propositioned Isa Hackett, executive producer of a thriving Amazon series who also happens to be a married lesbian with children. After she repeatedly rejected Price's advances, he allegedly told her, "You will love my dick" and later shouted "Anal sex!" loudly in her ear when surrounded by fellow execs at an Amazon party (Kim Masters, *The Hollywood Reporter*).

Inappropriate sexual advances and assaults also were Matt Lauer's M.O. during his lengthy tenure as the star host of NBC's *Today* show. While he was in Russia covering the 2014 Sochi Olympics, for example, the seemingly friendly Lauer was said to have lured young NBC staffer Brooke Nevils to his hotel room only to anally rape her (Ronan Farrow, *Catch and Kill*). Lauer allegedly also kept an office in a secluded area of NBC where he would summon women colleagues and demand they perform oral sex (Ramin Setoodeh and Elizabeth Wagmeister, *Variety*).

Unwanted sexual attention in the workplace doesn't just happen in Hollywood or the media. According to an expansive 2019 survey by the American Economic Association, nearly one hundred women economists said a peer or colleague had sexually assaulted them, some two hundred reported experiencing attempted assaults, and hundreds said they had been stalked or inappropriately touched. Rosette Pambakian, Tinder's former marketing chief, says she was groped and forcibly kissed in 2016 by then CEO Gregory Blatt. In 2019, Army Colonel Kathryn A. Spletstoser came forward with allegations that Air Force General John E. Hyten (her boss) had tried to kiss and hug her several times at the office until he finally assaulted her in December 2017 by forcibly kissing her on the lips while pressing himself against her, before ejaculating onto her through his sweatpants (Helene Cooper, *The New York Times*). Sexual harassment is everywhere.

Although men often perpetuate it, they're not immune to unwanted sexual attention or assault. Comedic actor Terry Crews, for instance, revealed in October 2017 that talent agency executive Adam Venit had groped the forty-nine-year-old former NFL player's genitals in 2016 at a Hollywood party. What was perhaps one of the more extreme male-on-male cases to hit the media occurred some two decades before and involved a young man named Joseph Oncale. Oncale said he was terrorized by his male coworkers while stationed on an eight-man offshore oil rig in the Gulf of Mexico in the early '90s. They taunted Oncale, put their penises on his neck while holding him down, sodomized him with a bar of soap, and threatened him with rape. When he went to management, the supervisor reportedly failed to help, instead suggesting Oncale was gay and welcomed the behavior. In 1998, his case produced the landmark U.S. Supreme Court decision acknowledging same-sex sexual harassment.[22]

Category 3: Sexual Coercion

The last category of sexual harassment is sexual coercion, which involves strong-arming a person into sexual activity by threatening to professionally punish them if they do not submit, bribing them with a professional opportunity, or giving someone else opportunities because that person does submit. Examples include a coworker refusing to share a file unless you show him your breasts, a supervisor demanding oral sex in exchange for a promotion, and an HR employee accepting a hand job in exchange for a job. The transactional nature can be implicit or explicit.[23]

While political news director for ABC, for example, Mark Halperin reportedly engaged in implicit sexual coercion by encouraging his women subordinates to meet him for drinks after hours if they wanted his approval to travel to big political events that would advance their careers (Oliver Darcy, CNN). Weinstein, on the other hand, was reportedly notorious for explicit sexual coercion, as the producer openly offered movie roles in exchange for sex and allegedly blacklisted actresses who dodged or refused his advances, à la Ashley Judd.[24]

The first major sexual harassment case to reach the U.S. Supreme Court involved explicit sexual coercion of a teen bank teller in Washington, DC. In 1974, Mechelle Vinson was a nineteen-year-old recently divorced high school dropout who had been juggling two part-time jobs. She was relieved when Meritor Savings Bank vice president and branch manager Sidney L. Taylor hired her and mentored her like a father figure. The former military man was married with seven children. Vinson trusted him—that is, until one night when Taylor reportedly told her something to the effect of, "If you don't sleep with me, I'll destroy you." He knew she needed the job.

Taylor coerced the young woman into sex some forty to fifty times, she estimated—not including the times she said he raped her in the bank vault. In 1978, after she was fired allegedly for getting a serious boyfriend, Vinson courageously took the case to court. In 1986, when her case finally made it to the high court, the U.S. Supreme Court declared that sexual harassment *is* a form of sex discrimination under the Civil Rights Act—forever changing the game for women and marginalized groups in the workplace.[25]

WHAT FORMS OF HARASSMENT HAPPEN MOST OFTEN?

Now that you know what sexual harassment looks like, let's talk about the forms of harassment that are most likely to occur. Here's a hint: It's not the stuff you see in movies or on *Mad Men* reruns. Research reveals that the *more* severe the sexual harassment, the *less* frequently it will occur. In order of most to least common, here are the forms of sexual harassment that typically occur in the workplace:

- Staring
- Suggestive comments
- Attempts to talk sex
- Offensive images
- Repeatedly asking out
- Trying to initiate a sexual relationship
- Unwanted touching

Simply because unwanted touching happens less often does not mean you're in the clear when it comes to getting groped. It just means it is less likely to happen, which is a good thing. However, you do *not* want to underestimate the impact of ogling, offensive comments, and other types of harassment that occur more frequently.

Gender harassment, which is the most common type of sexual harassment, may seem inconsequential in comparison to unwanted sexual attention and sexual coercion, but the impact of enduring gender harassment alone may take the same toll on your health as other forms of harassment, which we discuss further in chapter 9. Bottom line: Sexual harassment is bad for you no matter its form.[26]

REPLAY

* Sexual harassment is gender-based behavior that the recipient finds offensive, threatening to her well-being, or beyond her resources to shut down.
* Sexual harassment is not about sexual desire or attraction. It is about reinforcing the traditional power structures in society and enjoying the benefits that come from those structures. Men are the main beneficiaries of our society's gender hierarchy. Whites are the main beneficiaries of society's racial hierarchy, which may interplay with gender.
* There are three categories of sexual harassment: gender harassment (sexist remarks and behavior, as well as bullying because of gender), unwanted sexual attention (inappropriate and offensive sexual advances, and sexual assaults), and sexual coercion (coercing sexual activity by threatening punishment or bribing).
* Unwanted sexual attention and sexual coercion are come-ons geared toward sexually exploiting you, and gender harassment are put-downs geared toward ostracizing and humiliating you.[27] Gender harassment is the most common but can be equally harmful as the other forms of sexual harassment.

CHAPTER 3

Harassholes and Targets

Identifying Harassers, Who Gets Harassed, and Knowing When You're Harassed

....

Some of us are becoming the men we wanted to marry.
—*Gloria Steinem, fierce feminist and cofounder of
Ms. magazine and the Women's Media Center*

LORI FRANCHINA WAS FAR from a Hollywood starlet. The western New York native was a former all-American softball star and a butch lesbian with her eyes set on becoming a firefighter. In 2002, her dream finally came true: Franchina finished tenth in her in class of eighty at the Providence Fire Academy in Rhode Island and subsequently joined the Providence Fire Department, the second largest in New England. She stood out—not only because she was one of the few female firefighters in the department but also because she happened to be exceptionally talented and professional. Quickly rising through the ranks, Franchina was promoted to acting rescue lieutenant after four years with the department. This put her in charge of the medic van.

During a night shift in 2006, Lieutenant Franchina was working with Andre Ferro, a firefighter medic whom she had never met and happened to outrank. The events of that night would forever change the course of her career and her life. Within moments of meeting her, Ferro said to Franchina that he didn't "normally like to work with women." He asked Franchina if she was a lesbian and, over the dispatch radio, offered to impregnate her if she wanted to have children. While rubbing his nipples, Ferro called Franchina his "lesbian lover" in the company of their firefighter crew, later repeating the reference in the company of patients at the hospital. Through the night, Franchina remained professional. After their shift ended, she was undressing in her quarters when Ferro barged in wearing just boxers and claimed to want to apologize, only to put his feet up on her desk and ignore her orders to leave. For his antics, Ferro soon faced disciplinary charges at Franchina's request. For her unwillingness to endure Ferro's harassment, Franchina faced all hell.

Once word got out that Ferro was disciplined, Lieutenant Franchina's coworkers—subordinates included—started calling her "bitch," "cunt," and "Frangina" (slang for a woman with untrimmed pubic hair). On the firehouse message board, they wrote numerous obscenities, from "Frangina leads Team Lesbo to victory" to "You get what you get, bitch." Male subordinates told her that they would never take orders from her, while flicking the pin on her collar. When she entered a room, firefighters made statements like "affirmative action's killing this fucking job" and "[t]he bitch is in the house." The firehouse chef yelled at Franchina in front of others, asking if she was trying to get Ferro fired. Soon enough, she started feeling ill after eating the communal meals the chef prepared. She secretly switched plates with a coworker, only to later see him go home sick while she felt fine.

Things were bad for Franchina in the field too. The men under her command abandoned patients, refused to lift stretchers, shoved her into a wall, flung blood and brain matter on her face. They terrorized her. And they did not stop. At one point, Franchina had to get a restraining order against a fellow firefighter.

Seven years later and some forty written harassment complaints after the 2006 night shift with Ferro that started it all, Franchina finally retired. Suffering from severe post-traumatic stress, she went out on permanent disability in 2013.[1]

Lieutenant Franchina's colleagues were never pursuing her romantically, as they did many of the other female firefighters in the department. Their sole mission was to push her out of the workplace. They succeeded.

Men like Ferro and his fellow firefighters often inflict sexual harassment on women like Franchina—that is, women who don't "know their place." This chapter helps you detect who is more likely to be a harasshole and who is more likely to suffer harassment. It arms you with information that will assist you in anticipating threats and uncovering hidden truths. Even if you're not vulnerable to harassment, you'll want to stay mindful of colleagues who are. We are truly in this together.

WHO ARE THE HARASSHOLES?

When the seriousness of sexual harassment finally registered with the American public in the mid-'80s, the leading thought was that harassers were either deviants with psychological issues or uneducated, uncouth men from lower classes. The public didn't awake from this "fantasy" until the early '90s, when now U.S. Supreme Court Justice Clarence Thomas, former Senator Bob Packwood, then President Bill Clinton, and several other "refined gentlemen," were exposed for allegedly engaging in lewd at-work antics.[2] Although decades have passed since then, research on harassers remains unreliable and nearly nonexistent. The lack of research certainly is not due to a lack of subjects. Rather, it's more a lack of candor.

⬆ HEADS-UP!

What is often covered by the media and what many people imagine is that the typical sexual harassment scenario involves a nefarious male boss coercing a female subordinate into a sexual tryst. That's not typically how things play out in reality. In the average workplace, one is more likely to be sexually harassed by a coworker than by a supervisor or subordinate.

A twenty-three-year study tracking a group of more than one thousand men and women found that coworkers were responsible for *three times* more reported incidents of sexual harassment than supervisors.[3] These stats are consistent with the fact that power is the goal of sexual harassment.

Of course, that does not mean you shouldn't be on the lookout for inappropriate advances or shady comments from superiors, subordinates, clients, or customers. Insecurity abounds. Stay alert!

According to sociologist and sexual harassment researcher Dr. Heather McLaughlin, it's hard finding people willing to admit to predatory sexualized or gender-based harassment.[4] Don't we know it! Since a September 2018 report in the *New Yorker* by Ronan Farrow, more than fifteen women have accused former CBS chairman Les Moonves of sexual misconduct, yet he denies any wrongdoing even after independent investigators found *all* the women they interviewed to be credible. More than one hundred women detailed sexual misconduct committed by Harvey Weinstein, yet the disgraced movie mogul adamantly maintains that *all* interactions were consensual. Since an explosive *Los Angeles Times* exposé (Glenn Whipp) on James Toback hit the streets in October 2017, at least 395 women have come forward with detailed allegations against the director, yet Toback stands by a profanity-laced denial. And so on . . . You see why getting a handle on the harasser prototype can be a doozy? That's why we rely on survivor accounts, which reveal that there's one common feature among nearly all harassholes: the Y chromosome.

Men Lead the Way

As you may have guessed, toxic men are the main culprits of workplace sexual harassment, accounting for some 90 percent of harassers targeting women and anywhere between 70 and 80 percent of those targeting men.[5] There's no prototype, but we do know that male harassers are more likely to have the following traits:[6]

- Support traditional gender roles
- Lack egalitarian attitudes toward gender and/or race
- Maintain a strong male identity
- Think men are superior to women
- Sexualize women and girls
- Believe men and women should be segregated
- Trivialize victimization or engage in victim-blaming

You may be able to determine whether a man has these traits based on what he says about the genders. Be on alert for these kinds of comments or thoughts:

- Men are better suited for traditionally male jobs and are the bread-winners
- Women should be in "pink careers" or stay-at-home moms
- Men have natural strengths like leadership, management, negotiation, etc.
- Women have natural strengths like support, organization, maintenance, etc.
- Terms associated with women demean men (such as "bitch," "pussy," "cocksucker")
- Activities traditionally tied to women are insulting for a man to engage in (for example, "If I'm wrong, I'll wear a wedding dress in public")
- Stereotypes about women as punch lines to jokes are entertaining

A harasshole can be further identified by the type of sexism he exudes—hostile or benevolent. As the name implies, hostile sexism is about dominating and denigrating women for fear that they will overthrow men's power through feminism or sexuality.[7] Translation: Hostile harassholes pathetically view life as a zero-sum game and women as opponents, and they're terrified by the idea of gender equality, so they go to great lengths to keep women "in their place" and tear them down. Hostile harassholes tend to view relationships between men and women as innately adversarial. They seek male dominance as the status quo and possess an intense drive to control women. This nonsense may manifest in crude comments, incivility, and underhanded tactics, much like what Lieutenant Franchina encountered.

On the other side of the broke sexism coin is benevolence (just not the kind you want). Benevolent sexism involves clinging to old-school notions of chivalry that assert men's power over women through paternalistic "affection" rather than hostile dominance. Translation: These dudes keep you out of the game by putting you on a pedestal and claiming it's in your best interest. Benevolent harassholes view women as "pure and warm yet helpless and incompetent beings who require cherished protection from men."[8] In their minds, women shouldn't be working in certain fields, *if at all!* Yuck! The ignorant and antiquated outlook of benevolent harassholes pushes women back into the kitchen while blocking access to the boardroom.

Both forms of sexism are problematic, but benevolent sexism is a tad more an issue. Why? Hostile harassholes are rude, distasteful, and easy to identify. Their behavior toward women is uncivil, to say the least, and thus offensive to most, making women more inclined to push back. Benevolent harassholes, however, are the sleepers. They appear nice and helpful, exhibiting caring behavior, but it *is* insidious. It keeps women in their place by limiting their professional opportunities under the guise that women are less competent and such limitations benefit them. Remember Laurie Chadwick, whose employer denied her a promotion and then told her she had a lot on her plate with four kids at home? That'd be an example of benevolent sexism. Research confirms that the more men and women are exposed to it, the more they'll try to rationalize sexist situations and the less likely women are to push for equality.[9] Stealthy shit, huh?

🛑 TIME-OUT

While harassholes are much more likely to be male than female, there is an exception to every rule—such as Dr. Avital Ronell, a world-renowned professor, who reportedly sexually harassed Nimrod Reitman, a male grad student who worked under Ronell at New York University. As reported in the *New York Times* (Zoe Greenberg) in August 2018, Professor Ronell was accused of kissing and touching Reitman repeatedly, blowing up his phone, sleeping in his bed with him, and refusing to work with him if he didn't reciprocate. Even though Reitman identifies as gay and Ronell as a lesbian, power is power.

Just like male harassholes, women who harass men can be hostile and/or benevolent. Hostile harassing women tend to resent men's societal power, use of force, historical exploitation of women, and so on. These women can be identified by their attacks on men that undermine the stereotypical male gender role and their harsh generalizations about men, like "all men are trash," or "men are pigs." Women engaging in benevolent sexism toward men may reflect a sense of maternal superiority and believe that women complete men. When in positions of authority, these women may hold men back in the workplace based on the belief that men are incompetent or simply because of insecurity.

   Women who sexually harass other women tend to demean and ostracize them. They're also more likely to engage in victim-blaming and embrace rape myths. Regardless of gender, harassholes are all part of the problem.[10]

Beware that a harasshole may engage in both types of sexism. It all depends on who they're targeting. For instance, one of my former colleagues was a benevolent harasshole to me, claiming to be overly protective of women, all the while being a hostile harasshole to our lovely lesbian colleague, denying her basic civilities and giving her undeserved shade. What can I say? Harassholes are shape-shifters.

   Whether they're hostile or benevolent or some twisted hybrid mix, harassholes of every walk of life support gender inequity and tend to believe harassed women bring it upon themselves by failing to know their place.[11]

WHO GETS HARASSED AND WHY?

No one is immune from sexual harassment. *Anyone* can be a target. There are factors, however, that make it more likely that certain individuals will be on the receiving end. Many of these factors have varying levels of influence and different degrees of interrelation that affect the likelihood of being harassed. But they all have one thing in common: vulnerability.

   Whether the person's vulnerability is particular to them as an individual or simply situational (such as economic, language, immigration, or right to work barriers), harassholes love to target the vulnerable as they're least likely to report the harassment or to be believed or supported in holding the harasser accountable.[12] With that said, broken into key categories on the following pages are some of the most significant individual factors that increase one's odds of being sexually harassed.

Youth and Inexperience

Younger workers and those new to an industry are more likely to be sexually harassed than older and more seasoned workers.[13] There are several reasons for this—and no, none have anything to do with taut skin.

First, younger people tend to be lower on the totem pole in the workplace, making them more likely to be seen as potential threats to those atop the hierarchy as these youths begin to rise.

A number of the women who spoke out against journalists Glenn Thrush (Laura McGann, *Vox*) and Mark Halperin, for example, said they were young and new to reporting when these prominent men reportedly harassed or assaulted them. I was targeted at a network when I was the bright-eyed newbie with no experience in broadcast or connections in the business. Producer Harvey Weinstein reportedly went after younger actresses who had no power and were looking to make a name for themselves in Hollywood— but he didn't necessarily target women like Nicole Kidman, who was married to a powerful man (Tom Cruise) during the years she was up-and-coming. Harassers truly do prey on the weak and vulnerable. Pathetic, right?

Second, harassholes target the young and inexperienced because with youth often comes ignorance, which can be bliss *except* for the fact that younger employees are less likely to see certain behavior as sexual harassment or feel they have the clout to speak up about it. Harassholes leverage this inexperience to conceal their misconduct and to further the culture of silence.[14]

Age-related vulnerability has serious long-term consequences on one's mental health later in adulthood. According to research, if you're sexually harassed before your thirtieth birthday, you're more likely to be harassed later in life, making repeat harassment a reality for many who got an early start in the work world.[15]

🛑 TIME-OUT

In addition to being susceptible to harassment, young workers also can be perpetrators due to a lack of knowledge about what behaviors are appropriate for the workplace.

In his six years creating content at *BuzzFeed*, author and online personality Saeed Jones often worked with younger team members and sometimes encountered inappropriate behavior. Jones used his best judgment to determine whether the behavior was rooted in inexperience, and if so, he approached it as a teaching moment, pulling aside his junior colleague and politely explaining why the behavior was offensive or not acceptable for the workplace.

If your instincts tell you that a young colleague's behavior is coming from a place of inexperience, consider whether it's an opportunity to mentor, and give it a go if you're comfortable!

Gender

The stereotype of the "traditional woman" conjures the image of a conservative housewife from the 1950s, waiting patiently on her man to come home from a hard day's work so she can serve him sirloin and massage his feet while he rests. She is deferential and delicate, compassionate and perky. She wouldn't dare be ambitious, assertive, or independent. Heavens no! The "traditional woman" knows her place. *Ick*.

By many women's standards today, this stereotype is neither realistic nor attractive. Yet researchers have confirmed that women who stray from this "traditional" feminine ideal are more likely to be harassed than other women. The further a woman strays, the more severe she'll be harassed. That makes sense, as sexual harassment is a weapon for policing stereotypical gender norms.[16] (Well, it makes sense in that oppressive, ignorant kind of way.)

With that in mind, here are some key traits that are more likely to incite a harasshole's insecurities:

Bawse Mentality. Women who show ambition, dominance, independence, or other stereotypical "male" traits are more likely to be sexually harassed *whether or not* they also display stereotypically feminine traits. That means that being compassionate, considerate, and chic will not spare you from degrading slurs or catcalls if you're also Ms. Independent.[17]

Traditionally Male Career Choice. Women in the military, STEM, sports, academia, finance, and other traditionally male careers are viewed by

Neanderthals as blurring the boundaries between stereotypical male and female behavior. And harassholes just won't have it. Really though, how dare a woman think she can pursue any profession she wants?[18]

Book Smart. If student loans weren't bad enough, you'll be disappointed to know that with more education comes more sexual harassment for women because they challenge the socioeconomic hierarchy traditionally dominated by men.[19] A 2018 Pew Research Center survey of more than 6,200 adults across the United States found that some 70 percent of women with at least an undergrad degree and 65 percent of women who had at least some college reported being sexually harassed, compared with 46 percent of women with a GED, high school degree, or less.[20] Evidently, the patriarchy prefers its women uneducated á la *The Handmaid's Tale.* #UnderHisEye

---

⚖ BONUS POINT

Even though harassholes are threatened by women who exhibit these traits, that doesn't mean you should play small or avoid doing you. It's not your job to make harassholes feel secure in their own insecurity. Shine bright and be the bawse you were born to be!

Single-Lady Status. To all the single ladies out there, you do not need a man. You do need to know that you're more likely to be sexually harassed than women who are married or living with a man, however. Unfortunately, harassholes see single women as "defying" traditional family structures and being less protected than married women.[21] Think about it: How many of Weinstein's accusers were married at the time?

Glass-Ceiling Breaker. Along with the perks of breaking that glass ceiling come the pains of added sexual harassment. Women supervisors are *significantly* more likely (138 percent) than other women and men of other ranks to be sexually harassed and to experience it at a sustained rate, reveals Dr. McLaughlin and her research team. When women are given authority in the workplace, harassholes use sexual harassment as an equalizer to effectively undermine the woman's power. In the harasshole's small mind, these women challenge the assumption that women should defer to men. As Dr. McLaughlin concludes, "The same forces that exclude women from management positions continue to operate even after women obtain supervisory authority."[22]

🛑 TIME-OUT

Turning to men, some studies suggest that men experience just as much of the behavior in the workplace that women find harassing. The difference is that men are less likely to be offended by such behavior.

A 2018 survey of more than three thousand adults in the United States revealed that only 49 percent of men thought asking a co-worker for a sexual favor "always" counted as sexual harassment, compared to 71 percent of women. Another study found that women are more likely to feel threatened by unwelcome touching in the workplace, whereas men tend to see it as a compliment or harmless fun! Isn't that nice? I guess if your gender largely has the upper hand in society, both physically and economically, you too may be more inclined to enjoy a casual grope or sexual request from the random guy a cubicle over. But women normally do *not* enjoy such behavior in the workplace—as it often is *not* harmless. Rather, for women it's a weaponized act that carries a degree of animus or is a veiled request, the denial of which has the power to ruin women's careers. Needless to say, women have it worse when it comes to the sexual harassment experience.[23]

While men may be the main culprits of sexual harassment, they're not exempt from being targeted. Same-sex harassment among men is the second most common form after male-to-female harassment.[24] But for men, the behavior is often dismissed as mere hazing or horseplay, although it is indeed sexual harassment intended to reinforce society's power structures and stereotypes.[25]

Under traditional "masculine" stereotypes, men are society's leaders, the sole providers and protectors of women. They're to be fearless, stoic, and all-knowing. Whether it's challenging other men to combat or pursuing women as sexual conquests, "real" men prove their masculinity through public demonstration. This alpha identity is not only tied to dominance and aggression, but it also hinges on the subjugation of women and anything associated with them. Men who fail to meet the mark find themselves facing harassment—for example, the guy who takes paternity leave, spends time caring for his children, is more in touch with his emotions or modest about his abilities. Even men who merely acknowledge male privilege and look to uplift women in workplaces are likely to be "punished" by being called degrading, heterosexist terms tied to not being "man enough."[26]

The more a man is expected to exhibit hypermasculinity in his industry yet diverges from that expectation, the more others may try to make him fall in line, possibly even resorting to sexual assault. This is what occurred in Joseph Oncale's case, where the young oil rig worker was targeted by his co-workers who claimed he displayed effeminate behavior—which is code for saying he transgressed masculine stereotypes that keep the gender hierarchy in place. Actor Terry Crews also may have been a casualty of this ignorant outlook when now-former William Morris Endeavor agent Adam Venit grabbed Crews's testicles at a Hollywood party in 2016. A few years before the assault, Crews had released a memoir titled *Manhood: How to Be a Better Man—or Just Live with One*, in which he advocated against men aspiring to be like the proverbial "Marlboro Man." As an open advocate against toxic masculinity, Crews bucked the alpha-male stereotype that steadies the gender status quo. This could've been why Venit openly groped him . . . Then again, at that Hollywood party it'd been two years since Crews's book came out, and several factors we'll discuss suggest that Crews exuded masculinity, which makes it less likely that Venit was looking to reinforce some aspect of the gender hierarchy. *But what about the racial hierarchy?* you ask. Read on.

LGBTQ+

Harassholes value clear distinctions between genders and their assigned roles, so when individuals blur the lines or deviate in any way, harassers will try to punish them into conforming. By their very existence and how they live their lives, however, members of the LGBTQ+ community blur these lines or deviate from assigned roles, making them targets of sexual harassment at higher rates than those reported by cis heterosexuals.[27]

On the matter of sexuality, a federal appellate judge poignantly explained why harassholes take issue with those identifying as lesbian, gay, bisexual, or anything that's not strictly heterosexual:

> Lesbian women and gay men upend our gender paradigms by their very status—causing us to question . . . antiquated and anachronistic ideas about what roles men and women should play in their relationships. Who is dominant and who is submissive? Who is charged with earning a living and who makes a home? Who is a father and who a mother? In this way the roots of sexual orientation discrimination and gender discrimination wrap around each other inextricably.[28]

When it comes to gender identity, the struggle for harassholes is also rooted in antiquity and ignorance. As harassholes see it, trans women don't want to live as men, thereby giving up their "birthright" to be the "superior" gender. This really upsets harassholes because nothing says "your shit's not that hot" like other people passing on it. In that same vein, harassholes view trans men as an affront because, by going from being a lowly woman to a totem-pole-topping man, they're advancing in the gender power structure—something harassholes cannot allow. As for those who aren't here to be boxed into identifying as a man or a woman, harassholes just don't like it because they don't know whether you're staying in your place and can be punished for failing to do so. As you may have noticed, for harassholes it's all a self-absorbed exercise in insecurity.

👍 **BONUS POINT**

Intersectionality is central to the sexual harassment conversation involving members of the LGBTQ+ community and people of color.

Intersectionality refers to the interrelation between an individual's social identities that cannot be mutually exclusive from one

another, such as race, sexuality, and gender orientation. The definition is more complicated than the concept. To explain by way of
example, consider Lieutenant Franchina's situation. She was attacked both because of her gender (woman) *and* her sexual orientation (lesbian), right? That's because "queer women cannot
separate their queer identity from their womanhood because it
defines their relationship with the world in a way that straight or
cisgender women do not experience," explains queer and feminist advocate Rosalind Jones, who's written for outlets such as *Ms.*
magazine.[29]

We often see intersectionality play out when women of color
are harassed while others engaging in the same activities are not.
As Jones explains, women of color "face specific forms of harassment that target their identity as women of color—forms of harassment that white women do not have to deal with because of
their whiteness."

Keep an eye on intersectionality, as it may increase one's likelihood of being harassed.

Drían Juarez, a global consultant who helps make workplaces trans-
inclusive and the founder and manager of the Los Angeles Gay and Lesbian
Center's Transgender Economic Empowerment Project, publicly speaks
about the horrific workplace discrimination that trans people face every day
in corporate America. As a proud transgender woman and Latinx, Juarez
knows the struggle firsthand, having endured hateful remarks, obscene
questions, and offensive behavior in work environments. She's had male coworkers pull out their penises in front of her and make crude comments
while management looked the other way. While recovering from gender
confirmation surgery, she worked for a major company that hosted an anti-
trans speaker who basically called her an abomination. Along her professional journey, Juarez has suffered and then some—yet she courageously
refused to hide her true self, even if doing so would've made it easier for her
to navigate the work world.[30]

Some members of the LGBTQ+ community do hide their true selves in the workplace in hopes of avoiding harassment. Even though he's had the good fortune to work in inclusive environments, such as at *BuzzFeed*, where he launched content specific to LGBTQ+ issues in 2013, Saeed Jones has seen friends conceal their sexual identity from coworkers for fear of homophobic harassment. The author of *How We Fight for Our Lives* recalls how a gay colleague teaching at a Texas public high school kept a sticky note at his desk bearing the word "fraud" as a reminder that he was deceiving everyone at the school by pretending to be heterosexual.[31]

When out in the workplace, members of the LGBTQ+ community are often subject to a range of mistreatment. For example, they may be implicitly or explicitly shamed out of doing things many cis heterosexuals take for granted, such as placing a photo of their partner on their desks, bringing their significant others to company events, being addressed by their preferred names and pronouns. They're also often policed for straying from stereotypical gender norms and hypersexualized, receiving inappropriate comments and perverse questions about their bodies and sex lives— inquiries cis heterosexuals would *never* be expected to tolerate in the workplace. This was the case for Lieutenant Franchina, who (as a butch lesbian firefighter) failed to invite men's sexual attention, something traditional gender norms encourage women to do.

Unfortunately, rather than correct their workplace culture, employers often will not hire qualified LGBTQ+ candidates because they know their employees will harass them and management doesn't want to do anything about it, keeping a number un- or under-employed.[32]

Race

Let's be real: The color of your skin impacts how people in our society treat you. The workplace is no exception. When it comes to sexual harassment, people of color are harassed at higher rates than whites.[33] These rates aren't the same across all races of color, however; nor are they the same across genders among these groups. With less institutionalized power overall on account of their race *and* gender, women of color experience more sexual harassment than men of color and a racialized form of sexual harassment distinct from what white women experience.[34] In addition to a wealth of sociological research confirming these facts, we have government statistics to back them up. A recent review of EEOC charges filed from 2012 to 2016 found that although women of color comprise just 37 percent of the workforce, they filed 56 percent of all the sexual harassment charges filed by women.[35] Bottom line: Being a person of color makes you a target for harassholes, particularly if you're a woman of color.

RATE OF EEOC SEXUAL HARASSMENT CHARGES
FILED PER 100,000 WOMEN WORKERS BETWEEN 2012 AND 2016

Race	Rate
Black	15.3
Latina	5.2
White	4.7
Asian	2.1

National Women's Law Center, 2018[36]

Before we get into the interplay of racial stereotypes and sexual harassment, bear in mind that these stereotypes are rooted in centuries of oppression and have profound complexity. Needless to say, this section cannot cover every nuance of these multifaceted issues, but it can give you a brief overview of why you or your coworkers of color are particularly vulnerable to the power play that is sexual harassment.

Asian. East Asian American men and women are fighting very different yet equally destructive labels in the workplace. Asian men are stereotypically desexualized and often deemed inherently misogynistic. As a result, they may be excluded from opportunities in work environments where masculinity is revered, such as in sports news coverage. When it comes to their female counterparts, Asian American women are seen as exotic. They're often stereotyped as either infantile, submissive "China dolls," or aggressive, money-hungry "dragon ladies."[37]

Asian Americans have battled gendered and sexualized racism for centuries, yet they're often the forgotten minority in society *and* also in sexual harassment research, leaving us largely uninformed about what they endure in the workplace. Still, we know that Asian Americans face significant hurdles when it comes to rising professionally due to intersectional stereotyping. As a group, Asian Americans make up 27 percent of the professional U.S. workforce yet are in less than 14 percent of executive positions.[38] That's an issue for which we deserve an answer. We also know that Asian American women are often undermined in business. A 2018 Center for Talent Innovation survey of more than 3,200 full-time, college-educated white-collar workers (ages 21 to 65), for example, found that Asian women (31 percent) were most likely to report being sexually harassed by colleagues who are *junior* to them compared to white (15 percent), Latinx (11 percent), and Black (22 percent) women.[39] This is also an issue, and there are many more that must be explored to get a complete picture of how sexual harassment impacts the Asian American professional experience.

Indigenous. If Asian Americans are the forgotten minority, what does that make Indigenous peoples? Academic research is practically nonexistent on the sexual harassment rates of the Indigenous. Yet they're far from insulated from sexualized stereotypes and disparaging caricatures. Indigenous women are labeled as exotic and submissive, while the men are made out to be violent and savage, a play on the heathen trope used to justify the mass rape and genocide inflicted by European colonization.

Although specific stats on workplace sexual harassment of Indigenous peoples is lacking, we do know that the group is especially vulnerable to sexualized violence, particularly the women—they're 2.5 times more likely to be sexually assaulted than women of other races and 65 to 70 percent of their assailants are non-Indigenous men. Let that sink in.

Despite the known high rates of sexual violence, "[t]he #MeToo movement has skipped Indian Country," said Amanda Takes War Bonnet, a public education specialist for the Native Women's Society of the Great Plains.[40] This isn't acceptable. We need and deserve research on the workplace sexual harassment experience of those in Indigenous communities, as we're all in this together.

Latinx. From actress Sofia Vergara's character on *Modern Family* to singer Jennifer Lopez's signature asset, the hot-blooded Latina stereotype thrives in mainstream pop culture *and* permeates the workplace. Latinas are deemed exotic and desirable, fetishized and hypersexualized. Harassers latch on to this derogatory and limiting stereotype, seeing it as an invitation to sexually harass Latinas in the workforce, who are already especially vulnerable as they're paid less on average than employees of every other race and gender.[41] To make matters worse, research reveals that the more educated a Latina employee, the greater the wage gap between her and white male colleagues.[42] Seriously.

Latinx men too face a range of stereotypes, from the misogynistic and perverted "Latin lover" to the sexually threatening assailant. Donald Trump leveraged this stereotype during his 2016 presidential campaign by calling Mexicans "rapists." Such labels work against members of the Latinx community when it comes to productive workplace dynamics. There must be more research on how sexualized and derogatory stereotypes hamper Latinx professional advancement.

Brown. As far as sexualized stereotypes are concerned, the outlook for those who are of Southwest Asian, North African, and Northeast African heritage (collectively, "Brown") is also bleak. Dr. Maytha Alhassen, a historian who studies race and ethnicity, explains that Brown women often face a struggle similar to the twisted, contradicting stereotypes that East Asian women encounter. Brown women are either oversexualized, belly dancing sirens or disconnected, submissive harems. On the other hand, unlike East Asian men, Brown men are sexualized to the point of perversion. They're labeled aggressive, domineering misogynists to whom a woman should never say no unless she's prepared to face violence. These sexualized stereotypes play out in who harassholes target and how they target them in the workplace. As you may have guessed, we need more research on the Brown professional's experience.[43]

Black. Although slavery ended more than a century ago, the taint of enslavement has left Blacks battling destructive and hypersexualized stereotypes that follow them into the workplace.[44] Fortunately, the research on the workplace experiences of Black women is improving, albeit data on the experiences of Black men is lacking. In the work world, Black women fight the label of the promiscuous Jezebel without sexual boundaries, expected to be sexually available at all times.[45] Although they also combat nonsexual, negative stereotypes such as the "angry Black woman," the Jezebel stereotype often leads, making Black women more vulnerable to harassment that is sexualized rather than gender-based. In fact, a survey of women in the military found that white women received more insulting and hostile comments, while Black women were subject to more unwanted sexual attention and coercion.[46] In that same vein, Black women also report receiving more inappropriate questions and lewd comments from coworkers, such as inquiries into their sex lives or sexualized remarks about their wardrobe.[47] This bolsters researchers' conclusions that Black women tend to be seen by peers largely as sexual objects rather than professionals.[48] The insanely high rate of sexual harassment Black women experience is evident in the fact that they file nearly three times more sexual harassment charges with the EEOC than white women in *every single industry* despite representing a smaller percentage of the workforce.[49] Then again, it all makes sense when we keep in mind that harassholes are intent on holding down those beneath them in the gender *and* racial hierarchies.

Despite being atop the gender hierarchy, Black men too suffer greatly given their position on the racial totem pole. In addition to being stereotyped as violent and aggressive, Black men are labeled "hypersexual, sexually knowledgeable and physically superior for sex."[50] Due to the dual legacy of being feared and desired, Black men are more likely to be sexually harassed by colleagues than white, Latino, or Asian men. In the expansive 2018 Center for Talent Innovation survey, 21 percent of the Black men surveyed reported being sexually harassed at least once by a colleague, while just 13 percent of white, Latino, and Asian men reported experiencing the same.[51]

Likewise, researchers at Columbia University and Michigan State University found that Black men in the military experienced far more sexual harassment than their white male counterparts across the board, regardless of whether it was disparaging gender-based comments or unwanted sexual attention.[52]

Turning back to hotshot agent Adam Venit's assault on actor Terry Crews. At that Hollywood party in 2016, Crews was the epitome of masculinity—a chiseled, six-foot-three, 245-pound former NFL player and married father of five—who was enjoying an exclusive evening among A-listers with his beautiful and talented wife on his arm when Venit, who is white, walked up to Crews, who is black, and gripped Crews's testicles in front of their colleagues. "Venit may have felt threatened by Crews's masculinity, and Venit's perceptions of the racial status quo; in that regard, he responded by groping Crews," explains Dr. Brenda L. Russell, a Pennsylvania State University psychology professor who has published research on aspects of male-on-male sexual harassment. Dr. Russell says, "People have a desire to protect or enhance their own social status against any perceived threat to their social identities, race being among them. They defend it by derogating the victim, demeaning or humiliating them."[53]

Indeed, Venit may have consciously or subconsciously seen Crews, a black man minding his own business, living his best life, as a threat in need of being reminded of his place in the racial hierarchy, so the exec used sexual harassment to get the job done. Cosigning this conclusion, sexual harassment researcher and professor Dr. Debra L. Oswald of Marquette University reminds us of this pivotal fact: "[S]exual harassment is used as a way to 'keep people in their place'—specifically 'uppity women' and people from ethnic minority groups."[54]

ARE YOU BEING SEXUALLY HARASSED?

You now know some of the leading research on sexual harassment, which will be extremely helpful when it comes to beating harassment like a bawse. But in all fairness, it can be difficult to recall the details of a study when a handsy colleague is crowding your space. Given that, if you're uncertain of whether you're being sexually harassed, focus on your feelings.

Instincts are your first line of defense. That still, small voice inside that lets you know when something isn't right. Never ignore what's going on inside. Trust yourself . . . and if you're still unsure, ask yourself some of the following questions:

- Do I feel anxious or uncomfortable around a certain colleague?
- Am I consciously ignoring a colleague's behavior?
- Am I avoiding certain areas or certain people?
- Am I telling myself that something is not as bad as it seems?

- Do I feel ashamed telling someone else about what's going on?
- Am I presenting myself differently than I once did?
- Do I enjoy my work but am still looking for another job?

The answers should help guide you. Good luck and Godspeed!

REPLAY

* Harassholes aren't deviants with psychological issues or uneducated, uncouth men. They're our coworkers, friends, family members, individuals from all walks of life who consciously or subconsciously seek to reinforce our society's traditional power structures.

* Although women can harass, the typical harasser is male. These toxic men are more likely to favor traditional gender roles, maintain a strong male identity, and think men are superior to women. Be on the lookout for those who are hostile toward women or indicate that women are inferior beings in need of care.

* Anyone can be sexually harassed, but individuals are more likely to be harassed if they're young and/or inexperienced, a woman who challenges traditional gender norms, a man who skirts stereotypical notions of masculinity, a member of the LGBTQ+ community, and/or a person of color. Never forget that sexual harassment is not about lust or desire—it's about maintaining traditional power structures by any illegitimate means necessary.

* When it comes to sexual harassment, you may not know it when you see it, but you will know it when you sense it. Trust your instincts. Ask yourself the right questions, if need be. But do *not* try to override your intuition.

CHAPTER 4

⁣||||||||||||||||||||||||||||||||||||||||||||||||

Recon Like Ronan

Determining Whether an Employer Is
a Sexual Harassment Hotbed

....

*We are grappling as a culture and as a world with our collective failure
to create a space that treats men and women equally.*
—*Ronan Farrow, investigatory gangsta and #MeToo game-changer*

RONAN FARROW APPRECIATES an egalitarian culture. You know Ronan,
right?... Satchel Ronan O'Sullivan Farrow of the House *New Yorker,* First of
His Name, the Unphased, Prince of the Pulitzer and the First Decent Men,
Farrow of the Unforgettable Weinstein Exposé, Breaker of NDAs, and
Spiller of Teas? Since journalistically drop-kicking Harvey Weinstein in
October 2017, Ronan has built a reputation for piercing the veil of big companies to expose powerful people reportedly engaged in sexual misconduct.
The man has gotten individuals of all walks to speak both on and off the
record about what's really been going on behind closed corporate doors. For
those paying close attention, Ronan and his team have revealed to the world
some common traits shared by employers that happen to be sexual harassment hotbeds. Early in my career, if I'd had Ronan the Rhodes Scholar's insight into what to look for when it came to company culture, it would've
saved me considerable headache.

At the end of my first year of law school, for example, I took a summer job
working in a small law office owned by an old, white, male attorney who'd
been around DC politics for decades. As a poor law student blinded by the
promise of a five-thousand-dollar summer salary, I ignored my Spidey-
senses in the interview and didn't bother talking to any of his former employees. It only took about a week for me to discover that the "happily"

married, AARP-aged practitioner liked a little bit of "brown sugar" in his coffee—*and vodka too!* Instead of learning more about the practice of law, I spent nearly the entire summer trying to evade an ogle-happy, inebriated old man who seemed more interested in my physical presence than my legal acumen.

Ultimately, the stress earned me an ulcer-in-progress and a doctor's note giving me good cause to leave the summer job sooner than he'd anticipated and later than I'd hoped. On my way out, this man who was slated to be my *only* professional reference for my summer legal work expressed concern that I couldn't "cut it" in law because I bowed out of the job early. Fortunately, a phenomenal law professor let me finish out the summer as his research assistant (shout-out to Professor Paul D. Butler), so I could omit that horrid summer work experience from my résumé and never need to rely on the Intoxicated Esquire for a reference.

From the old lawyer's bloodshot eyes before lunch to the half-naked and wholly unprofessional receptionist (who openly nicknamed herself "moist and meaty"), there were a litany of signs that the office culture was a tad toxic and would *not* be a good fit for me. But at that time, I didn't know what signs to look for other than dollar signs.

Taking a page out of Ronan's Pulitzer-winning investigatory playbook, in this chapter we discuss indicators of sexual harassment hotbeds. We talk peer-reviewed research on toxic workplace cultures, and I give you the intel on what Ronan would likely look for, inquire about, and wisely avoid getting into business with. Even if you don't fear being a target of sexual harassment, you'll want to pay attention because being a bystander still could be threatening to your conscience and career. You've seen what can happen to companies with CEOs on Ronan's hit list, right? (Let's just say there's a chapter 7 in this book *and* in bankruptcy court.) All right, time to put on your Ronan Reconnaissance hat, and put aside the allure of big paydays and free-latte Fridays, so we can focus on finding what truly matters—a healthy, harasshole-free workplace.

WHERE DOES SEXUAL HARASSMENT OCCUR MOST OFTEN?

Workplace sexual harassment is not limited to what happens within the four walls of your office building. It happens everywhere. In fact, when it comes to sexualized harassment, colleagues will most likely try to shoot their shot when you're away from the office, according to a recent Pew Research Center report. Translation: Sexual harassment knows no bounds.

Harassed women said it happened . . .	
In a professional/work setting	69%
Outside of professional/work setting	85%
Both in *and* outside of a professional/work setting	55%

Harassed men said it happened . . .	
In a professional/work setting	61%
Outside of professional/work setting	80%
Both in *and* outside of a professional/work setting	42%

2018 Pew Research Center national survey of the workplace experiences of 6,251 adults.[1]

A few years back, a friend who was a doctoral candidate at the time was speaking to a group of colleagues at an academic conference when one of her very-married professors suddenly swept up behind her, placed his hands on her hips, and pulled her into him while nestling his nose into the side of her neck. *Yes*, in front of everyone. It was as though her professor were reenacting scenes from *Dirty Dancing* like a low-grade Patrick Swayze, rather than interacting with a colleague in a professional space. My friend, who was new to academia, was thrown off guard by her professor's antics. She didn't feel as though she could check him without checking out of the opportunities that she needed to succeed on her path to PhD status. So she played nice, pulling away and greeting her professor professionally, despite knowing his actions likely sent the wrong message about her to their peers.

In the aftermath, my friend could've avoided off-campus engagements where her professor would likely be, but that would have kept her from valuable networking opportunities. For numerous reasons, women already tend to avoid socializing with their superiors outside of the workplace, even though employees who do are more likely to be content with their jobs and to remain longer, so says the 2018 Lean In study.[2] But what's the point of "leaning in" if it means leaning into demeaning nonsense like daily forced hugs? Ick. Just remember that sexual harassment, whether sexualized or otherwise, can and does go down anywhere.

IN WHAT JOBS IS SEXUAL HARASSMENT MORE LIKELY TO OCCUR?

While sexual harassment can and does happen in every profession, certain fields are more likely to attract it. That doesn't mean you should choose another career path. Rather, if a particular field of interest feeds your passion or your employment prospects, you should go in with a complete map of the land mines so you're not caught off guard. Here are the types of jobs more likely to attract sexual harassment:

- **Historically Masculine Jobs.** As suggested in the previous chapter, jobs that are historically masculine, like STEM and public safety, tend to bring out the harassholes. These jobs often have a gender imbalance, which alone is a Michelin-star recipe for harassment of all genders. Plus, individuals in these jobs are more likely to support traditional power structures, making those who don't fit gender or racial stereotypes for the job prime targets for harassment.[3]
- **Customer Satisfaction Jobs.** Where pleasing the customer is paramount, sexual harassment often appears. Between 2005 and 2015, nearly 28 percent of sexual harassment complaints filed with the EEOC came from workers in food service, hospitality, and retail.[4] The fear of losing sales, tips, or commissions pressures employees to tolerate inappropriate or harassing behavior from customers and management.[5] In 2019, former medical device saleswoman Kathryn Boston said she had this experience while working for Options Medical, where Boston said she was often sexually groped and

subject to lewd comments from Florida neurosurgeon David Greenwald, a company client. Upon notifying her employer, Boston reportedly received dismissive responses, like "surgeons are wired differently" and "grabbing a butt or grabbing a breast means nothing to them, so you either like it or you don't."[6] In sum, beware the "customer's always right" mentality.

- **Low-Wage Jobs.** Given the significant power imbalance, sexual harassment often occurs in jobs that don't pay well, according to an analysis of unpublished EEOC data. Women of color also tend to be disproportionately employed in low-wage industries, like service and retail, where women filed three times as many EEOC claims as those in higher-paying fields like finance and insurance.[7]

- **Monotonous/Low-Intensity Jobs.** Beware of boring and repetitive jobs, as sexual harassment may become an outlet for frustration or boredom. As sad as it is, people *will* undermine your dignity because they have nothing better to do.[8]

HOW DO YOU IDENTIFY SEXUAL HARASSMENT HOTBEDS?

As we'll discuss at length in chapter 6, sexual harassment is incredibly bad for business *and* "a preventable, if not always predictable, occupational health problem."[9] Yet so many companies still haven't gotten the memo and continue to maintain predatory environments or look the other way despite knowing there's a problem.

STOP TIME-OUT

Other than an individual's propensity to harass, company tolerance for sexual harassment is the single-most powerful factor in determining whether sexual harassment will occur and the extent of the damage it could cause. Organizational tolerance is so impactful that even those with a propensity to harass can be deterred if management is strict in setting the norms and creating a climate that won't tolerate it.[10]

With arbitration agreements and NDAs often concealing misconduct from the public, it can be challenging to determine from the outside whether a company's culture is problematic. Accolades labeling employers as "industry best" and declared commitments to diversity never tell the full story. Likewise, those on the inside of a company may not be candid with you about their employer for fear of compromising a paycheck. And even after leaving a company, former employees can be reluctant to be real with you if their former employer has an industry stronghold. Fortunately, as with dating, there are red flags when courting a company. Whether the potential employer is waving a dangerous red, cautionary yellow, or good-news green flag can be easily discovered via publicly available online data, intel obtained while interviewing, or innocuous inquiries of former staff. Take it all in!

Red Flags

The following red flags are powerful indicators that an employer is likely to be a sexual harassment hotbed. Should you choose to ignore any of these flags, proceed at your own risk!

Dude Overload.[11] Sexual harassment of women *and* men most often occurs in workplaces where there's a *significant* imbalance in the gender ratio, with too many men and too few women. For women working in homogenous male workplaces, their "otherness" stands out, making them appear as vulnerable targets *and* threats to established social norms. Gender imbalance was a noticeable issue at Uber in November 2015 when engineer Susan Fowler joined a department that was just 25 percent women. On Fowler's very first day, she said her manager made one of what would be many sexual overtures toward her. She'd later leave the rideshare company in 2017 after she says Uber threatened to fire her for complaining about the harassment. By the time she left, Fowler's department had dropped to 3 percent women. Apparently, Uber's HR tried to justify this pitiful percentage of women engineers by claiming that "sometimes certain people of certain genders and ethnic backgrounds were better suited for some jobs than others" and suggesting that women "needed to step up and be better engineers."[12] (Isn't that fascinating? Of course, by "fascinating" I mean sexist and racist. Anyway...) Yale researchers had a different explanation, concluding that "sex-segregated employment is typically tied to discrimination, not choice."[13] I think Yale overrules Uber's HR on this one. Bottom line: Too many men in a workplace is a hot mess and more.

⬆ **HEADS-UP!**

It says a lot about toxic masculinity that men are more likely to be vicious Neanderthals unless a sufficient number of women are present. Alas, I have more bad news for you: Hostile women harassholes often appear in dude-dominated workplaces, as these women are likely to embrace a power scarcity mind-set, feeling the need to compete for power and using stereotypical female traits to do so. The experience Anne Durkin described during the last two years of her two-decade stint at Verizon is a good example.

After Durkin, an office technician, transferred to a new office, she said three of her new female coworkers harassed her. They spread rumors about Durkin, claiming she was "loose" and referring to her as "Trailer Park Anny." When she confronted and reported them, they upped their game, going so far as tearing open Durkin's blouse at the office, exposing her breasts in front of their male colleagues, and suggesting that she used her bosoms to get ahead in the workplace. Durkin said these women made crude remarks about her breasts on a daily basis, locked her out of the building, and withheld her mail and messages. For Halloween, she says they stuffed their bras at the office, wore "Anne" name tags, and had a male coworker take photos of them in suggestive poses. Durkin ultimately went on sick leave until it was exhausted and Verizon removed her from the payroll.

Mean Girls may have been funny in theaters, but they can be a career killer in real life.[14]

Embraced Bad Boys.[15] Speaking of career killers . . . Management may simply say, "He's just having fun!" or "He's harmless!," but workplaces that tolerate employees who openly tell raunchy jokes, treat others with disrespect, or engage in "horseplay" are a definite red flag. You don't want to be in this type of culture, because if you object to the behavior, you'll be challenging the company's social norms, making yourself an easy target for abuse. No one should have to endure harassment merely because they want to work in a civilized environment where everyone is treated with respect. Consider asking former employees about "horseplay" and culture.

Big Power Imbalances.[16] Beware of workplaces with significant power disparities among workers, with men concentrated atop the hierarchy, as this increases the likelihood that lower-ranking employees will be exploited to the tune of sexual harassment. Indeed, rainmakers—such as high-earning execs and highly regarded talent—tend to feel like they don't have to follow the rules and can evade accountability for sexual harassment.[17] And they typically do. Prime examples include high-profile news anchors like now-former NBC *Today* host Matt Lauer and now-former CBS *This Morning* host Charlie Rose (Irin Carmon and Amy Brittain, *The Washington Post*). Both men were faces of their respective networks while they reportedly preyed upon numerous women over the course of decades without consequence. You can tell if an employer hosts a workplace conducive to sexual harassment if it selectively enforces rules, where certain people are punished for misconduct and others are not. Pay attention to how individuals of different genders and races are treated. The problem is real and it's everywhere— particularly where power imbalances reign. Check what's in the press and get a good look at the execs.

Isolated or Remote Workplaces.[18] Where employees work alone much of the time or in a geographically isolated environment, sexual harassment may be normalized as harassholes have easy access to their targets with few witnesses and few professional opportunities in the surrounding areas. A friend once worked on a college campus–like environment in rural America where leaving the job required her to uproot her entire life, making her more likely to stay with her employer and endure the harassholes who leveraged the isolation against her.

In that same vein, where corporate offices are far from front-line supervisors and employees, individuals are more likely to engage in sexual harassment due to the lack of oversight. Remember Joseph Oncale, the lowest man on the totem pole, spending weeks at sea interacting solely with the seven other men aboard an offshore oil rig? Exactly.

Discrimination Lawsuits or Fines. Companies are often sued for a range of things. But if the employer has been sued or fined a lot for sexual harassment (or racial discrimination), it's a red flag because such lawsuits are especially rare. You can get this info online by searching in the media and on the EEOC website. If something pops up, try to obtain a copy of the complaint or charging document to review the allegations and assess whether those involved are still with the company. Bear in mind that the absence of lawsuits or government fines does *not* mean the employer isn't a sexual harassment hotbed. Many companies keep sexual harassment out of court and out of the media by way of arbitration agreements, NDAs, and good ol'-fashioned threats to blacklist.

🛑 TIME-OUT

How many discrimination lawsuits and fines are too many? There's no set number. Consider factors like company size and type of suit or fine.

A single class-action lawsuit, a shareholder lawsuit, or a lone EEOC penalty may be enough to wave a red flag because it could speak to rampant sexism in the company. In March 2018, for example, a class action was filed against Microsoft in which the tech giant was accused of mishandling more than 230 sexual harassment complaints between 2010 and 2016, and in April 2019, a leaked ninety-page email chain from women working at the company alleged even more sexual misconduct that Microsoft reportedly ignored. Yikes!

Consider all the circumstances—including how the employer responded to the allegations. Specifically, look at whether the employer did any of the following:

- Admit fault and plan for change
- Fire the harasshole(s)

- Publicly speak ill of the accuser(s)
- Create or destroy evidence
- Hire a third party to conduct an internal investigation and publicize the results
- Make transparent changes in business practices

Answers to these questions will speak volumes about whether the employer has an unmitigated sexual harassment problem.

Alcohol and Drug Flow.[19] Unless you're looking to sling bottles *Coyote Ugly*–style or operate a cannabis dispensary Cali-style, you'll want to avoid workplaces where alcohol and drug consumption is tolerated or encouraged. Sexual harassment abounds when inhibitions are lowered and judgment is impaired. I presume that's because people are trifling and don't know how to act. You could say this was the case for former Vox Media editorial director Lockhart Steele, who *The Awl* (Silvia Killingsworth) reported was relieved of his duties in October 2017 when the public learned that Steele allegedly got handsy with a subordinate after drinking too much at a company event. The next month, Vox announced it would no longer host open bars at its holiday party. Smart. The media outlet wasn't alone, as a number of employers stopped serving alcohol at holiday parties post–Weinstein exposé. Apparently, since the #MeToo movement surged, employers are finally appreciating how problematic intoxicants can be in workplaces. Cheers to that!

High Turnover.[20] High turnover can be indicative of serious workplace issues, including sexual harassment. Think about it: If management can't keep an office occupied for longer than the standard ninety-day review period, it's unlikely they can keep a harasshole in check anytime you're within an inch of his office. Ask about the tenure of the last person who had the position, or perhaps check with a headhunter in the area. Indeed, if workers are frequently leaving your prospective employer, it's safe to assume *you* will be leaving too. It's just a matter of time. A high-turnover employer is kind of like that insanely attractive, well-educated thirtysomething who's been divorced four times but is convinced you're "the one." Be smart: Run far, far away.

Yellow Flags

Not every employer is insanely toxic when it comes to sexual harassment; some are just teetering on toxicity. They're kind of like most contestants on *The Bachelorette*—they could go either way. Here are some indicators of questionable companies you may wish to approach with caution.

Sketchy Job Posting. If you look at the job description and are left with way too many questions, this job is probably a bad bet, if not a hot mess. Whether there are too many or too few requirements, unmeetable demands, a wide salary range, or a missing company name, this employer does not have it together. You can't really expect that employer to police sexual harassment when it can't even put together a decent job posting, right? That's just basic logic.

#MeToo Response. The #MeToo movement has been game-changing. If the company you're looking at has done absolutely nothing to reevaluate itself, you may be looking at a crummy workplace. Did the company fire or retain any "problematic" employees? If it let go of Moonves-like rainmakers or high-level Lauers, did it use the "bad apple" excuse or sincerely invest in addressing its toxic culture? Did the executive team issue any statements about the company's commitment to ensuring a harassment-free workplace, input new safeguards, or kill mandatory arbitration agreements? A company that does nothing but rest on a "zero-tolerance" sexual harassment policy is touting nothing short of bullshit, as we all know revenue generators frequently get passes and vulnerable employees frequently get harassed. Let's not pretend every employee is treated equally or that every executive's misconduct doesn't have a trickle-down effect. Pay attention to whether the prospective employer has been paying attention.

Too Close or Too Cold. How do people in the office interact? Do they smile, hug, scowl? Are all the office doors closed? Are the races or genders segregated in the lunchroom? A healthy workplace, where there is solidarity among coworkers and sympathy offered by supervisors, reduces instances of sexual harassment.[21] On the other hand, workplaces where employees are too cozy or too detached can be quite problematic. When coworkers are too intimate, people often cross the line when it comes to acceptable professional behavior. When coworkers are too detached and isolated, employees become more vulnerable to harassment due to a victim-blaming mentality and lack of empathy. Monitor if a vibe is too hot or too cold, as it may be indicative of bigger issues.

Rainbows and Unicorns. If all of the employees you talk to before taking a job *only* have positive or ambiguous things to say about the workplace, run. Like Olympian Usain Bolt, run! Those employees are hiding something. This isn't about rejecting positive energy. It's about getting a candid look at corporate culture before joining the ranks. Sure, before you run away, try asking questions from another angle, see if you can candidly speak with the person you're replacing, and scour LinkedIn to connect with former employees of that office. Do what you can to get the info you need to sincerely feel comfortable with your decision. That being said, be on the lookout for people using seemingly innocuous descriptors like "special," "interesting," "unique." These are abstract terms individuals use to avoid feeling like they're lying to you about a work environment without being 100 percent direct about its shittiness. It's subtle code. I've been guilty of using it myself, describing a past employer as having "potential," "talent," "a lot to offer." It just seemed a lot simpler than saying "most of the people there are ashy and management is filth." A good rule of thumb: If the person you're speaking with describes an employer like a Realtor would describe a money-pit property, do like Ariana Grande and "Thank you, next!"

Beautiful-People Problem. If the office has a solid number of employees and access to a range of prospective employees yet there are no attractive men in sight or nearly all the women are extremely attractive, it may be a sexual harassment hotbed. Hear me out on this: Researchers have found that, because men typically make hiring and promotion decisions and they generally dislike competition, they're less likely to hire or promote men who are *too handsome*.[22] Translation: Unsavory decision makers will likely block dudes who look like *Thor's* Chris Hemsworth because he'd hurt most mortal men's chances of hooking up at the office holiday party. This same rule doesn't apply to women, interestingly enough, as attractive women are less likely to be seen as threatening in the eyes of a male decision maker. Still, if there are too many conventionally attractive women in a workplace where looks play little to no role in performing the job, proceed with caution, as someone may be making their staff pool into their dating pool. Journalist

Mark Halperin was implicitly accused of doing just that when he was the political director at ABC News. On one occasion Halperin reportedly interviewed roughly sixty people, selecting attractive, young women to fill eleven of the thirteen open positions.[23]

Certainly, a lot of factors could account for a company's complete absence of Michael B. Jordan doppelgängers, or unreasonable abundance of Gigi Hadid look-alikes. But all things being equal, be mindful if the employer has a "beautiful-people problem."

⬆ HEADS-UP!

Some workplaces deal with sensitive subjects, like sex and abuse. Good employers recognize that these topics can be addressed in a professional manner, and they invest in ensuring employees have safe spaces to do their job without making the workplace toxic.

For example, I once worked on a legal case where a group of artists said an obscenity law violated their right to free speech because it discouraged them from producing their art, which was graphic smut and hard-core porn. Let's just say the exhibits in that case were NSFW+. Knowing this, my employer added a lock to my office door and required that I review the material in private spaces. Likewise, a friend who worked at a progressive media outlet for years and wrote on sex-positive topics said his employer designated web workrooms for his team to generate ideas and adequately warned any employees before they entered the workroom to prevent them from stepping into a space where they may be uncomfortable.

Indeed, even when dealing directly with sensitive issues, good employers will take the necessary steps to make the workplace comfortable for all. If your prospective employer has departments dealing with sensitive subjects, ask about the safeguards in place before joining that workplace.

Green Flags

Just as there are signs of toxic workplace culture, there also are indicators of decent workplace culture more likely to be hospitable to those who aren't fans of sexual harassment. Look for companies waving these green flags!

Tailored Training with Incentives and Fewer Videos. Those mandatory anti–sexual harassment training videos alone are mere window dressing that can work against stopping sexual harassment.[24] Researchers have known this for some time—and companies know it too! A good company will replace or supplement training videos with in-person bystander training, workplace- and industry-specific education, and incentives that encourage *voluntary* training attendance. To help foster an inclusive workplace, a green-flag employer will dispel any notion of "boys will be boys" and will invest in training employees on all forms of harassment—sex-based, sexualized, same-sex, sexual orientation, gender identity, and stereotyping.

Innovative Complaint Options. As we'll cover in more detail in chapter 8, old-school complaint procedures that haul you and the harasshole in front of an HR disciplinary body are not effective and can discourage you from reporting.[25] According to the *Harvard Business Review*, after establishing these types of procedures, companies see significant declines in white women in managerial roles and in minority women in all roles, likely due to departures caused by retaliation or fear of retaliation should they report harassment.[26] But employers that use both formal and informal approaches to harassment complaints, however, have less women turnover and fewer repeat offenders. From confidential electronic reporting systems to allowing supervisors to play informal mediator, there are oodles of effective options out there that good employers explore and implement.

⬆️ **HEADS-UP!**

The little things can say a lot about how a company treats women. Here are several things that stay on my radar when scouting an employer:

- **Bathroom Business.** Are there toilet seat covers and free feminine hygiene products in the women's bathroom? Are there gender-neutral restrooms?
- **Pay Scale and Benefits.** Is the company transparent with pay? Are the benefits progressive and trans-inclusive, such as coverage for IVF treatment and gender confirmation surgery?
- **Life Stuff.** Are there pregnant women around the office, private lactation rooms, on-site childcare, or paid vacation time? Does the parental leave policy extend beyond legal requirements and include pay?

These progressive practices and convenient amenities speak to whether the employer embraces women and diverse groups in their workplaces. While each individual, their circumstances, and their life goals differ, working for an employer that offers *options* outside the status quo can make a world of difference.

Mentorship and Sponsorship. Companies that are invested in your future have informal and formal mentorship and sponsorship programs, not just because they recognize the value of good professional guidance but also because they know that women and men network differently, which can leave women behind in male-dominated environments where people tend to mentor and sponsor those who look like them.[27] According to the 2018 Lean In study, women often have less access to senior executives, which hinders their professional growth because those with more access are more likely to receive promotions and remain with the company.[28] Companies looking to break up the "old boys' club" that fosters sexual harassment will proactively invest in ways to ensure you're connected with the right decision makers and leaders so you can rise to the top!

Women in Leadership. Speaking of rising to the top . . . Gender balance is an essential part of eliminating workplace sexual harassment, which is less likely to occur when there are more women in management and core positions.[29] Although women leaders are underrepresented in nearly all industries in the United States, look for workplaces where there are women in leadership roles—not just in finance and legal, where they're often relegated.[30] If your goal is to wait for an employer to promote women, you may be waiting awhile, as research confirms that the number of women in management will increase by just 1 percent over the next decade if women continue to be promoted at the current pace.[31] As of early 2019, women held a meager 16 percent of board seats at three thousand of the largest U.S. public companies, of which 624 have no women on their boards whatsoever.[32] That's problematic because women are unlikely to be promoted to leadership roles unless the company already has a significant number of women in management.[33]

Leaders with a Strong Public Stance. C-suite execs who consistently, publicly, and sincerely push an anti–sexual harassment message lead companies with fewer issues.[34] These leaders put actions behind their words by attending regular training *with* their employees, chairing committees that *actively* solve problems, and the like.[35] In conjunction with many of the previously discussed other approaches, the U.S. Armed Forces used this tactic to reduce its insanely high rate of sexual harassment. In subsequent years, women in the military who felt supported by their leaders reported experiencing less harassment.[36] That's a good thing.

⭐ **PLAYBOOK PRO TIP**

A healthy workplace culture isn't just about gender parity but also diversity in race and ability, particularly as sexist environments also tend to exclude other marginalized groups. Bärí Williams, a diversity, inclusion, and equity advocate who has written for numerous outlets including the *New York Times*, recommends you keep the following factors in mind when determining whether a company has the type of toxic culture that fuels sexual harassment:

- **Four-Legged Stool.** Check out the diversity of the company's four core elements: the board of directors, customers, employees, and suppliers. Are they homogenous, nationalistic, underutilized, traditional? Diversity can be indicative of progress, ingenuity, and growth. A company that merely gives lip service to diversity is more likely to align with the old-school mind-set that limits women in the workplace.

- **C-Suite Lineup.** Does the company have a leader devoted to improving corporate culture or diversity? If so, you can see how serious an organization is about diversity based on how far down the reporting chain the head of culture or diversity is from the CEO.

- **Concentration.** Are women or minorities concentrated at a particular professional level within the company? Where do you begin noticing fewer women or minorities in the ranks? Where there are fewer members of a marginalized group, there is likely a glass ceiling holding them down. A good company should be making a sincere effort to hire, retain, and promote diverse candidates.

- **Advocacy.** Does the company advocate for issues that are important to you? Affinity groups can be good for an organization, but they need legitimate support and backing from management to advance and address issues important to the group. Be mindful!

Anti-Retaliation Best Practices. Retaliation is insanely common, as some 75 percent of women who file sexual harassment complaints with the EEOC also allege retaliation. A good employer uses the EEOC's recommended best practices to curb the practice, including establishing and communicating a clear anti-retaliation policy, training employees at all levels on that policy, paying individualized attention to supervisors accused of retaliation, following up with complaining employees, and providing high-level oversight of any major employment decisions affecting harassed employees. An employer should be invested in preventing your oppression, not enabling it or looking the other way.

No Arbitration Agreements or NDAs. Because arbitration agreements and NDAs impose a veil of secrecy and further the culture of silence, it's a green flag if companies don't use them.[37] Fortunately, lawmakers in several states are advocating for legislation to prevent employers from using arbitration agreements to limit employees, as well as NDAs that shield misconduct from becoming public. Such a move could have a big impact when it comes to exposing companies that keep predators employed. Think about it: *The O'Reilly Factor* likely wouldn't have risen in the cable ratings had the public known sooner that host Bill O'Reilly and Fox News had allegedly shelled out over $45 million to settle the conservative host's numerous accusations of sexual misconduct. If a company offers you either an arbitration agreement or NDA, consult an attorney or your union representative first and do not sign it if you're not comfortable.

Unions and Union-Like Protections. Unions can be essential to protecting employees from sexual harassment and advancing their interests. If your industry is conducive to unions, keep an eye out for employers who recognize and work with unions. Even if there's no union, green-flag employers will implement union-like protections, such as sexual harassment complaint protocols where you and the accused may have an employee advocate present during the complaint and investigation to ensure fairness and preserve confidence in the process.

REPLAY

* ✳ Don't be blinded by the title, money, or prestige offered by an employer. As we discuss more later in the playbook, nothing can repair the damage caused by working in a sexual harassment hotbed.
* ✳ Sexual harassment is not limited to what happens within the four walls of your office building, as it can and does go down everywhere, from inside your DMs to outside your cubicle. In fact, as it concerns sexualized harassment, colleagues will most likely try to shoot their shot when you're away from the office.
* ✳ Certain fields tend to attract the most harassholes, including professions that are historically masculine, customer-satisfaction oriented, pay low wages, or involve monotonous or repetitive work.

* Red-flag companies, those that are high-risk for being sexual harassment hotbeds, often have significantly imbalanced gender ra-
tios with more men higher up than women, a practice of embracing
employees who skirt the rules, significant power disparities among
workers, isolated or remote work environments, free-flowing intoxicants, and/or high employee turnover.

* Yellow-flag employers that you should be cautious of may have
sketchy job postings, questionable responses to #MeToo, too hot
or too cold employee interaction, the appearance of rainbows and
unicorns, no physically attractive men or too many physically attractive women, a number of workers from vulnerable demographics,
and/or an absence of safe spaces despite the prevalence of sensitive issues.

* Green-flag attributes that are ideal in companies you want to court
include incentives to participate in voluntary training, innovative
complaint options, mentorship and sponsorship initiatives, women
in leadership, a strong stance on all forms of diversity, anti-
retaliation best practices, and no arbitration agreements or NDAs
on the table.

CHAPTER 5

NSFW Coworkers

Identifying and Avoiding Toxic Colleagues

....

In fairy tales, the bad guy is very easy to spot. The bad guy is always wearing a black cape, so you always know who he is.
—*Taylor Swift, singer and LGBTQ advocate with a winning "reputation"*

PRODUCER HARVEY WEINSTEIN championed Gloria Steinem, fund-raised for Planned Parenthood, and donated millions to promote women in film. CBS's Les Moonves was a founding member of Hollywood's Commission on Eliminating Sexual Harassment and Advancing Equality in the Workplace. Louis CK spouted woke stand-up routines and uplifted the work of his fellow women comedians. At face value, none of these accomplished men looked anything like the "bad guys" we're taught to avoid, or even those T-Swizzle talked about. Then again, this is real life, where bad guys aren't in capes; they can be hard to detect and even harder to get away from—especially in the workplace.

Fortunately, when it comes to sexual harassment, the bad guys aren't very original. They're pretty typical to the point where we can throw them into categories of five types of harassholes (typically men) and five types of enablers (typically women) who seem to cause real trouble for professionals at work. These ten types aren't textbook. They come from my interviews with women and men from all walks of life and from years spent working in male-dominated spaces. That being said, these ten categories are not the final word on problematic people in the workplace. Keep your eyes open—*and your mind too!* Workplace personalities are often dynamic, and people are complicated. The goal is for you to be aware of these common types of problematic people, so you can keep them at arm's length. Enjoy!

FIVE TYPES OF HARASSHOLES TO AVOID

As we've established, men are more likely than women to be harassholes. But that doesn't mean all men are bad news. I repeat, not all dudes at work suck. Some are legit champions of women. Veteran anchor Scott Pelley said CBS demoted him because he wouldn't stop complaining to management and Les Moonves about the news division's sexist work environment. I've had a number of amazing male mentors with a seat at the table and no ulterior motive, who were my advocates, allies, confidants. I may not have thrived in the workplace without them. Dope dudes are out there, and they may not look like what you'd expect. Also, even if a man's not "mentor material," there are some men at work who are simply there to do their jobs and don't have issues respecting you or your contributions. They may not help you get that pay raise and could mansplain concepts on occasion, but there's no reason to believe they present a threat when it comes to sexual harassment. Outside of men like Pelley, Mr. Amazing Mentor, and Mr. Just Doing His Job, there are *other* types of men in the workplace that you definitely want to avoid.

Without further ado, here's the harasshole starting lineup: Asshole Adjacent, Ulterior Motive Mentor, Shameless Dude, Flexor, and Fake Ally.

Asshole Adjacent

We all know Asshole Adjacent. He's that borderline inappropriate guy. This is the guy who always "accidentally" brushes up against you when grabbing a file or claims to be admiring your necklace when he's really eyeing your rack. He's the quintessential "Where's my hug?" man, the "I was just joking" guy. One Asshole Adjacent I knew gave me a gift certificate for my birthday in the amount of a one night's stay at a *local* hotel—a hotel that did *not* have a restaurant, spa, or any other amenity that could be enjoyed without a mattress. Cute, huh?

Not every Asshole Adjacent is about making come-ons, however. Some sneak in put-downs, like the guy who "mistakenly" calls you the intern for the umpteenth time or frequently "forgets" to invite women in the department to important meetings.

Whether he's engaged in sexual innuendo or career sabotage, Asshole Adjacent's antics are always super shady. This creates two big issues for you. First, because he's subtle, Asshole Adjacent's behavior is unlikely to ever cross that heightened legal threshold for sexual harassment, even though his antics are distracting, demeaning, and inappropriate. Second, given his intentional slyness, Asshole Adjacent will play dumb when his behavior's questioned. This is beyond annoying because, while your instincts tell you he's up to no good, he'll tell you his actions are innocent or that you're reading into things that aren't there. Asshole Adjacent will try his damnedest to make you think you're crazy. He's a walking gaslighter (a topic we discuss more in chapter 10).

If you can't avoid the gaslighting that is Asshole Adjacent, you may want to consider lighting his ass up. What do I mean by that? This is the type of guy who thinks he's stealth, so if you're up for confrontation, start calling him out on his antics to make sure he knows he's not as clever as he thinks. Maybe hit him with an "It's clear that you consistently find a way to touch me when [insert scenario], and that's not okay." Or, "This is the third project email you've left me off of, which is unacceptable." You'd be well served to log his actions so you can refer back to specific dates when he engaged in the same behavior and describe the similarities between the circumstances. (See chapter 7 for how to keep receipts.) Don't necessarily feel the need to give an explanation as to why Asshole Adjacent's behavior isn't cool. He knows better. Plus, you don't need to worry about his feelings as he clearly doesn't give a damn about yours. If you do try to explain *why* he needs to stop the behavior, he may just think that it'd be all right under different circumstances, that there are exceptions to respecting you, or that you care more about his feelings than requiring him to treat you like a professional. All of those are no good . . .

But as I mentioned earlier, be prepared for Asshole Adjacent to play dumb or try to convince you his actions are innocent. Don't let it bother you. You're not here to cleanse the world of his kind. You're here to get a job done, and you can't do that when you're fielding covert comments about your dating habits ten minutes before a department meeting.

If you're not up for confronting Asshole Adjacent yourself, you may wish to ask a reliable third party to call him out, or you can go directly to HR or management if you trust them. If your employer allows for anonymous reporting of sexual harassment, that may be an option as well. Either way, Asshole Adjacent needs to know the jig is up.

Ulterior Motive Mentor

Good mentorship is like good sex: life-changing and rare. While I can't speak to your typical sex life, I can confirm that young professionals in the workplace often do not get enough good mentorship . . . In walks the Ulterior Motive Mentor! He's the guy who knows you're naive and hungry for information, so he looks to leverage his experience and industry insight to get some action. Yes, he's a true capitalizing creep.

The Ulterior Motive Mentor typically seeks *you* out, touting a wealth of knowledge and promising to let you in on the "secrets" to success in your industry. (Spoiler alert: Those secrets are in his pants.) He seems super nice at first, and you feel fortunate to have his insight and attention. After he builds rapport to gain your trust, he starts looking for opportunities to be alone with you, suggesting meet-ups after work over drinks or offering you invitations to exclusive events. Then he starts testing your boundaries by turning the conversation from something professional to something personal, maybe moving into your physical space, pretending to need your help on a private matter, or "accidentally" shooting you questionable texts. The jump may be subtle or sudden, but ultimately *any* relationship with an Ulterior Motive Mentor *will* go from LinkedIn to Tinder. Before you know it, you'll be sending distress signals like you're aboard the RMS *Titanic*.

Speaking of drowning at sea . . . Navy Auditor General Ronnie J. Booth's reported misconduct offers a prime example of an Ulterior Motive Mentor in action. According to Congresswoman Jackie Speier, multiple women accused the thirty-two-year-Navy man of engaging in the following "pattern of behavior": "Booth offers to mentor female subordinates, suggests he meet them, outside of work hours, arranges travel with the women and subsequently makes inappropriate advances on them." Not surprisingly, many men manipulating the mentorship angle portray themselves as champions of women in the workplace. That's what a twenty-three-year-old aspiring journalist remembered about accomplished reporter Glenn Thrush, who reportedly "tried to make himself seem like an ally and a mentor," all while leveraging his reputable position to put young women in compromising positions.[1]

↥ **HEADS-UP!**

Ulterior Motive Mentors come in many forms, but they all seem to be working off the same pathetic play that involves praise and professional opportunity as a precursor to acting inappropriate.

South Dakota school superintendent Robert Bordeaux reportedly ran this play on repeat with teacher Sarah Sunshine Manning, who is half his age. Speaking to *Indian Country Today* (Mary Annette Pember), Manning recalled:

> He would praise my work and offer me professional opportunities but follow up with these increasingly inappropriate messages and requests to meet for dinner.

Some Ulterior Motive Mentors will run this play with a little extra manipulation to build rapport before being inappropriate. A *BuzzFeed News* report (Patrick Strudwick) on now-former *Billboard* executive Patrick Crowley provides an example. Here's how *BuzzFeed* described Crowley's messages with vulnerable artists looking to break into the music industry:

> Crowley used humour. He self-deprecated, in an attempt to provoke pity. He spoke in metaphor, he generalised and used emoji. All serve to disguise his intentions: softened, and couched in playfulness before the direct, unquestionable command: Send naked pictures.

An Ulterior Motive Mentor I encountered made a similar play on me: he first spoke to my talent and offered me guidance, then whined about his divorce and asked for help before sending foul photos and feigning an apology and, after I recoiled, repeating the play again. Beware!

Given his clout, you may fear upsetting the Ulterior Motive Mentor and possibly ruining professional opportunities for yourself if you outright reject him. I'll let you in on a little secret: Many—I repeat, many—people in your industry know he's filth, and you're not the first young professional he's played this game with. Think about it: There's a reason he targets newbies. Women who've been in the game for a while are hip to *his* game. Also, if other people know he's unsavory, wouldn't they assume you're down for *that* kind of thing if you're *his* "mentee"? Exactly.

I wish I had known this when a notorious Ulterior Motive Mentor some two decades my senior invited me out to "talk shop"—only to use the meeting to corral me into helping him with a side business, only to segue that into shooting his shot (albeit with the tact of a failed geriatric gigolo). It was quite disturbing, and utterly bizarre. Being young, fierce, and fabulous, I had no idea this basic, past-his-prime huckster with a bunch of baggage and kids thought he could somehow seduce me—especially when I'd already told him I wasn't interested. But that's something important to remember: An Ulterior Motive Mentor is not a rational thinker. He's a manipulator. Do yourself a favor and drop him. Stat.

Other than reporting him to HR or management, you have a few good options for shutting down an Ulterior Motive Mentor. First, you can directly communicate to him that the way *he's* acted is *not* okay. Here are two examples: "Your behavior isn't appropriate for a mentor relationship. I'm moving on and wish you the best." And "Your behavior is unprofessional. It is not what I need from you. Nor is it acceptable. Take care." Just know that whatever his "excuse" is, you must ignore it. He had an agenda that, much like his fake apology, is far from sincere. Second, you can also do away with the Ulterior Motive Mentor by professionally ghosting him—that is, never respond to him ever again. This works very well if you don't work directly with him and need not interact on a daily basis. If you end up seeing him again in a professional setting, treat him like the sinister chump he is and ignore him. Should he have the audacity to question your whereabouts, you can embarrass his ass with the truth, generate a nonspecific excuse for your sudden departure, or simply act like there's nothing to discuss and keep it moving. Your choice.

⬆ HEADS-UP!

Be prepared when you walk away from the Ulterior Motive Mentor. He'll likely try to entice you by offering guidance or some professional opportunity, hoping it'll draw you back in, only for him to later engage in more antics. He's *not* sincere. It's a game, and it's one you need not play.

Shameless Dude

If fortune favors the bold, Shameless Dude's a legend at the bank. He's *that guy*. He slaps asses as if he's reenacting scenes from *Mad Men*. He talks about women like he's reciting R. Kelly lyrics. He calls you a "cunt" during a client conference call. He's degrading and insulting and hostile. Shameless Dude is the embodiment of blind, unapologetic misogyny—and he's your co-worker. Congrats!

Unlike most harassholes, Shameless Dude doesn't try to hide his antics. Nor does management try to rein him in. Colleagues may try to justify Shameless Dude's nonsense by saying, "Oh, that's just the way he is," or "He's harmless," or "It's annoying, but you'll get used it." Yeah? No. He's a problem—and so is the company culture if they're condoning that kind of bullshit.

🛑 TIME-OUT

Should Shameless Dude or any dude *ever* put his hands on you in an inappropriate way, just remember that being nice is overrated and that a good police officer *and* prosecutor are just a phone call away. Seriously, no one has a right to touch you. Be as unapologetic in enforcing your worth as he is in trying to diminish it.

I once worked with a Shameless Dude who had this nasty "signature move" he'd unleash on you out of nowhere. This dude would walk up behind an unsuspecting young professional at the office and grind his crotch against her backside like he was in Miami turning it up on the dance floor. You'd just be standing at the copy machine and *BAM!* The poor man's Marc Anthony is gyrating against your favorite Zara skirt. So gross! This Shameless Dude got served eye rolls and occasional audible objections, but it did *not* deter him or the swivel in his hips. *No bueno.*

When it comes to Shameless Dude, the best thing you can do is document, document, document . . . and report. Yes, even if management knows how he acts, you should still give the powers that be a play-by-play *in writing*, detailing Shameless Dude's shenanigans so management can pretend this is their first "chance" to do something about it. But the reality is, if management's willing to keep a troll like him on the payroll under the "boys will be boys" excuse, the employer's probably trash too. #RealTalk

Also, if you're comfortable, don't hesitate to tell Shameless Dude what the score is. This is the kind of bro who likely gets slapped often in public, so he's no stranger to getting read the riot act. Telling him his behavior is not okay doesn't mean he'll change how he treats you or other women in the workplace, but at least you'll have it on record that you weren't down for his misconduct should you need to go to DEFCON 1.

Shameless Dude is a reminder that not every man is clandestine when it comes to sexual harassment—and that society really hasn't come *that far* since passing the Civil Rights Act of 1964. Some dudes will always be as bold as they come when it comes to disrespecting you. The good thing is you're as bawse as they come, and this won't break you.

Flexor

The Flexor is a power player who plays dirty when it comes to young professionals he wants to dominate. He's the dude who leverages his authority so he can harass you, offering to create or threatening to kill professional opportunities unless you entertain his advances, even shifting schedules to gain more access to you. The Flexor may have supervisory authority or just wield serious clout in your workplace. He's toxic and he's a powerhouse—a filthy combination.

The Flexor doesn't always come on forcefully, nor is he always explicit. He may appear to be a gentleman by politely initiating the chance to work together, offering you opportunities, and making you feel it's your choice or that you're specially chosen. He builds your trust before peppering you with passive-aggressive power plays that leave you at his will.

Case in point: A Flexor at a law firm started assigning my friend to work on his cases, eating all of her time so she couldn't work with anyone else but him. Initially, she thought it was great for her career—that is, until he started making his true objectives known. The Flexor would call closed-door meetings where he could ogle her and keep her in the office late at night so she couldn't live her best life. Conveniently, several of the Flexor's cases would require just the two of them to take overnight business trips where he'd find ways to ensure he sat beside her on flights to invade her space. He'd later try to get her to review case files with him over dinner in his hotel room. When this Flexor didn't get the response he wanted, he'd casually remind her of his role in her annual review and pay raise. Yep, this man had a Weinstein Starter Kit.

While the Flexor will put in some real effort to be near you, don't be flattered—and do *not* catch feelings. (It'd be borderline Stockholm syndrome anyway, and that's not a good look.) This trash of a man feeds off abusing power. He knows how to holla at a woman if he's interested, but he'd rather force you into sick situations where he can control you and prey on you. The Flexor is Fifty Shades of Fucked-Up. Fortunately, no matter how powerful he is, you *always* have options, and options are power.

First, should you find yourself working with the Flexor, you definitely want to try to get away from him. That may require asking to be reassigned or building alliances to change departments or expressing interest in working in a different area. If you're familiar with the relationships in the office, you could also consider going to a more powerful person you'd like to work with and seeing if that BFD would pull rank to bring you under their wing. (I've done it before. It requires a good amount of gumption and emotional intelligence to get a good read on the power dynamics. But it can prove to be worthwhile!)

Second, if you can't break free from the Flexor, you can try to get him to back down by ignoring his advances and pretending to have a man or partner in your life (aka a decoy dude). While we shouldn't have to play these games, some men won't respect your "no" but will value that of another man. Power players like the Flexor generally do *not* respond well to rejection from a woman, so if he doesn't take the hint, he may try a more aggressive approach or punish you by taking away opportunities. Be on the lookout for how his "frustrations" manifest.

And third, you can always report the Flexor to HR or management—just be ready for a fight. Even in the face of serious financial loss, employers often foolishly side with the party with the *most* power, which would be the Flexor. That's a bummer because letting go of toxic stars translates to huge savings for companies, as we'll discuss in the next chapter. Indeed, these employers can be nonsense. But that doesn't mean you should suffer in silence or compromise your dignity just so some pervert on a power trip can shoot fish in a barrel.

Fake Ally

The Fake Ally is a sleeper. He talks a good game about protecting you from predators, advancing women in the workplace, and using his male privilege to put bad guys in their place. He seems super progressive, passionate about equality, and invested in your success, unlike Mr. Just Doing His Job. The Fake Ally restores your confidence in mankind—that is, until it actually comes time to act.

The Fake Ally fakes the funk. Despite all he says, this is the type of guy who does *nothing* when he has a chance to help you. That's because the Fake Ally isn't really here for you. He's here for you to *think* he's here for you.

⬆️ **HEADS-UP!**

The Fake Ally doesn't necessarily have to be a dude. It can easily be the woman seated next to you.
  Be mindful!

Although he won't sexually harass you, the Fake Ally can be dangerous because he creates a false sense of security when it comes to combating harassment. He leads you to believe that you have his support, someone to validate your experiences, a *man* to back your play. But when you have the Fake Ally on your side, you're really just alone—or better off that way. In short, he's all talk. He also could be talking to your detriment.

A friend of mine had that happen to her. While in the web of a Flexor, she began airing her grievances to a friendly coworker, who turned out to be a Fake Ally. She never saw it coming. He was so encouraging. He'd speak life to her face, and talk the #TimesUp movement and more—only for her to later learn he'd been sharing details about her personal life and re-airing her grievances with the Flexor. SMH.

Although my friend didn't see it coming, the Fake Ally can be easily detected—just ignore his words and watch his actions. Does he stay silent when Shameless Dude starts talking sexist trash about Paige from personnel? Does he look away when Ulterior Motive Mentor locks in on the new hire? When he gets a new project, does he assign you to his team to protect you from a Flexor? It's checkers, not chess.

The hard part is accepting that the Fake Ally's not in your corner despite all his talk. That's tough because you wanted to believe he was decent. We all did. But the reality is, whether he's walking weakness or just a fraud, he can't be trusted. It's better to break from him now than when you're standing in front of Helen from HR, counting on him to live up to his hype.

Sure, you can always challenge the Fake Ally. Ask him why he sat quiet when Asshole Adjacent tried to make you think he was harmlessly reaching for the highlighter when your left breast suddenly jumped in the way. The only problem is that the Fake Ally is all talk, so you might as well disregard any excuse he gives you and keep him at arm's length. Definitely open up to loved ones or other colleagues you trust, but don't confide in the Fake Ally about harassholes or rely on him to stand by your side. He may not let you down on group projects, but he'll sure as hell leave you high and dry when it comes to defending your dignity.

All said, good intentions aren't good enough. Leave Fake Ally "on read" and keep it moving.

FIVE TYPES OF ENABLERS TO AVOID

According to the Department of Labor, women make up nearly 47 percent of the U.S. workforce, and some 74 percent of HR managers are women.[2] Yet sexual harassment continues to thrive in workplaces across America. That should tell you that not every woman is looking to put an end to sexual harassment. In fact, when it comes to perpetuating and concealing it, women often play a supporting role. We saw that in Ronan Farrow's exposé of Weinstein, where female assistants and execs admitted to luring actresses into hotel rooms, knowing what would go down and that their presence as women put the actresses at ease. That's just one example, but there are many—and many reasons why women hold other women *and themselves* back. While you likely can't save those lost souls, you can learn to identify and avoid them. The five types of enablers you want to avoid in the workplace are the Handler, the Mercenary, the Cool Chick, the Seller, and Ol' Girl.

Handler

She's warm, friendly, sympathetic. She listens to you. She laughs along with you. She's the perfect person to coddle you out of being pissed. Meet the Handler. She's the employer's first line of defense when it comes to hushing women who've been sexually harassed. The Handler typically works in some supervisory capacity (possibly in HR), and she's probably been with the employer for a long time. She's survived layoffs and other corporate casualties because she has a valuable skill: The Handler will lie to you—and you'll feel good about it.

⬆ HEADS-UP!

You could already know the Handler and just not know she's *it*. She could be your best office buddy and suddenly whip out shenanigans when necessary.

Remember: Be careful who you trust at work. #StayWoke

The Handler's approach is brilliant. She'll share intimate, personal stories to gain your trust, feign interest in your experiences, and verbally take your side without question. She'll make you feel seen, using her emotional intelligence to infiltrate your feelings. When you're harassed, the Handler will be adamant that you're entitled to justice and that she's committed to doing something about it. But guess what? She's just stroking you. Her role is to make you *feel* like something will be done so you go away without the company actually having to do something about the ol' boy's behavior. (As I'm sure you've guessed, that's not helpful when it comes to accountability or stopping the harassment.)

The good news is that the Handler won't seek you out unless you've already raised an issue. When that happens, don't get distracted by how nice and sincere she seems. This woman will do all she can to manipulate you and to play on your emotions.

One Handler I dealt with went as far as unleashing full-on crocodile tears as a last-ditch effort to manipulate me into dropping my complaint about a harasshole. She was an executive pushing sixty, yet out here crying in the office like a toddler caught in a lie. Make no mistake, the Handler carries a Coach bag o' tricks.

The Handler *is* great at what she does. That's why the company keeps her around. One thing she doesn't do well is put actions behind her words, but she'll have to if you press her and insist she make good on her promises. If you have to deal with the Handler, don't hesitate to push. You're entitled to work in a safe space, and she needs to do her damn job.

Mercenary

Coming from a twisted mind-set that women *must* compete in the workplace, the Mercenary is the proverbial worst. She actively looks to suppress and oppress other women, particularly those who are on the rise. This is the woman who intentionally puts you in sexual harassment situations because she knows its toxicity will throw you off your game, eliminating you as competition. Sounds wild, but these types are very real—especially in male-dominated arenas.

The Mercenary can be tricky to spot. She usually seems to be cool with you and always puts on a good face for the boss. Everybody seems to like her! What they're not telling you is that she runs hot on the competitive, insidious side—a side they may have yet to see. But it's very much there. The moment you start to shine, her shade and fierceness come out. For the Mercenary, sexual harassment is just another hurdle she can erect to block your path to success.

An encounter I had a few years back is a good example. I heard from several colleagues that a certain dude was known to be an Ulterior Motive Mentor who targets new hires. Like clockwork, within months of my joining the company, he reached out to me, speaking to my potential and offering unmatched guidance to help me take my career to the next level. Without saying what I'd heard about this Ulterior Motive Mentor, I asked an established woman "friend" at the company what she thought of him. She enthusiastically recommended I take him up on his offer and make him my mentor. Seriously. After unleashing some real side-eye, I realized she was a Mercenary. You may say to yourself, "Maybe she didn't know about him?" Nah, she knew. Everyone knew. In fact, when I directly confronted her about what I'd heard about him, she admitted to knowing he was trash.

You don't have to be as direct as I was when dealing with a Mercenary, but you'll want to keep her at arm's length because she's actively operating as your frenemy. Don't give her information, and don't rely on anything she tells you without corroboration. The Mercenary will set you up so long as you're a threat to her game, going as far as sexualizing you in the workplace to play you as a pawn. That doesn't mean you should dim your shine or play small. It's tough being a bawse, but someone's gotta do it. Might as well be you!

Cool Chick

When ol' boy openly mocks Equal Pay Day, you can always count on her to join in. When Mark from marketing wants to play a round of "Who Would You Rather?" she offers up the first set of names. When Shameless Dude calls you a "bitch" for the umpteenth time, she'll hit him with the high five. This is the Cool Chick, the woman who's All-Team Bro!

The Cool Chick can show up anywhere and through any means. She has an attractive personality because she's full of laughs and mad fun. The problem is that the Cool Chick refuses to see inappropriate behavior for what it is—harassment. She only sees it as good times. She's also willing to diminish her self-worth to fit in—or to "survive," depending on how you look at it. She may even participate in the harassment, all in the hopes that the patriarchy will embrace her as one of their own (*insert sigh*). You kind of feel bad for the Cool Chick because she's been brainwashed by the patriarchy or may be going along to get along. We've all been there, but I'd like to think most self-respecting women have also evolved past that point.

🛑 TIME-OUT

It's not uncommon for women to adopt sexist attitudes toward their gender. They're internalizing the misogyny, oftentimes unknowingly and sometimes as a means of coping. In one toxic workplace, for example, I reduced myself to trash-talking another woman in an effort to bond with a Cool Chick, as misogyny was the only language she seemed to speak. It was a low for me. Don't lower yourself. Do better!

A Cool Chick I once worked with was so bent on bonding with the boys that *she* would sexually harass and occasionally assault men in the open. On one occasion, a young male production assistant was bent over a computer desk, just doing his job, when this gem of a woman felt it necessary to trot over in her five-inch heels and squeeze his backside while announcing something crude within earshot of others. This Cool Chick took advantage of the fact that she ranked higher than the poor lad in hopes of sealing some perverse connection with the harassholes at work.

At the end of the day, the Cool Chick is not here for the struggle or for you. Like the Fake Ally, she's likely not an enemy as much as a nuisance. But if you're not careful, partnering up with the Cool Chick could bring you trouble in a few ways. First, she actively tries to be "one of the boys" and is eager to please men, so it's unlikely she'll be loyal due to your gender. Second, the moment it looks like you want to advance women, or that you're *not* down with putting down women, the Cool Chick might drop you. That makes ties with her a wasted professional investment. And third, her willingness to take part in disrespecting herself suggests she probably doesn't have the best grip on boundaries. So if you ride with the Cool Chick, you may find that dudes will try to treat you the same way they treat her. #HardPass

Seller

As you know, men largely have had control over the business game. To buy their way in, some women seek to leverage *all* of their assets—including their bodies. Those are the Sellers. These are women who excessively flirt, needlessly touch, and purposefully get physical to get ahead. Sometimes it works. According to the Center for Work-Life Policy, 34 percent of women executives surveyed said they knew a female coworker who'd had an affair with a married power player, and one-third of them said the affair resulted in a promotion for the woman.[3] The woman reportedly on staff and on call to perform oral sex on then CBS president Les Moonves was said to have job security and to be shielded from discipline. A British actress was getting roles and introductions around Hollywood in exchange for sex with then Warner Bros. CEO Kevin Tsujihara, according to the *Hollywood Reporter* (Tatiana Siegel and Kim Masters). Sellers are everywhere.

They may not be uncommon, but Sellers can be hard to identify unless the sexual interactions are publicly displayed, or they admit to it. You'll have to use your best *unbiased* judgment in determining whether a woman is a Seller. Don't fall for baseless, unfounded rumors about another woman at work though, as it could be slut-shaming, which holds women back just as much as a Seller's actions do.

🛑 TIME-OUT

Let's quickly talk about women who publicly defend men accused of sexual harassment—you know, they sign letters and make statements like "He was always professional with me." These women are a variant of the Seller—but they're not selling their bodies; they're selling nonsense.

We all know that an individual's behavior changes around different people and under different circumstances. People are fluid, dynamic creatures. Simply because a man was professional with one woman (maybe you) doesn't mean he's treated all women that way in all settings. Women who betray that basic, universal truth are selling out common sense and other women. They may be doing it to stay in their employer's good graces and for the comfort of thinking they know someone (see chapter 10 for more on cognitive dissonance). Regardless, don't be among them.

Should you ever be in a position where a man you know is facing accusations, think about that universal truth before you cape for him. If for some reason you still want to publicly run to his defense, maybe ask yourself the following questions first:

1. Was I present for the alleged misconduct?
2. Is there a chance he didn't find me threatening, or didn't bother me because he couldn't have gotten away with it?
3. Is it likely he's a harasshole and I'm just late to the party or blinded by "good guy" goggles?
4. Do I like issuing public apologies or looking really damn foolish, like several people at Fox News did after Gretchen Carlson's receipts confirmed former CEO Roger Ailes was indeed trash?

In sum, don't interject your opinion about the side of a man or any human you've never seen in circumstances for which you were not present. Don't be a Seller and don't sell out others.

Stand-up comedian Marcella Arguello often watches Sellers at work. While the eye-catching, six-foot-two headliner has no issue shutting down chauvinist comments and sexual advances, not all of her fellow female comedians follow suit. In her years traveling from city to city and club to club, Arguello has seen some colleagues flirt with talent bookers and go further to get stand-up time and break into the male-dominated space. She doesn't shade the Sellers because she gets the game—despite the fact that she relied solely on her comedic chops to earn her way onto HBO, Starz, and other networks. Arguello does, however, acknowledge the harm Sellers cause on a larger scale. The politically conscious comedian, who recently released her debut comedy album, *The Woke Bully*, theorizes that Sellers are part of the reason why there are fewer women in positions of authority in the workplace. According to Arguello, Sellers know how to use their "talents" to get things out of men, but because their talents are not likely to manipulate a woman, Sellers advocate to keep men on top. Misogyny's no laughing matter.

The Seller doesn't necessarily believe she's holding back women by using her body as currency. Although these transactions were legally taken off the table years ago, she simply sees sex as part of the game. Sexualizing herself may help in the short-term, although she likely won't get very far in the long run. According to the *Harvard Business Review*, many Sellers are treated like poison in the workplace, with nearly half of male and female colleagues despising them.[4] Although Sellers may gain promotions, professional opportunities, and job security, their skills go only so far and their protection lasts only so long.

A friend once worked with a Seller, for example, who had climbed high in finance and seemed happy on the surface. But she was insecure and ashamed, knowing it wasn't her intelligence or her business skills that got her opportunities. Also, knowing that her colleagues were aware of what she'd done to get ahead must've been horrible. Management ultimately used layoffs as an excuse for disposing of her.

Unless you're an exotic dancer or sex worker, adding your body into the equation only lowers the bar and invites disrespect. The Seller doesn't understand this. She may be a wonderful person at heart, but her illegitimate path to success likely clouds much of what she may have to teach you. You're better off wishing her the best and hoping someday she learns there's a better way.

Ol' Girl

What can I tell you about Ol' Girl? She's got miles on her. She remembers the days when young women went to college for their MRS degree or sought to be secretaries simply to get a company man. Ol' Girl has been propositioned, offended, fondled. You name it! She's been through it *all*—and she suffered in silence and thinks you should too.

⬆ HEADS-UP!

Ol' Girl isn't always carrying an AARP card or enjoying an early Sunday supper at Sizzler. She may be *any* age. Many women coming up in heavily dude-dominated fields still see sexual harassment as a "rite of passage" or just part of the job. Keep an eye out for them, as they're just as problematic as an older Ol' Girl.

To Ol' Girl, sexual harassment is a rite of passage for young women in the workforce. It's not a problem but a small price to pay if you want to work in a man's world. That's why Ol' Girl will tell you, "Just get used to it," or "Let it go." That's what one Ol' Girl said to me when I complained about an Ulterior Motive Mentor. She was a high-level person in the company's HR department who knew the sexual harassment laws like the age spots on the back of her hand. This kind of woman could quote from Anita Hill's '91 Senate testimony like I could quote from *The Devil Wears Prada*. Even so, it was ingrained in Ol' Girl that women shouldn't complain when filthy dudes pursue them in the workplace. As you can imagine, self-respecting Adrienne *and* attorney Adrienne didn't take Ol' Girl's "get used to it" too well.

You too should ignore Ol' Girl's advice and not waste your time trying to educate her. She didn't somehow miss the feminist movement or #MeToo. Ol' Girl's been exposed to enough in her life to have the opportunity to change her way of thinking and embrace gender equality in the workplace. At this point, she *chooses* not to fight sexual harassment for whatever reason that's not your problem.

Don't feel bad for Ol' Girl either—and do *not* get too close to her. She may be super nice, rock that mom vibe at times, and know plenty of stuff. But her outdated outlook and unwillingness to hold bad guys accountable is nothing a progressive professional like yourself needs to latch on to. Plus, when it comes to sexual harassment, Ol' Girl will *always* side with the patriarchy over you. She couldn't imagine responding any other way to something she thinks is good for you to endure.

Ol' Girl misses the mark. Internships build character; not sexual harassment. Quote me on that.

REPLAY

* There are five types of harassholes and five types of enablers commonly found in the workplace. You want to avoid them, as they can be problematic when it comes to sexual harassment.
* Asshole Adjacent is the borderline inappropriate guy who "accidentally" or "unintentionally" engages in offensive behavior. He'll play dumb when confronted about his antics, but he needs to know that you see it is inappropriate and it must stop.
* Ulterior Motive Mentor is a colleague who seeks a sexual relationship under the guise of mentorship. He'll seem great at first and then manipulates you to take the relationship from professional to personal, testing your boundaries in the process. You're better off cutting ties with him.
* Shameless Dude is a bold misogynist who engages in hypersexualization and hostility toward women. He may be physical with you. Confronting him may be your only option, although that too may be ineffective, as his overt antics are likely indicative of a toxic workplace. You may want to consider updating your résumé.
* Flexor is a BFD who leverages his power and authority to harass you. He's a power player who likes to control and doesn't like to hear "no," which is why confronting him can be hazardous. Consider doing everything possible to avoid working with him.
* Fake Ally is a sleeper who talks a good game but doesn't really have your back. He's just blowing smoke and would never join you

on the picket line. Keep him at arm's length, and if you're not 100 percent certain he can keep your confidence, tell him nothing.

* Handler is a warm, friendly, and sympathetic person who will coddle you out of being pissed about a harasshole. She'll tell you what you want to hear, but nothing will be done. If you have to deal with her, stay on her to do her job and do not get manipulated.

* Mercenary actively looks to subjugate and oppress other women, particularly those who are on the rise, because she thinks she has to do whatever it takes to compete against them. Avoid her at all costs.

* Cool Chick is a lot of fun but not someone in whom to invest professionally. She refuses to see sexual harassment for what it is and is too busy trying to be one of the guys. Keep her at arm's length.

* Seller is a woman who leverages her body to get ahead by excessively flirting, needlessly touching, and getting physical. She may be nice and think she's taking advantage of the patriarchy, but she's holding women back. Keep her at a distance.

* Ol' Girl sees sexual harassment as a rite of passage for young women in the workforce; it's not a problem but a small price to pay if you want to work in a man's world. She's toxic to the core. Avoid her.

CHAPTER 6

Paying the Price

The Costs of Sexual Harassment
to Employers and to You

....

The most influential institutions in America have long had serial sexual abusers and deep misogynists at their apex. Those abusers didn't just shape their workplaces or their industries; they shaped our politics, our culture, and our country.
—*Ezra Klein, speaker outer and Vox Media founder*

WHETHER BUSINESSES SELL services or products, you would think they were in it to make money. Here's a bit of harsh truth that goes directly to the bottom line: Companies can be quite complicit when it comes to sexual harassment. They'll try to convince you otherwise, talk a good game about equal opportunity, and put on a helluva show to make you believe they're bias-free employers, but don't be fooled.

Many employers are star players in the workplace oppression game. From intentionally ignoring complaints to quietly paying out settlements to holding on to harassholes, businesses continually place bad bets on sexual harassment, many just hoping the public never finds out. What these employers foolishly refuse to recognize is that gambling with sexual harassment isn't like gambling in Las Vegas: With sexual harassment, the house never wins. In 2018, one of the world's most elite gaming and hotel empires learned this the hard way.

Wynn Resorts entered the 2018 New Year with the number one casino on the Las Vegas Strip. Raking in billions in profits, the company's share values were up nearly 87 percent from that same time the year before. Wynn Resorts was riding an unprecedented and insanely profitable hot streak—that is, until January 26. That morning, just a day before CEO Steve Wynn's seventy-sixth birthday, the *Wall Street Journal* (Alexandra Berzon, Chris

Kirkham, Elizabeth Bernstein, and Kate O'Keeffe) released a bombshell report, detailing a "decades-long pattern of sexual misconduct" and alleged cover-ups involving Wynn. According to dozens of people who worked for Wynn, the casino mogul repeatedly abused his power over the years, pressuring employees to perform sexual acts, including one incident in which the very married Wynn allegedly impregnated a manicurist after forcing her to disrobe and bullying her into sex. He reportedly paid $7.5 million for her silence. Former female employees recounted other disgusting encounters with the Ivy League–educated billionaire, who was said to have exposed himself regularly and made countless sexual advances. So as not to jeopardize their employment, the women responded by creating fake appointments and physically hiding in back rooms to dodge Wynn whenever he was in the building, heading their way.

In the *Journal*, Wynn was portrayed as a power-hungry sexual predator, free of accountability and devoid of conscience. Within hours of the report's release, Wynn Resorts skidded over 10 percent on NASDAQ, shaving off more than $2 billion from the company's value.

Wynn was facing multiple accusations. He had appeared to violate the law. He reportedly entered NDAs. He allegedly paid out settlements. Nevertheless, he persisted . . . to deny, deny, deny. But the downward spiral didn't stop. Wynn Resorts shares took another nosedive, dropping some 9 percent more. The company had now hemorrhaged $3.5 billion in value in less than ten business days. The gambling empire Wynn had meticulously built went from being a sure bet to a big bust, now facing the threat of a potential hostile takeover.

Just when Wynn Resorts had been badly wounded, along came the *Las Vegas Review-Journal* (Carri Geer Thevenot and Arthur Kane), a small publication owned by one of Wynn Resorts' business partners and arguably one of its competitors. For twenty years, the local paper had been sitting on an exposé detailing *more* sexual misconduct allegations against Wynn reaching way back into the '80s. On February 5, 2018, the *Las Vegas Review-Journal* finally sent that story to print, explaining that the exposé had been killed back in '98 (see chapter 13 for more on the media tactic known as "catch and kill"). It took less than twenty-four hours for the disgraced Wynn to resign as CEO and to turn the company over to his ex-wife. In the following months, Wynn Resorts' share values struggled to rebound while the company defended itself against government investigations and numerous class-action lawsuits claiming Wynn's sexual harassment and cover-ups squandered company resources.

Ultimately, Wynn was ousted from the empire he created, reportedly losing at least $412 million of his personal net worth. His board of directors was broken up, and his once flourishing company closed out 2018 in the red, only for it to enter 2019 with a $20 million regulatory fine for failing to address decades of sexual misconduct.

There are two universal truths at play here: (1) What happens in Vegas *never* stays in Vegas; and (2) Sexual harassment is bad for business. Not only can sexual harassment kill careers, but it can kill companies. This chapter dives into the costs borne by employers, individuals, and others. When it comes to workplace sexual harassment, you can rest assured that the house will never win.

HOW MUCH DO EMPLOYERS PAY TO HOLD ON TO HARASSHOLES?

Most employers have anti–sexual harassment policies that talk the talk of the anti-discrimination law we dive into in chapters 11 and 12. Too often, however, these policies are nothing short of lip service. Employers tend to be more invested in touting workplace policies to reduce legal liability than in stopping harassholes from harassing. But symbolic compliance is simply costly shenanigans. Unsupported policies do not and will not shield employers from the unnecessary and high costs that accompany holding on to harassholes.

Harasshole Costs. No matter how you look at it, harassholes hurt the bottom line. Research reveals that, on average, companies lose $27,800 in productivity per harassed employee.[1] But harassed employees generally don't hang around long, as they're 6.5 times more likely than others to leave a job. In fact, employee turnover generates the largest sexual harassment economic costs for employers. As reported by the Institute for Women's Policy Research, the average costs of employee turnover resulting from sexual harassment is 16 to 20 percent of a standard employee's annual salary, reaching as high as 213 percent of the salary for experienced managerial and professional staff.[2] What's that look like in dollars? The International Center for Research on Women estimates that range to be anywhere from $5,300 to $225,000 per lost employee depending on their level and industry.[3]

BTW, none of those numbers include the average cost of lost productivity per bystander or the average costs of recruiting, hiring, and training *each* new employee needed to replace the ones scared off by a harasshole. That is data researchers have yet to be able to quantify. Even without those unknown costs, it's clear that keeping harassholes around is expensive—and bringing in a top performer won't change that.

In a fascinating large-scale study of more than fifty thousand employees working across eleven different companies, Harvard Business School looked at the comparative cost of employing a toxic worker—that is, someone who engages in sexual harassment and other forms of misconduct that hurts the business. The 2015 study revealed that, even though toxic workers tend to be more productive than the average worker, they gravitate toward using unethical means and adversely impact those around them, making them problematic for net profitability. In fact, avoiding a toxic worker generates nearly twice the amount of returns of simply hiring a high-performing superstar. You don't need an economics degree to know that two-to-one returns don't suck—but holding on to a harasshole definitely does.[4]

Reputational Damage. In addition to suffering financial costs associated with keeping harassholes around, an employer's reputation can take a costly hit. In a 1,500-participant survey discussed in the *Harvard Business Review*, researchers found that even a single sexual harassment claim can dramatically impact public perception of how fairly an organization treats men and women. In such cases, the company is seen as less equitable than a company accused of economic misdeeds, like fraud. Researchers also revealed that the "bad apple defense" isn't fooling anyone: people see a single sexual harassment claim as an *overall* culture problem.[5]

As you may imagine, because people prefer to support fair and decent organizations, the damage sexual harassment does to a company's reputation *will* resonate at the bank. The numbers are difficult for researchers to quantify, as the loss varies per industry and employer. Nonetheless, there's no dispute that sexual harassment allegations drive away customers, investors, and talent.[6]

Take CBS, for example. On a Friday in July 2018, the media giant's stock plummeted some 6 percent in response to the mere rumor of Ronan Farrow's upcoming exposé on then company chairman and CEO Les Moonves. That same night, the *New Yorker* published Farrow's piece. By COB on Monday, financial outlets reported that CBS shares had shed more than $1.5 billion. Not million. *Billion.*

What happened to American clothing brand Guess in early 2018 is another example. Just hours after model Kate Upton fired off a tweet accusing the brand's cofounder Paul Marciano of abusing his power to "sexually and emotionally harass women," the company dropped $250 million in the market that day as its shares tanked some 18 percent. Reputational losses tied to harassment are real.

Not every company takes a quantifiable hit in value when its toxic culture becomes public, however. Shares of Netflix, Amazon, and NBC (via its parent company Comcast), for instance, were neither shaken nor stirred when news broke in 2018 that the companies were harboring harassholes. That doesn't mean these companies went unscathed though. Netflix said it lost at least $39 million upon cutting ties with actor Kevin Spacey after more than a dozen men levied sexual misconduct allegations against the *House of Cards* lead, with whom Netflix was also producing a now-never-to-be-seen movie titled *Gore*. Later that year, Netflix likely absorbed more loss when it had to write off Danny Masterson's character from *The Ranch*, after years of multiple rape allegations against the actor resurfaced. Indeed, doing business with harassholes can be very expensive—and we have yet to look at the costs coming out of the legal system.

Settlements and Jury Awards. When it becomes a legal issue, the costs of holding on to harassholes are compounded for companies as they fork over millions to pay out settlements and satisfy jury awards.

In May 2019, for example, producer Harvey Weinstein and his former board members reportedly reached a $44 million deal to resolve sexual misconduct lawsuits brought by the New York State Attorney General and a number of women. Similarly, 21st Century Fox shelled out at least $100

million in connection with sexual misconduct allegedly committed by former Fox News CEO Roger Ailes and former host Bill O'Reilly, plus a whop-
ping $90 million to shareholders who sued Fox for mishandling sexual
harassment. No wonder 21st Century Fox fell short of meeting Wall Street's
profit expectations during 2017. Yikes!

Most companies likely don't spend as much on sexual harassment claims
as Fox has for a decade. On average, each sexual harassment settlement costs
an employer $75,000.[7] That may not sound like a lot to you, but it can add up
for employers. From 2010 to 2017, employers paid nearly $1 billion to settle
sexual harassment charges brought by the EEOC, which litigates only a
small number of cases.[8] That ten-figure price tag doesn't even factor in any
of the following:

- Fines from state regulatory agencies (like the $20 million the Nevada
  Gaming Commission fined Wynn Resorts)
- Payments employers made to employees who settled before or after
  seeking legal action apart from the EEOC
- Payments to employees who won in court or through private dispute
  resolution (like arbitration)
- Costs businesses paid in insurance premiums for employment practices liability insurance coverage (which averages anywhere from
  $1,000 to $1,000,000 a claim)[9]
- Legal fees paid to attorneys and costs associated with litigation, which
  isn't nominal either, assuming the company hired a medium-sized law
  firm.[10]

Legal Fees and Court Costs	
Out-of-Court Settlements	$10,000–$50,000
Dismissed Cases	$10,000–$15,000
Cases That Go to Trial	$150,000–$200,000

Although only a small number of sexual harassment cases go to court and
even fewer ever see a jury, companies can end up paying considerable
amounts if they're found liable under state discrimination laws. The average
jury award in sexual harassment cases is $217,000—*not* including legal

fees.[11] Some of the biggest sexual harassment jury verdicts have come out of cases where employers ignored or failed to properly handle complaints.

In 2012, for example, a California jury awarded a physician's assistant $3.5 million for lost wages, $39 million for mental anguish, and $125 million in punitive damages, all against a hospital that ignored her repeated complaints about surgeons sticking her with needles, calling her a "stupid chick," saying she performed surgery "like a girl," and greeting her with "I'm horny."

An employee of lease-to-own retailer Aaron's Inc. was awarded $95 million in 2011 after she was sexually harassed and assaulted by her supervisor. When she reported him to the corporate office, they did nothing but notify him to keep an eye on her because she was complaining.

A few years later, in 2016, a New Hampshire jury awarded a Walmart pharmacist $164,000 in back pay, $558,000 in front pay, $500,000 in compensatory damages, plus $15 million in punitive damages for gender bias and retaliation when management selectively punished and fired her for blowing the whistle about unsafe pharmacy conditions.

Don't let the dollar signs distract you. These women didn't necessarily get to keep *all* of that cash, *and these results are rare*, especially considering the total number of actual and potential workplace sexual harassment claims that could be filed. Still, these cases speak to the risks companies take by giving lip service to anti–sexual harassment policies.

WHY DO COMPANIES TOLERATE HARASSHOLES?

Companies are supposed to be in the business of making money, not enabling employees to release insecure angst at the expense of their colleagues. So, why do so many employers tolerate sexual harassment? Good question. Here are three very sad yet real reasons why.

First, many companies allow sexual harassment to flourish because they're basically incentivized to do so. Check this:

- **Tax Benefits.** The U.S. tax code allows companies to write off the legal fees incurred in fighting sexual harassment claims and any settlement payments (so long as neither is attached to an NDA entered after January 1, 2018). That above-the-line deduction can actually *shrink* the company's tax bill. In a sadistic world like ours, this tax setup incentivizes employers to some extent to allow misconduct.

▪ **Insurance Covers It.** Large employers often have insurance plans that will cover their legal defense and the cost of paying out sexual harassment claims. If someone else is picking up the bill at the end of the day, how concerned would you be about the underlying issue?

▪ **Arbitration Advantage.** Many companies force employees into arbitration, a courtlike proceeding that typically sends the employee home with a lot less money than if they were able to sue in court. We talk about this more in chapter 12.

▪ **Money Limits.** There's a good chance you may not take home much in a sexual harassment lawsuit thanks to Congress. The legislature has capped the amount of compensatory *and* punitive damages you can receive if you prevail on federal sexual harassment claims to a *total* of $300,000— that's *if* the company has five hundred or more employees. If less, the cap falls. (This doesn't mean you can't win more money under *state* claims, however, as shown by the multimillion-dollar jury verdicts we discussed earlier. But again, those are rare.) We also talk more about the available remedies in chapter 12.

Second, most major U.S. companies allow (if not enable) sexual harassment because they're merely an incorporated reflection of society's traditional power structures, which we know are founded upon subjugating women and members of marginalized groups. Translation: Dudes run the show and typically like to keep it that way. While women make up nearly half of the workforce, most *Fortune* 500 companies were founded and are led by men, with a meager 6 percent led by women as of mid-2019.[12] As we've established, men have more to gain from maintaining the status quo and tend not to be offended by harassing behavior, giving them no reason to try to stop harassholes—that is, so long as the public doesn't find out.

And third, companies allow sexual harassment because they arrogantly think no one will ever find out about it. Seriously. No matter what a woman says or whether she openly outlines her action plan, these fools do *not* believe she'll publicly speak about the harassment given the hurdles the system has set before her. Just ask me. I know. And think about it: Before Gretchen

Carlson publicly outed Fox News and #MeToo put on blast the misconduct of many, numerous companies knowingly and unapologetically harbored harassholes for decades, paying them big bucks while paying out big settlements. Corporate America intentionally elevated harassholes over profits while good talent suffered because nearly all of those suffering were women. These companies didn't value women in the workplace—rather, they valued the clout they got from *appearing* to value women in the workplace. When their duplicity became public, their reputations took a hit that materialized on Wall Street and Main Street as stocks dropped and advertisers boycotted. With the advent of social media and change in times, women have options and they're no longer staying silent. Yet so many employers will still harbor or hire harassholes—that is, until the public finds out.

⬆ HEADS-UP!

As often as they like to use the "bad apple" excuse, companies love to feign ignorance when it comes to sexual harassment. But don't be fooled. They're *never* in the dark. Per research studies, it's nearly guaranteed that those on the inside know about their harasshole problem.[13]

Case in point: Remember *Today* host Ann Curry, who left NBC in 2012 purportedly because she didn't get along with cohost Matt Lauer? According to a 2018 piece in the *Washington Post* (Sarah Ellison), before leaving the network in 2012, Curry told two members of NBC management that a young staffer said she was "physically sexually harassed" by Lauer, yet management did nothing other than silence Curry with an NDA and send her on her way. That was *five years* before NBC finally fired Lauer in 2017, based on what the network said was the first and only complaint it ever received about its star host. That complaint, which Lauer vehemently denied and NBC supposedly spent just one day investigating, was made by a young staffer named Brooke Nevils. And even after *Variety* published a litany of other sexual harassment complaints against Lauer that same day he was fired, NBC

> maintained that it was completely clueless about the predatory nature of the man it paid more than $20 million a year. Riiiiight . . . It takes a village to cover up sexual harassment, but it takes some real fucking gall for NBC to say it didn't know.

You can see why companies elect to have Adam from accounting watch an ineffective sexual harassment video and run amok instead of spending the money to effectively educate him and actually enforce anti-harassment policies. Businesses will *never* admit this though. It's safe to say some companies are making a *conscious* decision to invest in office-wide Thirsty Thursdays rather than proactively creating a safe workplace.

WHAT COULD SEXUAL HARASSMENT COST YOU?

No matter what industry you're in, sexual harassment is costly to all exposed. In addition to the stress and psychological toll that we'll discuss in chapter 9, sexual harassment has professional and financial costs that impact both targets and bystanders. These costs can be felt immediately or over time. Either way, they're not good.

When it comes to professional consequences, here are some of the typical costs:

Reduced	Increased
Job satisfaction	Coworker conflict
Commitment	Absenteeism
Performance	Tardiness
Productivity	Neglect

These professional consequences can make *you* look bad by giving the impression that you're a difficult, unproductive, or unreliable employee, when in fact, you're really just trying to survive a psychologically and possibly physically detrimental experience while tending to your work obligations. This can make it challenging to advance in your career and keep your networks open. Said another way, sexual harassment can tank your entire professional brand.

As for financial costs, exposure to sexual harassment makes you more likely to use sick leave or vacation time to avoid being at the workplace. You're also more likely to prematurely leave your job, which sociologist Heather McLaughlin, PhD, says can have an adverse impact on your long-term career trajectory, particularly if you're a woman in your late twenties and early thirties.

In the 2017 research report "The Economic and Career Effects of Sexual Harassment on Working Women," Dr. McLaughlin explains how sexual harassment knocks women targets *and* bystanders off course during a formative time in their careers in a way it does not impact men. While men are likely to remain in high-paying jobs after their professional climb is disrupted, women are often held back, ultimately suffering long-term economic injury upon leaving a sexual harassment situation. Eight in ten women who are sexually harassed leave their employers within two years of the initial harassment, and they're more likely than men to suffer greater financial stress in the twenty-four months that follow, as they become more likely to accept lower-paying jobs or avoid their preferred industry out of fear of further harassment.[14] Dr. McLaughlin finds that this unfortunate outcome occurs regardless of whether the woman is in a white-, pink-, or blue-collar profession.

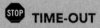

TIME-OUT

People who work with harassholes also suffer financial consequences when allegations of misconduct make their way into the media. Case in point: Do you remember the 2017 dramedy *I Love You, Daddy* with an all-star supporting cast that included Chloë Grace Moretz, John Malkovich, Rose Byrne, Charlie Day, Edie Falco, and Helen Hunt? Probably not—because a week before the film was to be released in theaters, the entire movie was canned. Why? Well, the film's lead actor, producer, screenwriter, *and* editor was comedian Louis CK, who had *just* been exposed for exposing himself regularly to women in his industry, among other things.

I Love You, Daddy banked zero dollars at the box office, and the film seems to be somewhat of a stain on the résumé of its accomplished cast. Moretz told the *New York Times* in August 2018 that she would prefer the movie "just kind of go away," and Byrne publicly supported the women who came out against her producer and costar Louis CK. The cast undoubtedly lost a fair amount in a film in which they made a considerable investment.

Award-winning actress and Dame Emma Thompson avoided the same fate in early 2019 when she pulled out of the animated movie *Luck* because Skydance Animation hired filmmaker John Lasseter, who was on a leave of absence from Pixar and Walt Disney Animation Studios due to decades of sexual harassment allegations against him that had become publicly known. Thompson passed on a paycheck that could have cost her more in the long run.

The lesson: Be smart. Know who you're working with. Don't look the other way. And don't do business with known harassholes. It will only cost you in the end.

After unexpectedly being forced out of a toxic workplace, I stayed away from the practice of law for a solid six months because I was afraid of further sexual harassment in my beloved industry. With two advanced degrees in tow, I dabbled in bartending craft cocktails and took a job as a hostess at one of LA's hottest restaurants, dealing with occasional drunk folk and burning through my savings until I was mentally prepared to practice law again. When I did join a new law firm, I started at a lower salary than my counterparts, likely given my time away from the practice and the then-depressed state of the economy. Either way, it wasn't awesome for me or my IRA.

Indeed, a sudden job change not only stifles your professional trajectory but may also lead to stretches of unemployment, financial stress, inferior job opportunities, lower earnings, and increased debt. These consequences can easily derail your long-term career potential, making financial stability and retirement far more challenging.

Ultimately, the consequences of sexual harassment put women exactly where harassholes want them to be—economically insecure and out of the workplace.

REPLAY

* Sexual harassment can cost you and your employer a considerable amount. Unfortunately, most employers often do not seriously invest in prevention methods that work.

* Although they tend to be more productive than average, toxic workers are problematic for net profitability, because they increase costs associated with employee turnover, lost productivity, regulatory fines, legal fees, settlements and jury awards, insurance premiums, reputational harm, and more. Employers who hold on to harassholes despite these financial costs are *not* in the business of making money.

* Despite the costs, companies hold on to harassholes because employers are practically incentivized to do so, most company leaders are men who happen to benefit from maintaining the status quo, and companies arrogantly think the public won't find out they're really not here for women in the workplace.

* Sexual harassment can adversely impact workplace performance and relationships with colleagues, harming your professional reputation, ability to advance, and access to important networks, among other things.

* Sexual harassment also can stifle your long-term career trajectory by forcing you to leave an employer, resulting in stretches of unemployment, financial stress, inferior job opportunities, lower earnings, and increased debt.

CHAPTER 7

Keeping Receipts

Documenting Sexual Harassment, Preserving Evidence, and Building a Record

People are afraid to be themselves because people are afraid to be recorded.

—Cardi B, elite rapper and Bronx-built bad bitch

IF HARASSHOLES KNEW they were being video and audio recorded, what are the chances they would harass? Probably slim to psychopath. You may not always be able to record a harasshole in action, but you should keep good receipts nonetheless. Documentation is an essential precaution, as no one ever expects to end up fighting their employer. I never did. Lara Carlson likely didn't either.

Carlson, an award-winning physiology professor at the University of New England, was on track for tenure and a rising star in 2011. Then Paul Visich was hired as chair of the Exercise and Sport Performance department. He was tasked with supervising Carlson's research, something that should've been smooth sailing given her accomplished track record. It turned out to be treacherous waters.

Shortly after he joined the university, Visich started sending Carlson inappropriate emails. The married department chair would make sexualized statements, such as, "I am home in my PJs sipping tea and watching porn!" and "[Your husband] told me he was shopping the other day and got you some real sexy panties, what a man!" He didn't stop at just talk. Carlson says Visich also put his hands on her legs during meetings and ogled her breasts. She started avoiding being alone with him after he forcefully grabbed her by her upper arm. Carlson wasn't the only woman Visich made uncomfortable.

He reportedly targeted female students too, once telling them to pack color-ful bras for a class field trip, and he took shirtless photos with the under-grads.

Given his authority over her, Carlson was reluctant to call out Visich directly, so she followed university protocol and called HR. She also sent HR copies of his emails in an organized binder before meeting with their officials on November 20, 2012.

On that day, she sat down with HR director Sharen Beaulieu and interim dean Timothy Ford, who Carlson said both acknowledged that Visich's be-havior was sexual harassment. Yet, instead of discussing how his behavior would be corrected, they ambushed her. Before Carlson knew it, Visich was in the room. She felt shock and betrayal as she learned HR never called the meeting but merely functioned as a conduit for Visich, who arranged for the four to meet *after* HR warned him that Carlson sought to file a complaint about his behavior.

Visich, the HR director, and the interim dean refused to even acknowl-edge or look at the emails, Carlson said. Rather, *his* concerns about *her* be-havior dominated the conversation. Carlson was told she had "to figure out a way to make this work," insisting she improve her "communication" and be a better "team player." She left the meeting feeling defeated, as Visich re-mained her supervisor. He would go on to rate her poorly on her next review, hurting her chances at tenure. But like the bad bawse that she is, Carlson went on to file a federal lawsuit in which she provided copies of Visich's emails, his shady performance review, *and* audio recordings of that Novem-ber 2012 meeting.[1]

As Carlson's situation demonstrates, keeping receipts on sexual harass-ment is about staying one step ahead of harassholes and heinous employers. This may include maintaining documents, emails, text messages, social me-dia posts, recordings, and more. In this chapter, you'll learn not only why you need to document and how to do it successfully but also tips and tricks for stealth follow-ups and recording conversations. Keeping receipts helps ensure your experience is backed up by more than your memory, and your recollection is bolstered by more than your word.

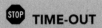 **TIME-OUT**

You could be scared to document for fear of what others may think about it. But who cares what others think? Others don't have to endure degrading behavior and pay your bills. *And* others damn sure don't need to know you're documenting sexual harassment.

Documentation is something you do for *you* and *your* professional well-being and future. It doesn't require anyone's approval or judgment.

If someone later learns you've been documenting behavior and isn't pleased about it, take that as a red flag. As Cardi B intimated, the person's salty likely because they're afraid to be held accountable for their behavior. That's a *them* issue. Not a *you* issue. Keep it moving.

WHY DO YOU KEEP RECEIPTS?

Let me be straight with you: You need to document sexual harassment for four reasons that may sound harsh but are reflective of reality.

First, documentation is necessary for monitoring harassholes. You'll see if certain behavior is repetitive or follows a pattern, which can tell you when the misconduct is likely to reoccur and whether it's escalating. Staying abreast of what threatens your professional and personal well-being can be helpful in getting out in front of harassment so that the harasshole doesn't take it to the next level. Safety first!

⬆ **HEADS-UP!**

When the first inappropriate comment is uttered or contact is made, we want to think it's a one-off and hope to forget about it. With harassholes, however, it *is* just the beginning.

Sexual harassment is never a one-off. It's a behavioral practice used to marginalize you in the workplace so that you play small or quit. That behavior will not change on its own. So as soon as that first instance occurs, be sure to document, document, document.

Second, when it comes to holding men accountable for sexual misconduct, a woman's word alone doesn't hold much weight in this world. As you may know, our society clings to an institutionalized and unfounded distrust of a woman's account of events as one of the many means of maintaining the power imbalances that favor men. We see that in how hordes of women must come forward against *one* man in order for society to even *question* his conduct. It took more than fifteen women to get former CEO Les Moonves moved out of office, and some CBS board members reportedly *still* didn't want to remove him regardless of whether the allegations were true. Although more than sixty women have accused President Donald Trump of sexual misconduct, those accusations didn't keep him from office. So, while your word may be good enough for me and your mom, our society is set up to doubt it. That's why you document, document, document.

Third, documenting sexual harassment is a must because recall can be flawed and memories faulty. Recollection fades over time, especially when the event involves something you may not have fully appreciated at the time or that involves trauma you'd rather forget. Sure, sometimes trauma etches memories into our minds, as it did for Dr. Christine Blasey Ford, who testified before Congress in 2018 about her memories of being attacked by then Supreme Court nominee Brett Kavanaugh. Even so, trauma may also encourage the mind to erase memories. All said, hard evidence corroborating our memories is more reliable and less likely to be questioned because it cannot be easily changed.

The fourth reason you should document is that you never know when things could go south with your employer. You may be the prized employee one day and the adversary the next. While working for a company, I saw a talented and well-liked woman go from being their "it girl," loved, well-paid, and praised for years, to being laid off in the cruelest of ways like she didn't even matter—simply because she objected to apparent pregnancy discrimination. Things can change and change quickly. You can't rely on your employer to provide documentation of other employees' misconduct or your good deeds.

In that same vein, we document sexual harassment because employers and harassholes may destroy or manipulate evidence. This is especially likely if your situation goes legal or involves a big name. The two law firms CBS hired to investigate Moonves found that the former CEO destroyed evidence in efforts to thwart detection. This isn't shocking, as manipulating evidence happens all the time and, as you'll read in chapter 13, it happened to me.

These people won't lift a finger to stop sexual harassment, but they'll move mountains to cover it up. Don't give them room to lie. Document. Document. Document.

WHAT TO DOCUMENT

Think about what it's like to write a screenplay for a movie. You'd need to map out a narrative description of the events, background, dialogue, and all other details to help clearly set the scene for the audience, right? *That* is the level of detail you should be documenting sexual harassment—the who, what, when, where, and how, with as much specificity as possible.

> ### 🛑 TIME-OUT
>
> Whenever you're documenting sexual harassment, stick to the facts. Keep it dry and opinion-free. Someone may be reading your notes in the future. The last thing you want is to make it look like you're rivaling J. K. Rowling as opposed to providing a neutral recounting of the facts. On that same note . . . Never lie. Your employer may be trash incarnate, but never lower yourself to lie. The truth always comes out. Believe me.

For example, let's say at the monthly meeting Mark from marketing ranted about how having a vagina got you the job. At a minimum, you should document the following:

- Date, time, and location of the meeting
- Full names and titles of Mark and the other attendees
- Where each person sat in the room (including anyone who witnessed his behavior and/or talked to you about it—in the latter case, include what they said)
- What Mark did and said, down to the most minute detail
- How you responded, how anyone else responded, and how it made you feel

If you're unsure of whether an experience *should* be documented, here are two tips to help guide you.

Tip #1: Trust Your Instincts. Document anything that instinctively makes *you* uneasy in any way. Pay attention to how a comment, photo, question, or look makes you feel. Were you offended by a colleague's email? Was there no way your supervisor was looking at your necklace because you weren't wearing one? Trust your instincts. How someone "intended" something is not relevant. Do *not* try to talk yourself into minimizing the situation or thinking you must be misinterpreting things. If something inside tells you that an incident may be an issue or may *become* one, document, document, document.

Tip #2: Performance Issues. Document anything about your performance, *good or bad*. Once confronted with sexual harassment, employers in "retaliation mode" love to claim that you were a mediocre employee or poor performer and that you had issues. Believe me, I know. Professor Carlson also knows, as the University of New England made that reach about her (meanwhile she was out here being nominated for the 2018 National Strength and Conditioning Association Educator of the Year Award—*for the third consecutive year*). Indeed, employers always turn trifling, which is why you need to document everything over the course of your employment that is related to your performance. This includes feedback, performance reviews, recommendations, copies of your personnel file and reviews, awards, emails of praise, and so on. You also want to document any criticism, complaints, uncertainties about your abilities, or issues you may have while with the employer. Documenting the bad can be just as important as documenting the good, as employers will not hesitate to mischaracterize situations or blow them out of proportion to mask the retaliation. These people do not play fair, and they're not your friends. Be sure to document, document, document.

HOW DO YOU DOCUMENT?

Gathering evidence can be easy. Building a record on the sly, however, is more of an art. The former involves assembling evidence already in existence, such as copying the proverbial "smoking email." The latter requires seeking out evidence that doesn't exist yet, like sending a stealth follow-up email that gets your harasser to admit to his misconduct in writing. Both are key to documenting sexual harassment, so you're not left high and dry when the employer and harasshole start telling lies. Let's talk about the types of documentation you may encounter, need, or want in such cases.

Sexual Harassment and Performance Logs. A sexual harassment log and a performance log are basically workplace diaries that you keep in real time, or in as real a time as possible. But they're not basic at all. Anyone who takes their career seriously should be tracking both sexual harassment and performance, to keep a running account of what's going on.

A harassment log should include all types of harassment, both sexualized and gender-based, experienced by you and your coworkers. Other employees' experiences are very relevant to you as a bystander, as we'll discuss later in the book. A harassment log also is especially ideal for day-to-day gender harassment, like degrading remarks and threatening body language, as these things could be hard to recall at a later date because much has become normalized by our society. Ugh.

A performance log is for recording events that go to how you do your job, such as client feedback, annual reviews, team comments, times your supervisor spoke to your value, and so on. *Any* performance issue—good or bad—goes here!

Harassment Log	Performance Log
All types of harassment experienced by you and your coworkers	All positive, negative, or neutral comments about your work performance

Rule #1: Write *everything* in the appropriate log, even if you have the evidence in another form. For example, if a coworker sends you an offensive DM or your boss sends you a praiseworthy email, enter the details in your performance log (noting that there is other documentation) *and* save a copy of that DM or email for your personal files. By entering the details into the log, you're keeping a running account of the event, making an über-useful chronology, and creating a backup should the DM or email suddenly disappear.

Rule #2: Enter the events in the log as close to the time they occurred as possible—and don't forget to include the full date!

It may sound like a lot of work, but it doesn't have to be. Here are the steps for creating and maintaining stellar contemporaneous logs:

1. Using the security tips outlined in chapter 14, open an **encrypted** email account using ProtonMail or another provider. (Encryption is a nonnegotiable. Without it, your log might as well be posted in your office breakroom.)
2. Create a new email. Put "July '22—Sexual Harassment Log," "March '21—Workplace Performance Log," or something to that effect in the subject line so you can easily identify the log's contents.
3. In the body of the email, write that real-life screenplay! Using the advice in the previous section, detail the events surrounding the harassment or the commentary on your performance.
4. In the "To" line, address the email to that account (that is, email yourself), and then send the email, which should pop up in your inbox.
5. Create a specific folder in that email account and move the email from your inbox to its designated folder.
6. When the next incident occurs, go to that folder and reply to that same email detailing the latest sexual harassment or performance situation. Do this each time there's an event to document.

Voilà! You've got a contemporaneous log with time and date stamps that records key events and is accessible no matter where you are! If you find that your log is getting too long, you can always start a new email chain. If there's a document you mention in your log that day, you also can attach it, adding it to the record and keeping it all in one place. If you forget to record something, input it ASAP with as much detail as you remember, updating the information with an additional entry if something later comes to mind.

Contemporaneous logs are a simple yet extremely reliable way to document evidence. You'll thank me when you can cut and paste from a meticulously maintained log instead of having to go through your emails, Instagram feed, and all else to create a reliable timeline of events.

> ### ⌃≣ BONUS POINT
>
> A performance log is not only helpful if your employer later tries to say you were bad at your job but also extremely helpful to have during bonus and pay raise season, when some employers conveniently forget your many valued contributions over the course of the year.

Stealth Follow-Ups (SFU). Sexual harassment doesn't always happen in email, text, or writing; sometimes it's verbal or physical touch. When that's the case, in addition to documenting it to your sexual harassment log, you should go for a stealth follow-up—SFU. I'll explain with an experience . . .

A prominent businessman (let's call him "Jim") approached me after one of my speaking events, expressing interest in collaborating with me on a joint venture and offering to meet up in two weeks to discuss details when he would be visiting my city. I agreed and was pumped about the potential partnership. When the time came, I had heavily researched Jim and the company he had just sold, and I arrived at the restaurant on time, wearing strategically selected social-professional garb, 100 percent ready to talk research-backed facts and financials. Instead of the night ending on a handshake marking the creation of the next billion-dollar enterprise, it ended with a friend—who I had to call for backup—throwing a handsy Jim out of her car.

Although my friend is a respectable member of the U.S. Armed Forces and could've attested to Jim's sexual harassment that night, I decided to build a record just in case it became an issue later on. I pulled an SFU via text. It went something like this:

JIM: Thank you for meeting me for dinner last night. I had a great time!

ME: Really? So, you had a great time misleading me into thinking we were meeting to discuss a business venture only for you to come on to me, grab at my legs and private parts, speculate on my "pussy," and act up in such a way that I had to threaten to scream for the waiter to intervene if you didn't stop touching me? Wow. We have different definitions of a "great time." Take care.

JIM: (calls although I do not answer) Sorry about that. I had too much to drink. How about we work together on publishing an article?

ME: Yeah, sure. I get it. Thanks.

Jim and I never worked on that article, but I did get him to acknowledge his misconduct. Working with this caliber of man would have been a hazard, but I didn't need to make him my enemy—although I *did* need to document his actions just in case something went down at a later date. *That's* an SFU— it's where you initiate a written interaction to generate a response that will confirm what did or did not happen. It's the best way to handle a potential he said/she said situation by creating irrefutable evidence that your version of the events is the true and only version. Execute an SFU by simply following up in writing with the harasshole or employer, asking questions or attesting to facts in a way that would provoke a response. Audio or video recording also may be an option, should you confront them in person.

I once had a direct supervisor admit in writing and on an audio recording that my performance was spectacular and that my contract was not being renewed *solely* because of layoffs. *I knew* what was really going on, but I wasn't going to raise the issue of retaliation until *after* my supervisor admitted the truth—that I was a talented and devoted employee and that my performance had absolutely nothing to do with the reason I wasn't being retained. Why did I get that evidence before raising the issue of retaliation? Because 99.9 percent of the time, once you've called them out on their misconduct, employers *will* lie about your performance and about the events. And I was right: The first thing my former employer tried to do in legal proceedings was attack my performance. #Predictable

An SFU may come in handy if a colleague gets handsy and then tries to create a career-damaging narrative about you. In her first-person exclusive for *Vox*, journalist Laura McGann shared her account of being forcibly touched and kissed by *New York Times* reporter Glenn Thrush, who had sent her an empty apology the next day. McGann said her gut told her that Thrush was spreading a "rosy version" of their encounter when she saw him chatting up her male colleagues a few hours after emailing her.[2] McGann would've been well served to hit Thrush with an SFU, so she could combat his "rosy version" with the truth. Of course, hindsight's 20/20, and if harassholes and employers didn't lie so much, you wouldn't have to SFU.

Electronic Evidence. Whether dealing with emails or text messages, you may come across various types of evidence in electronic form that you may wish to document. Cybersecurity expert Satnam Singh Narang shares these four options for documenting electronic evidence:

1. *Saving.* If the option is available, the best choice is to save evidence on a personal thumb drive or external hard drive. This may help preserve any data stored about the evidence's creation and use, among other things.

2. *Forwarding.* Forwarding a copy of the evidence to yourself via encrypted email or text is also an option. While forwarding may remove data, such as email header info, it can be helpful if saving directly to a personal drive is not an option.

3. *Screengrab/PDF.* If neither saving nor forwarding is available, you can screengrab it on your phone or use a tool with a built-in screen capture function, or create a PDF. Be sure to include the email header if you opt to screengrab. Screengrabbing and creating PDFs can be helpful but are not preferred, given that the evidence will become detached from any originating data.

4. *Print.* If the evidence is connected to a printer, and none of the other options are available, print on! Just take note that hard copies require physical storage space, can be damaged or lost, and don't preserve originating data.

When looking at electronic evidence, consider which of these options are available to you and take advantage of the best one. You may even use all four options if you want a backup, as you can never really overdocument.

Regardless of the option(s) you choose, it's better to have something than nothing. Take all that you can get!

Video Recording. Social media shows us the power of visual evidence to exonerate and to condemn. With a few exceptions, most video recording is legal with or without the consent of the party you're recording. Also most public and many private places have signs indicating that video surveillance is ongoing, which usually serves as sufficient notice.

By virtue of the modern-day mobile phone, we all have video recording devices at our fingertips. If you can make it happen absent detection or otherwise, please do! It can be game-changing evidence to combat that near-guaranteed future lie.

Audio Recording. In-person audio recording raises more legal issues than video recording does but may still be a viable option for you depending on your state law. Some states require just one person being recorded (you) to consent, and other states require the consent of all parties being recorded. Some states will penalize you for recording without the required consent, and other states simply won't allow the recording to be used in a court of law—although it can always be used in the court of public opinion! The Digital Media Law Project keeps an updated list of each state's laws on audio recording.

↥ **HEADS-UP!**

When dealing with shady people, avoid phone conversations at all costs. Recording a call can be difficult, and the law varies from state to state on whether you need one-party or all-party consent to lawfully record phone calls.

Unless you're certain that you're in a one-party consent state *and* the caller is as well *and* you have the equipment to stealthily record the call, the best practice is simply to avoid taking the call.

Just send the call to voicemail. If you accidentally answer, tell the caller, "It's not a good time," and hang up. Then, text or email the person, explaining that it's best to correspond in writing. Also keep your phone records by taking a screenshot of the call to show the originating number, date, and length of call time. It's harder for a harasshole or employer to misrepresent what happened on the call, if you can show you didn't answer it or the call lasted no more than three seconds.

Notwithstanding the legal complexities, audio recording can be extremely beneficial when it comes to building a record. Just ask Professor Carlson! Plus, audio recording is a lot easier to do on the sly than video recording. When you're heading into a meeting or other engagement, here are the steps to getting decent audio of your harasshole and/or employer:

1. Put your phone on airplane mode.
2. Turn on the audio recording feature.
3. Turn the screen brightness down low.
4. Once you enter the room, place the phone near where you plan to record (without it looking suspect, of course).
5. With the mic facing the direction of the speaker you're recording, place the phone facedown on a desk, upward in a purse or pocket, or hold it in your hand.
6. When you're done recording, add the relevant details to the appropriate log and attach the audio file to the entry, in addition to saving the audio file in a secure place.

Those are six easy steps to building an audio record on the sly. Audio recording is what likely saved Professor Carlson's case, what reportedly got former Fox News anchor Gretchen Carlson a $20 million settlement and a vague public apology, and what you should have in your arsenal should your employer or harasser later deny the facts (as they likely will).

♪≡ BONUS POINT

As mentioned, an audio recording may not be admissible in a court of law, but it is always admissible in the court of public opinion! If you opt to go public, use the tips in chapter 13 to share your recording with a journalist you trust to tell your story.

If you're unsure of whether to audio record, always err on the side of recording. Also do not selectively record people based on gender or your history with that person. Just because the HR official is a woman or your supervisor has been super supportive for two years does not mean either of them wouldn't lie later on to save their jobs. I've foolishly thought otherwise before. Don't be a fool. It's better to have the audio record than not.

Witnesses. Witnesses can be an important part of documenting sexual harassment because they can offer a living testament of the events to corroborate your experience. But as with your own memory and biases, witnesses too can be limited in their ability to recall and in their interpretation of the events. For those reasons, you should approach witnesses based on their role as either a bystander or personal witness.

BYSTANDER WITNESSES. A bystander witness is someone with whom you have a professional relationship who was aware of the harassment. Because the bystander witness may not recall the incident years later or could be put in a "compromised" position (that is, being forced to choose between doing the ethical thing versus staying employed), your approach should be strategic and include an SFU.

Here's how to handle a bystander witness: After the incident, check in with him or her in person or by email to confirm that they too observed what occurred, their impression of the incident, and your respective feelings about it. Be sure to memorialize it in writing with an SFU, including as much detail as is appropriate for the communication method.

Email Example

Scott, I still can't believe Delaney said in front of everyone that I shouldn't be here because I'm a woman. It was demeaning and embarrassing. The fact that you heard it too and found it disrespectful tells me everyone at the meeting (McDougal, Johnson, Smith, Masterson) must have heard Delaney's comments too. I'm unsure of what to do at this point. Like I said when we spoke after the meeting, remarks like Delaney's are what make it hard to be the only woman in the office. But I'm here to do my best work and make a contribution. Your words of encouragement during our talk this afternoon make me feel less alone. Thanks for being there.—Robin

TEXT EXAMPLE

Thanks again for being there after Delaney's demeaning comments earlier today in the management meeting. I still can't believe he said I shouldn't be here because I'm a woman. But I'm grateful you thought Delaney was out of line too. You make me feel less alone. Tx for the support.

With this approach, you're able to memorialize the incident, its impact on you, and the bystander witness's impression at the time. Now you have hard documentation to corroborate your log entry!

BONUS POINT

Unless it would come off as weird, use last names in your follow-up because it'll make it easier to identify people at a later date. There are too many Johns, Michaels, and the like that can make it difficult to identify the attendee years down the line.

PERSONAL WITNESSES. Personal witnesses are those in your nonwork life. They may be close friends and family members you opened up to about the harassment. Their knowledge of the situation can be helpful should you later need someone to corroborate events and your feelings about them. You don't necessarily have to SFU with your personal witnesses, although you may do so inadvertently by way of everyday text messages and emails venting about what's going on in your life. Do bear in mind that personal witnesses are often seen as biased by outsiders, and they may have faulty recollection too. My mother, for example, has been along for the ride on a fair amount of the sexual harassment I've experienced in my work life. That doesn't mean she can recall each detail about every harasshole over two-plus decades, as she has a life too and other children to fuss over. In sum, personal witnesses are less likely to turn on you than are coworkers and companies, but personal witnesses may not recall everything. Proceed at your own risk! . . . Or document, document, document!

 TIME-OUT

Just as documentation can help you, it can be used against you. In fact, a number of men have tried to use friendly messages from women they allegedly harassed as evidence that they didn't harass them.

For example, when entrepreneur Laura Fitton accused venture capitalist Shervin Pishevar of trying to forcibly kiss her in a hotel elevator, Pishevar publicly flaunted kind cards she'd sent him as though it were exoneration. Roger Ailes and Bill O'Reilly did the same thing to former Fox News hosts Gretchen Carlson and Megyn Kelly. Earlier in my career, on the well-meaning advice of a female mentor, I played nice by buying a gift for a Flexor when he started messing up my future after I rejected him. Of course, all of these women and I were simply trying to preserve our careers, but our efforts were spun.

While you may fear alienating a harasshole could hurt your career, don't play into your fears. Err on the side of not offering unnecessary gestures of appreciation. Sending that thank-you card or going out of your way to buy a harasshole a gift won't make him respect you, your boundaries, or your contributions. All it does is give him leverage to try to later discredit you.

HOW TO KEEP DOCUMENTATION

What's the point of gathering a bunch of evidence if you ultimately lose it, right? Exactly. There's a right way to keep documentation, and following it is critical. There also are precautions you should take so as not to give your employer documentation to use against *you*. Here are some nifty notes with dos and don'ts from our cybersecurity expert, Narang, and me.

Electronic Storage. Store electronic evidence, including your contemporaneous logs, on your *personal* computer. *Never* keep any of that data on your employer-issued computer and device. The last thing you want is for your employer to go through your workplace logs or for the evidence to become their property. If possible, back up *all* electronic evidence on an external hard drive or thumb drive. You never know when your laptop could crash or be stolen or your cloud hacked. Have your back with a backup.

Hard-Copy Evidence. Store hard-copy evidence in an organized file away from the office, at home. Any evidence you have in hard copy needs to be in electronic format too. Consider creating PDF copies. If that's not feasible, consider taking a picture of the evidence using your phone. Regardless of which way you go, having a backup of hard copies is imperative, as the ink in documents fades over time, and paper copies are easy to destroy or lose. Have a backup.

Private Phone Calls and Conversations. If you're ever discussing your game plan for beating sexual harassment, do it away from the workplace on your personal time and on your personal device, without your employer-issued phone or computer in the room. It's the twenty-first century. Siri, Alexa, and a world of corruptible microphones are just inches away from the average American. Many employers can and do listen to calls and conversations on workplace premises, and some do elsewhere too. The legality of the matter is irrelevant when getting their hands on your evidence is their main concern. Be smart and box out.

⬆ **HEADS-UP!**

When it comes to sexual misconduct, the moment they see you as a threat, harassholes and employers *will* try to get a leg up on what information you have—and they'll do it by any means necessary.

After he went public about being groped by one of the founders of William Morris Endeavor, actor Terry Crews said his computer hard drive suddenly was hacked and his family was being followed. Actress and activist Rose McGowan reported that she had the same experience after she came out against producer Harvey Weinstein and began writing her memoir, *BRAVE*, exposing sexual misconduct in Hollywood. In 2017, former Fox host Andrea Tantaros accused the media conglomerate of listening to her cell phone calls and hacking her email after she reported sexual harassment by Ailes and O'Reilly. While my harassment complaint was pending before the EEOC, a series of disturbing events—all witnessed by third parties—led me to buy a burner phone. Then, after waking one morning to find several of my daily emails in my inbox had already been marked "Read," I had to move to an encrypted email account.

Our experiences could all be coincidental, sure—or they could be further evidence that harassholes and powerful entities will do what their resources allow them to get away with in their pursuit of covering up sexual harassment. Don't fall victim. Stay one step ahead. Chapter 14 teaches you how to protect yourself from digital surveillance and cyber warfare.

Email Exchanges. Like phone calls and in-person conversations, email exchanges about your strategy for handling a sexual harassment situation should be done over your personal encrypted email. *Never* email about your strategy using your work email or over your employer's email server; otherwise, you're just handing them your game plan. If you have access to your encrypted email through a phone app and happen to be at work, remember to log off of the employer-granted Wi-Fi before transmitting any information about your strategy.

Text Messages. When it comes to text messages, use the Signal app as your primary form of messaging because it offers complete encryption. iMessage and WhatsApp are solid alternatives, but bear in mind that Apple and Facebook can be subpoenaed to share metadata (who you messaged and when), and iMessages are encrypted only if the recipient is also using iMessage.

⬆️ HEADS-UP!

Given how common DMs and texts are, here are some tips on keeping good receipts on these platforms:

Screen Grabs. If a harasshole comes at you via text message or social media, screen grab everything for your records, ensuring that the phone number or social media handle is in frame. Wireless carriers and social media websites keep messages for a limited amount of time, so you may not be able to recover all data through the provider. That said, do *not* give in to the temptation to block the harasshole's messages, as you need to keep a record of the misconduct and to keep abreast of what the harasshole's doing. If receiving the messages becomes too much, silence/mute the harasshole and have a loved one review the messages to ensure you're not in imminent danger.

Read Receipts. When dealing with a harasshole, you should turn off your read receipts so he cannot see whether you've read his message. This can be helpful in terms of creating the space you need to deal with the harassment on your own terms.

HOW TO USE DOCUMENTATION

How you use documentation is all a matter of strategy that depends on what you wish to accomplish. Given that everyone's circumstances are different, here are three ground rules to help guide you in determining your strategy.

Rule #1: What documentation you have is your business. You may have documentation that the harasshole or your employer does not need to know you have. You don't have to show all or any of your cards. *You* get to decide what you plan to share with the employer and anyone else. Some-times a verbal accounting of the events or a description of the matter should suffice, and sometimes copies of emails and text messages are necessary. It may not be in your best interest to whip out an audio recording to prove you're telling the truth because some employers won't respond well to know-ing they're being held accountable for what they've said and thus have no room to lie. (It's funny how that works.) Decide wisely, but never feel pres-sured to put it all out there.

 TIME-OUT

Like in a lawsuit, some employers investigating a sexual harass-ment complaint require you to provide a certain amount of evi-dence to prove that sexual harassment occurred. This type of evidentiary standard is not required under the law; rather, it's something an employer creates for itself. If your employer has a standard that requires you to submit hard-copy evidence to prove the harassment, you should consider providing *some* documenta-tion other than your logs (as those are the equivalent of diaries). But even if you opt not to provide any documents, the law does require the employer at least investigate your complaint.

Rule #2: Keep the evidence to yourself if revealing it would do no good. Don't get me wrong: I'm not saying you shouldn't tell your employer about a harasshole's misconduct. I'm saying there are circumstances in which you may be better off withholding *the documentation* that supports your complaint until there's a more appropriate time.

Remember Professor Carlson's account of how the university's HR de-partment didn't give a damn about Visich's emails? The fact is that your em-ployer may unequivocally favor the harasshole, or it may have no intention of stopping the harassment, no matter the situation or the evidence. In such cases, you may wish to give them a verbal account but withhold your sup-porting documentation, as it would do no good to show them all of your cards—especially when they haven't asked for them.

When I complained to a former employer about an Ulterior Motive Mentor, for example, the HR director basically told me that the harasshole was her friend of twenty years and that I needed to "give him a chance." When I pushed back, the director then offered to review the harasshole's inappropriate text messages and photos that I'd already verbally described to her *and* two other company officials. Do you think I accepted her offer or shared anything else with her? No, I started audio recording conversations—regrettably far later than I should have.

Bottom line: There may be times when you're better off keeping quiet about what evidence you have, so you can use it as leverage in settlement negotiations, in the court of law, or in the court of public opinion.

Rule #3: Use your documentation to corroborate your account. You documented so that you would have a record of what occurred and be able to craft an airtight account and detailed timeline of the events. When it comes time to make a report to your employer or file a complaint in court, you should review the documentation to gather facts, dates, and details that bolster your report or complaint. You shouldn't necessarily attach the actual documentation but should use your best judgment based on Rules 1 and 2.

REPLAY

* Documentation is essential. It's something you do for *you* and *your* professional well-being and future. You don't need anyone's permission, approval, or judgment.

* You need to document, document, document because words are weak, memories fail, harassers must be monitored, and evidence gets destroyed. Need I also say it? Harassholes and employers will deny, deny, deny, and lie, lie, lie.

* With as much specificity as possible, document the who, what, when, where, and how about anything that instinctively makes you feel uneasy, as well as both positive and negative comments about your work performance.

* Several methods of documentation are effective, including keeping a sexual harassment log and workplace performance log; saving,

forwarding, printing, and taking screenshots of electronic evidence; executing stealth follow-ups; making video and audio recordings; and corroborating witness accounts. Also, ensure you preserve all documentation correctly, which includes keeping backups.

* Using documentation is all a matter of strategy. Remember that what documentation you have is your business, you need not (and may not want to) share with your employer or others the extent of your documentation unless it would be helpful, and it is important to review your documentation before filing a formal report with your employer or filing a legal complaint.

CHAPTER 8

Responses and Reporting

How Sexual Harassment Gets Handled

Upper management told me that he "was a high performer" ... and they wouldn't feel comfortable punishing him for what was probably just an innocent mistake on his part.

—Susan Fowler, tech industry game-changer and
Uber sexual harassment exposer

AFTER SHE REPORTED her new male boss Paul Evans to HR, Luisa Santana said she was told by a supervisor in the department that she needed to "learn to get along" with her fellow executives. Santana knew how to work with others in the C-suite. With more than three decades of experience in their industry, she had risen to vice president in the entertainment group at Marsh & McLennan Companies, the nation's largest insurer. But executive status didn't insulate her sexual harassment. She said Evans harassed her openly, both in sexual and hostile ways. According to Santana, Evans would comment on her breasts in front of other coworkers, opining aloud that she wore a DD cup. She also recalls how her boss falsely suggested that she was sleeping with their colleagues and used hand gestures to fake the act of fellatio in mockery of her—all in the presence of their staff. Evans referred to her as "Brown people," a "wetback," and "Mexican," she said, in addition to telling her, "You're only here because of affirmative action." Santana said she continued to complain to HR, and as she attests, another official responded by telling her that Evans was not "that bad" and tried to offer her solace by saying, "We can fix him." Nothing changed, Santana said, and HR did nothing to investigate until three other employees also came forward. Ultimately, Santana took unpaid medical leave after being diagnosed with post-traumatic stress disorder.[1]

Customer service agent Ashley Alford followed her employer Aaron's procedures when reporting Richard Moore, her store manager. The young employee received no response. According to Alford, in addition to demanding sexual favors in exchange for basic employee benefits, Moore would grope her breasts, jam his thumb between her butt cheeks, and comment on her looks while the other employees jeered. She said she repeatedly complained to her direct supervisor and called the furniture retailer's HR hotline—all to no avail. Her mother even called the hotline once on her behalf.

Around Alford's one-year anniversary with the company, things escalated. She says Moore grabbed her ponytail while she was seated, pulled out his penis, and hit her in the face with it. She complained again, yet nothing was done. Less than a month later, Moore reportedly cornered Alford in a back room, threw her to the floor, yanked up her blouse, pulled down his pants, and masturbated before ejaculating on her. This time Alford called the police. Only then—in response to a police investigator—did someone from Aaron's HR department come to the store to look into her harassment claim.[2]

I wish I could tell you that Santana's and Alford's respective employers' alleged failure to respond to their reports were a rarity. But I cannot. They'd be like most all employers—they had anti–sexual harassment policies and reporting procedures in place, but reportedly failed to abide by them. As aptly stated by Lauren B. Edelman, a professor and author of *Working Law: Courts, Corporations, and Symbolic Civil Rights*, "Sexual harassment policies and procedures can comfortably coexist in organizational cultures where women are regularly subjected to demeaning commentary, unwanted physical contact, and even threats or sexual assault."[3]

Policies and reporting procedures are important, but enforcing them is critical. While we have no control over whether employers actually enforce sexual harassment policies, we can talk about the legitimacy of those policies and procedures. In this chapter, we do just that, after addressing how individuals typically respond to sexual harassment, problematic responses from employers, and questions you should consider before filing a formal report. This chapter isn't fun, but it is fact.

HOW YOU RESPOND TO SEXUAL HARASSMENT

"Why didn't she just confront him? I would've done that!" People sure like to talk a good game when it comes to how they *would* respond to sexual harassment if *they* were in *your* shoes. Those fancifully distorted, self-inflated assumptions are as accurate as the presidential polls going into the 2016 election. Regardless of conjecture, everyone responds differently to high-stress situations, like sexual harassment, based on a host of factors that hinge on individual personality and external circumstances. How you feel in response to sexual harassment is unique to *you*. You are entitled to those feelings. Never feel ashamed or as though you must justify your response. Nor should you ever make someone else feel that way for their response. You don't know their background and past experiences. No one just shows up to a job baggage-free, devoid of history. A woman who's been abused, for example, may be triggered when someone crowds her space, or an older colleague may feel insulted when younger team members call her "betch." No matter the circumstance, we're all entitled to our own feelings when it comes to sexual harassment. Our feelings are manifestations of our instincts. We need to trust them. They're part of the process!

Let's talk about how people typically respond to sexual harassment and some of the factors that impact those responses.

The Range of Responses

From freezing up to formally complaining, there are a range of responses to sexual harassment. Responding is not so much a single act but a process, a series of acts. Here's the typical response process for most people:

TYPICAL RESPONSE PROCESS

Ignore ➔ Avoid ➔ Self-help ➔ Tell family/friends ➔ Tell coworkers ➔ Tell supervisors ➔ Contact attorney/government agency

Where you start in that process is an individual decision you make based on the type of harassment, surrounding circumstances, and your comfort level. You're entitled to respond in a way that makes you comfortable. You need not wait to be touched or for someone to get up in your face before you call them out or contact authorities, if need be. Respond as you see fit. (Of course, I'm not suggesting your coworker should catch hands for mocking #MeToo. I think you get what I mean.)

To give you an idea of how people respond, let's look at the range of common responses, which we can separate into three different categories: nonresponses, informal, and formal. Here are examples:[4]

Nonresponses	Informal Responses	Formal Responses
▪ Deny or downplay	▪ Confront harasser (in	▪ File a report with
▪ Ignore it	person or in writing)	employer
▪ Play dumb	▪ Threaten to tell	▪ File a complaint with
▪ Walk away	others	the EEOC (or state
▪ Avoid the harasser	▪ Seek bystander help	agency)
▪ Leave position/job	▪ Use humor/sarcasm	

Typically, the more severe the harassment (for example, sexual touching or propositioning), the more formal the response. That's not a hard-and-fast rule, however, as there may be other factors at play. For instance, if the behavior isn't severe but is reoccurring and offensive like sexist microaggressions, you may decide to stop ignoring it and go directly to filing a formal complaint. You get to decide what response is right for you based on your circumstances.

Nonresponses. The most common responses to sexual harassment are nonresponses, such as freezing up, giggling, walking away, conscious denial, and leaving the job.[5] Oftentimes, those using nonresponses know that they don't like the behavior but don't recognize the experience as "sexual harassment," instead coping by denial, downplaying, or simply tolerating the behavior. Trying to avoid a harasshole entirely isn't uncommon either. One of the dancers who reportedly worked with the opera icon Plácido Domingo (Jocelyn Gecker, AP News) called her technique "the bob and weave, the giggle and get out."[6] Who hasn't actively dodged *that person* at work with the creepy come-ons or insulting overtures?

Informal Responses. Informal responses include confronting the accuser, threatening to tell others, seeking a bystander to help, and using humor or sarcasm to indirectly address the offensive behavior.

Despite popular belief, confronting the harasser is extremely uncommon. Some suspect it's because women are afraid a harasshole will respond with a physical threat. While fear of violence may be a valid concern, this isn't the only reason why women avoid confrontation. Some women fear professional repercussions—Michelle Blanchard among them.

Blanchard, who portrays the Dagger on Women of Wrestling (WOW), an LA-based professional wrestling outfit co-owned by Lakers' owner Jeanie Buss, has *no* reason to fear physical threat from any man. Despite her sleek and stunning appearance, Blanchard is an accomplished mixed-martial arts fighter and trained Muay Thai kickboxer who also happens to be a competitive sharpshooter and tactical knives expert—and she's super nice too! (Read: Blanchard is *that* bitch, and we love it!) When it comes to fighting sexual harassment, she says she uses humor or sarcasm as her first line of defense, despite having no issue with direct confrontation that might escalate into a physical threat. Blanchard simply avoids directly checking harassholes because it could hurt her professionally. The accomplished everywoman and walking deadly weapon is not trying to do that.

Blanchard makes a good point with the comedic approach. I've directly confronted male colleagues about their inappropriate behavior, only to have them block me from future professional opportunities. Even so, I have no regrets. The appropriate response to sexual harassment is a personal decision for each individual to make for themselves. You may be quick-witted like Blanchard, or have a lethal tongue like me, or neither. Do what works for you.

🛑 TIME-OUT

Although confronting harassholes is not a common approach, it could be helpful not only in terms of stopping the behavior but also in documenting it. From least to most aggressive, here are some options for confronting a harasshole (which may be best done in writing or in person *and* followed up by an SFU).

ROUND 1

- "You may not mean any harm by it, but it makes me uncomfortable when you [behavior], like you did on [date]. I'd appreciate it if you would stop."
- "On [date], you [behavior]. This is not appropriate for the workplace. It also makes me uncomfortable. Will you please not do it again?"

ROUND 2

- "As we've discussed, it makes me uncomfortable when you [behavior], like you did on [date(s) and circumstance(s)]. I'm hoping we can resolve this without needing a third party to get involved. Please stop."
- "After I raised the issue on [date], I expected you to stop [behavior]. Yet your behavior continues to make me uncomfortable. On [date], you once again [behavior and circumstances]. Please stop."

ROUND 3

- "This is the third time I've asked you to stop harassing me. First, on [date] when you [behavior and circumstances]. Second, on [date] when you [behavior and circumstances]. And now third, when you [behavior and circumstances] on [date]. I'll have to file a formal complaint with management if you do not stop."
- "You have repeatedly ignored my requests to stop [behavior]. On [date(s)], you [behaviors and circumstances]. This is sexual harassment. It's offensive and degrading. I will report you to management and/or the EEOC if you do not stop now."[7]

Formal Responses. Formal responses involve bringing in a third party, such as making a report to management or filing a complaint with the EEOC.

Because a broader range of behavior is harassing to women, they're more likely than men to respond but are less likely to take the formal route unless the harassment is severe.[8] Unfortunately, that means women rarely ever report gender harassment. Men, however, are less likely than women to report harassment regardless of severity due to toxic masculinity and peer pressure.[9]

The stronger the company's stance against sexual harassment, and the more supportive your supervisor and colleagues, the more likely it is that you'll formally report sexual harassment.[10] This isn't surprising. A supportive supervisor wouldn't want you to suffer in silence, and a true team wouldn't want you to "take one for the team" by staying silent. In good companies, sexual harassment violates the written and unwritten rules defined by corporate culture—which starts at the top! I once worked at a law firm where my supervisor told me that the firm's chairman referred to me as "a hot piece of ass." After hearing that, do you think I reported to HR when my supervisor started coming on to me? Nope.

Formal reporting is the *rarest* of all response options among both men and women. Just an estimated 6 to 13 percent of employees formally report a harasshole to management, and most wait an average of sixteen months *after* the initial incident.[11] Typically, if an employee makes a formal report, it means all other avenues have been exhausted, or the harassment is severe, such as touching or sexual coercion. Even then, reporting rates remain low, as reports are made by only 8 percent of those physically touched and only 30 percent of those sexually coerced.[12] This is likely because formal reporting is risky. According to the *Harvard Business Review*, an employee who speaks up about sexual harassment is more likely to lose their job than one who stays silent.[13] (Harassholes know that.) In addition to retaliation, employees often fear not being believed, no action being taken, and ostracism from colleagues.[14] Those who are still brave enough to formally report are often left with a greater sense of organizational injustice, if not left unemployed altogether.[15]

Women's Responses to Severe Sexual Harassment

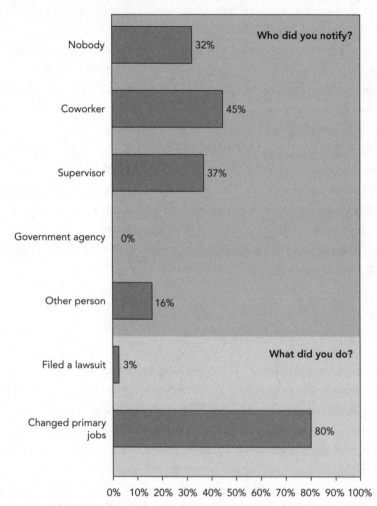

Ann Arbor, MI: Inter-University Consortium for Political and Social Research [distributor], 2015-12-18.

Ann Arbor, MI: Inter-University Consortium for Political and Social Research [distributor], 2015-12-18.

⅃ᗜ BONUS POINT

Spotting gender harassment can be difficult for many people because treating women as second-class citizens is ingrained into much of American culture. Think about it: How common are phrases like, "You play like a girl" and other gender-based insults?

If you're dealing with a colleague who's making gender-based slights and doesn't seem to fully appreciate the insult, here's one way you can help them see the offense: Ask your colleague if the comment would be offensive if it were made about a racial minority group. For example, if the colleague says to you, "Women aren't cerebral enough for that type of work," you could respond with, "I'm sure you didn't intend it this way, but that comment is offensive. What if you replaced the word 'women' with 'Blacks'— your comment would be insulting and racist, right? Hopefully, you can see why what you said is offensive and sexist."

Perhaps your colleague will apply that same logic before making gender-based remarks in the future.

HOW BYSTANDERS RESPOND

"Everybody fucking knew," Scott Rosenberg wrote in a Facebook post about his former boss Harvey Weinstein in the wake of the media mogul's undoing.[16] Bystanders aren't in the dark. Your colleagues know who the harassholes are. They just rarely do anything about it.

Women often don't speak up out of fear of harassment and awareness that they have less institutional power. Sociologist and sexual harassment researcher Dr. Heather McLaughlin says men often don't speak up about harassholes because they fear their own past behavior will be scrutinized. The mentality is, "If he goes down, I go down too." In fact, a 2019 online survey reported in the *Harvard Business Review* revealed that nearly half of the 1,100 men surveyed said they've done something in the past that today might be labeled as workplace sexual harassment or misconduct.[17] This self-preservation through silence must end. Mark Greene, author of *The Little #MeToo Book for Men*, explains why it's imperative that men use their male privilege to speak up when harassholes act up—regardless of whether women are present. Greene says:

Every male social space that exists has an impact on women's lives because our words as men go with us, change us, inform what we do next.

Our denigration of women, or our choice to remain silent when others do so, takes place in a world populated by the women and girls who must coexist with us, along with the words, ideas, and predators we grant refuge to.

Regardless of one's gender, bystander intervention can be one of the most powerful ways to shut down sexual harassment. Catalyst, a global nonprofit that advances women in the workplace, reminds us that bystanders can intervene using any of the four Ds:

- **Direct:** Directly confront the situation
- **Distract:** Create a distraction
- **Delegate:** Get help
- **Delay:** Touch base with the harassed later to offer emotional support or accompany her or him to make a formal report

Employers that invest in bystander training and incentivize employees to take action when they see sexual harassment are less likely to have a toxic work culture. If you're in a toxic workplace and don't feel comfortable intervening with the four Ds, consider other proactive steps you could take. For example, I worked at a company where many young women couldn't go to the workplace cafeteria without being preyed upon by harassholes who would lie in wait like vultures. Using their male privilege, some of my decent male coworkers proactively accompanied their female coworkers to the cafeteria as protective chaperones.

The little things you do can make a world of difference for a vulnerable coworker.

⭐ PLAYBOOK PRO TIP

As mentioned in chapter 3, the LGBTQ+ community is harassed at higher rates than other groups in the workplace and thus is in greater need for bystander assistance. Acclaimed diversity educator Scott Turner Schofield founded Speaking of Transgender, a consulting group that educates workplaces on trans-inclusivity and LGBTQ+ ally-ship. Schofield offers these five tips for those looking to up their LGBTQ+-ally game:

1. **Don't Ask.** A rando coworker asking you about your genitalia or sexual partners would definitely be disrespectful and invasive, right? Exactly. Be an ally and don't ask. You're not entitled to know about someone else's body or judge their private life. Just like you, your colleagues are there to work, not entertain inappropriate inquiries.

2. **Don't Assume, Educate Yourself.** Allies educate themselves. For general information about *something—not someone*, read a book or hit Wikipedia. Keep in mind that each individual is complex, making assumptions foolish. Do the work to overcome the oversimplification of humanity.

3. **Shut Down Gossip.** When someone starts talking about a trans person's body or a coworker's sexual interests, end the discussion immediately. Whether it's changing the subject or privately calling out the gossiper, be an ally and shut it down.

4. **Use Pronouns.** Misgendering and deadnaming (calling someone by a former name) is demeaning. It's not something to take lightly. If you hear either, immediately interject to correct a speaker using the wrong pronouns or name for an LGBTQ+ colleague. Also, put your pronouns on your email signature line to set the tone. Little things go a long way!

5. **Don't Sexualize or Accessorize.** Trans men and gay men are not somehow "safer men." So no, you don't get to flirt with them or befriend them as "safe space." Be an ally and don't sexually harass or use someone as an accessory.

HOW HARASSHOLES RESPOND

I'll just say it: Women lie about being sexually harassed by men as often as men tell the truth about sexually harassing women. Whether the accusations are levied by one woman, ten women, or ten thousand, a harasshole's go-to response is to deny, deny, deny. Do not take it personally. Do not be shocked. Just know a denial when you hear it.

From the passive-aggressive "I'm sorry she felt that way," to the egotistical "She's not my type," to the deflective "Social norms are changing," denials come in many forms, some more creative than others, but nearly all are insulting. Let's look at three entertaining "apologies" that came out of Hollywood in the three months after the #MeToo movement went mainstream.

First up, Kevin Spacey! The Oscar winner delivered a pathetic performance in October 2017, when actor Anthony Rapp told *BuzzFeed* (Adam B. Vary) that Spacey tried to pressure him into sex in 1986, when Rapp was just fourteen years old and Spacey was twenty-six. In his response, Spacey first claimed memory loss before asserting that *if* he did sexually assault his fellow actor, it would've been "deeply inappropriate drunken behavior" for which an apology *would* be necessary. Spacey then apologized *for Rapp's feelings*, before trying to change the subject by suddenly coming out of the closet as gay.[18] To call it a trash move would be kind.

About a month later, the *Hollywood Reporter* (Kim Masters) broke a story on John Lasseter, chief creative officer of Disney/Pixar, who gave us blockbuster films like *Frozen*.[19] Apparently, the then sixty-year-old, married Lasseter had a well-known reputation for grabbing and kissing women on the job and making inappropriate comments about their physique, so much so that, instead of checking Lasseter's misconduct, Disney/Pixar reportedly kept staff as "minders who were tasked with reining in his impulses." Upon being publicly exposed, in Lasseter's colorful mea culpa, he called his behavior "missteps" before telling his employees, "I deeply apologize if I have let you down." Does that "if" scream insincerity to you too?[20]

Lastly and possibly most appalling, we go to December 2017, when Mario Batali whipped up some real nonsense in responding to an *Eater New York* exposé (Irene Plagianos and Kitty Greenwald) that detailed decades of sexual misconduct allegations against the celebrity chef and cohost of ABC's

The Chew. Among the many allegations, Batali would reportedly grope employees' breasts and force them to straddle him.[21] How did the fifty-seven-year-old married father of two respond? By way of his weekly fan newsletter, in which he first apologized to his friends, fam, fans, and team—but not to any of the women who he reportedly assaulted and harassed. In fact he never even mentioned them or acknowledged their allegations. Instead, the Seattle-born Batali waxed poetic about the honor of cooking Italian food, promised to regain fans' trust, and then shared this gem: "ps. in case you're searching for a holiday-inspired breakfast, these Pizza Dough Cinnamon Rolls are a fan favorite," before inserting a link to the recipe.[22] FFS.

Why Harassholes Lie

Other than a desire to evade accountability, why do harassholes deny, deny, deny? Setting aside the possibility of a legitimate miscommunication and the ultra-rare false accusation, several things may be at play behind a harasshole's denial.

🛑 **TIME-OUT**

Although men are less likely than women to view certain behavior as harassing and could unknowingly engage in sexual harassment, it doesn't mean they're off the hook. We're well into the twenty-first century of a supposedly civilized society. If a harasshole can perform a job and take home a paycheck, he should know how to act appropriately in the workplace. There's also plenty of proof that harassholes know they're in the wrong. For example, the fact that a harasshole will lie about engaging in the behavior tells you he knows the score.

Not all harassholes run from accountability, however. Some get out in front of allegations with an apology, like *Supersize Me* director Morgan Spurlock. And others take full responsibility when confronted, like Barry Lubin, who played Grandma the Clown for nearly forty years with Big Apple Circus. Either way, a sincere and thoughtful apology can go a long way. It'd be good if more harassholes embraced accountability, even if they're all clowns.

Human Frailty. "Humans are wired for defensiveness," says Dr. Harriet Lerner, psychologist and author of *Why Won't You Apologize?: Healing Big Betrayals and Everyday Hurts.* This faulty wiring makes it hard for harassholes to admit fault for their behavior without blaming, making excuses, or muddling facts. According to Dr. Lerner, some men in the #MeToo era have put on a clinic in how *not* to apologize as they obfuscate and gaslight, as Disney's Lasseter did in his letter to Pixar staff. But we can't expect much from harassholes, especially when it comes to public apologies because they're simply a "performance" anyways. Dr. Lerner says, "It's an act of self-protection, an attempt to do damage control, to save one's reputation."[23]

Moral Licensing. Harassholes love moral licensing—that is, rationalizing behavior by thinking good deeds offset misdeeds, like when a harasshole thinks ruining your career with lies isn't a big deal because he buys jerseys for the local girls' soccer team or regularly visits his parents. Moral licensing is for punks. It's *not* how life works. Just because a man donates to causes that support women doesn't mean he should be absolved of sexual misconduct. Perhaps someone should've explained this to Weinstein before he tried to donate $5 million toward advancing women directors, thinking it'd sorta cancel out that whole "serial rapist" thing. Yeah? No.

Over-Perception Bias. A harasshole may deny sexual harassment accusations because his narcissistic mind-set actually thinks you liked him. Power can cloud someone's ability to appreciate another's perspective, making the powerful person more likely to think others are romantically interested in them when they're not. The *Harvard Business Review* says over-perception bias may partly explain why some harassholes underestimate how uncomfortable their unwanted sexual advances may make coworkers feel.[24] But that's a "harasshole" problem—not a "you" problem or a legitimate excuse. Harassholes are 100 percent responsible for checking their self-inflated egos at the door.

↥ **HEADS-UP!**

In a recent survey, the *Harvard Business Review* found that 65 percent of men think it's now "less safe" to mentor employees of the opposite sex since #MeToo. There's a lot to unpack there . . .

What kind of "mentorship" were they providing before #Me Too?! If these men don't know how to professionally interact with women *now*, there's a good chance they weren't acting professionally with women before—and you definitely don't want their advice. Also, as actor and everyman Idris Elba said, "#MeToo is only difficult if you're a man with something to hide." Perhaps that 65 percent of men need to draft their mea culpas, 'cause the past won't change and neither will 47 percent of the U.S. workforce (that is, women).

Fortunately, the decent men who were mentoring women *before* #MeToo are *still* mentoring women today. Those men who are unsure of whether they're acting appropriately won't alienate half the workforce but will invest in learning how to be a better colleague. There are decent male mentors out there. You can find one by having a candid conversation with a woman you admire and trust in your industry and who has similar characteristics as you. Ask who her male mentors have been and whether they're available. If she's worth being professionally prized, she won't lead you astray.

HOW THE PUBLIC RESPONDS

How the public responds to sexual harassment allegations varies depending on the parties involved and the evidence publicly known. All accusers generally receive the eye-roll-inducing *"Why didn't you just . . . ?"* conjecture, in addition to hurtful scrutiny. But women are treated far worse than men. Male accusers are publicly mocked for failing to fight the harassment in a way that aligns with toxic masculinity, but the criticism they face still tends to be less heinous than what women experience. For a woman accusing a man of sexual misconduct, the public response remains far more problematic for *her* than for *him* because she's effectively challenging the power structure that is the gender hierarchy. Unlike male accusers, women get inquiries into their appearance and are often accused of seeking money or fame. Women who speak out are often attacked, harassed, and threatened on social media, and accounts about them in the media may be skewed. Until we evolve as a society, the public will continue to doubt and ostracize the woman by default—all while giving the man the benefit of the doubt, which we see materialize in selective demands for due process and cries about *her* ruining *his* career.

What the Public Doesn't Know

The patriarchal bias is bullshit, but it's ever-present. As a member of the public, you too may find yourself playing into it. Don't get played, and don't play yourself. Here are a few things the public (and you) may want to keep in mind when sexual harassment allegations come out against men in power.

Play No. 1: Toxic Stars Are Virtually Untouchable. Under the language in almost all big employment contracts, employers can't fire a star without "cause"—a vague concept that is rarely defined by the employer. Because most sexual harassment is he said/she said, even good employers may struggle to amass sufficient evidence of "cause" to fire the star without facing a big lawsuit. Leveraging this little loophole, toxic stars are uniquely positioned to harass—and that's exactly what many of them do. Of course, there's a simple fix: In big contracts, employers could easily define "cause" to include specific forms of sexual harassment. But until that becomes the norm, toxic stars stay virtually untouchable.

👍 BONUS POINT

While things are a bit different for the common man who's an at-will employee without a secured contract, Everyday Joes accused of sexual harassment who don't get media attention still get a leg up over everyone else.

Even though they're not entitled to due process, these at-will employees on average get more due process in sexual harassment situations than they do when accused of theft, embezzlement, and other forms of workplace misconduct. Indeed, companies will fire a man on the spot when he's caught with his hand in the cash register, yet they'll give him a second chance when he's caught getting handsy with the intern.

Of course, due process and second chances aren't afforded to *every* common man. Research shows that companies may use sexual harassment allegations as a pretext for firing certain employees for discriminatory reasons, such as race or sexual orientation.[25] This puts men from marginalized groups in a tough position, as the allegation could stem from unfounded hypersexualized or aggressive stereotypes, which the employer may then seize as an opportunity to fire the man or to at least put him in his place.

Bottom line: If the public feels intent on advocating for due process, it should push for fair treatment of the everyman from marginalized groups, as he's more likely than toxic stars to be sexually harassed and to have sexual harassment weaponized against him.

Play No. 2: Toxic Stars Cash-In. These toxic stars also know they won't suffer when booted for sexual misconduct given their lucrative deals and payouts. For instance, Google reportedly agreed to pay two executives, Amit Singhal and Andy Rubin, a total of $135 million upon forcing them out when the public learned of the many credible complaints against them (Shannon Liao, *The Verge*).[26] But for the public outcry and shareholder class actions, Les Moonves (who was named Hollywood's highest-paid executive in 2017) would've walked away from CBS with a $120 million severance despite numerous allegations against him. The list is long, the denials plenty, and the public sympathy misplaced.

Play No. 3: Oodles of Undeserved Second Chances. What's also misplaced are public cries about women ruining a man's career, as most men rarely struggle to come back from sexual misconduct. Here are some examples: After Bernie Sanders reportedly fired him in January 2019 for allegedly kissing a subordinate and making crude sexual remarks, Robert Becker was hired that same year by Marianne Williamson to run her presidential campaign (Alex Thompson, *Politico*). On the eve of his antics becoming public in late 2017, Disney sent John Lasseter on a six-month paid "sabbatical" yet kept the *Frozen* filmmaker on the payroll through 2018, after which he was allowed to retire only to be quickly hired as an exec at Skydance Animation. After four women in media recounted sexual misconduct by journalist Glenn Thrush, the *New York Times* suspended its star White House correspondent without pay for some two months before simply reassigning him to another department as though problem solved! And my personal favorite: Eyal Gutentag! He was general manager of Uber's LA office until he reportedly forcibly groped the breasts and buttocks of a subordinate in front of multiple employees during a group outing. Four months later, in January 2016, Gutentag was hired by ride-hailing service HopSkipDrive as COO, only to hop on over to ZipRecruiter later that year in another executive spot, where he stayed until April 2019, when *BuzzFeed* put his misconduct on blast, after which he suddenly resigned (Davey Alba and Ryan Mac).[27] (To note: Between his hops, the married Gutentag started a foundation to give back to his community. Ahh . . . moral licensing much?)

Perhaps the public should cape for those who don't easily get second chances and *actually* suffer in sexual harassment situations—like the women and men who are harassed.

HOW EMPLOYERS RESPOND

In a perfect world, no employer tolerates sexual harassment, all complaints are swiftly and impartially investigated, all parties receive due process, and any misconduct is promptly and appropriately disciplined. Unfortunately, that's not the world we work in.

In our world, each employer responds to sexual harassment complaints differently, some better than others. Nearly all employers have some type of anti–sexual harassment policy, and a number offer related training—but not all (36 percent).[28] If employers do offer training, they're largely motivated because it may reduce their legal liability should they be sued. Not to be a buzzkill, but most employers are not seriously invested in doing anything about sexual harassment. We know this given its prevalence and the high rates of retaliation. Despite the many disappointments within our work world, let's talk about what you should expect from an employer in terms of complaint reporting and procedures, and potential problems that often arise in the process.

What You Should Expect

Not all employers have an HR department, but there are still a few things you should expect when reporting a sexual harassment complaint. Here are those baseline standards:

- Professional response upon receiving your complaint
- Appropriate questions geared toward gathering relevant information
- Prompt and fair investigation of your complaint
- Interviews of the harasser and any known witnesses
- Information about the outcome of the investigation
- If necessary, appropriate discipline of the harasser, such as oral or written warning, relocation, suspension, or firing
- No retaliation from your supervisor, harasser, or coworkers

Reporting Procedures and Handling Complaints

There's no uniform complaint procedure for sexual harassment. But many employers have recycled the same old-school approach for decades—and yes, this is despite advancements in research confirming what does and does not work. Those advancements have given us several informal yet effective new-school approaches that will hopefully gain traction in workplaces in the future. Before discussing the two approaches, I offer examples from my own experiences that may shed light on why reporting procedures are so important.

EXPERIENCE #1. While killing the game at one media company, I sat down with a supervisor I trusted and opened up about a high-level harasshole who had turned out to be an Ulterior Motive Mentor coming on to me and claiming to be dating me. That supervisor told me I had to use the company-mandated process to make a "formal complaint." In order to do so, I had to sit for an interview with a male HR screener whom I had never met or seen before. Several days later, I had to go to a different building to sit for yet another interview. This time the interview was with a female HR director, during which I learned that another woman had reported similar concerns with the harasshole just the year before. Days after that, I was asked to trek up to the office of a male HR director to sit for yet another interview. The formalized process was a dehumanizing waste of time meant to discourage me from ever complaining about sexual harassment again. I have few positive things to say about my time there. Shocker.

EXPERIENCE #2. While employed at an elite car dealership, a female co-worker and I walked over to our supervisor's cubicle and told her we wanted a rainmaking Shameless Dude to stop grinding up against us. (Remember the poor man's Marc Anthony?) After hearing our complaint, our supervisor simply walked across the showroom floor to the male sales manager and in so many words said, "Can you please tell Shameless Dude to stop touching the girls?" Without missing a beat, the sales manager summoned Shameless Dude via the PA system, and when he arrived, the sales manager unequivocally ordered, "Stop touching the girls!" Shameless Dude said, "Okay." We thanked the sales manager. Everyone dispersed. Problem solved. I think highly of that company to this very day. Not a shocker.

While these experiences involved two very different companies, both were male-dominated environments in traditionally male professions at high-level companies with anti–sexual harassment policies and training. In both cases, multiple women raised the same issue about a "superstar" harasshole with whom we would have to continue working. The media outlet's formal approach failed largely because it punished *me* for reporting the harasshole by putting me through a drawn-out and unnecessary process with people I neither knew nor trusted. The informal approach at the car dealer, on the other hand, was seamless, direct, and swift, making me feel comfortable and valued. Altogether, there was less perceived tolerance for sexual harassment at the car dealer than at the media outlet, which was evident in how each company handled the complaints. Now let's talk about the old- and new-school approaches to handling sexual harassment complaints.

Old-School Approach. The old-school approach touts a zero-tolerance sexual harassment policy. Employees must file a formal complaint, which could involve sitting for interviews with management and/or providing a written, signed statement outlining the allegations. After the official report is made, the employer decides whether the allegations amount to sexual harassment, and if so, the investigation begins. The harasser and any relevant witnesses are then notified and interviewed, and relevant evidence is collected. The employer may reinterview the complaining employee or invite her to submit any supporting evidence. After the investigation concludes, the employer decides whether the harasser violated the company's sexual harassment policies, and if so, whether and how the harasser should be reprimanded. Boring, aye? Sometimes employers using this old-school approach will try to appear progressive by throwing in a reporting hotline, like that helps.

The old-school process has some benefits, like allowing for greater accountability and corporate-sanctioned punishment, tracking repeat offenders, and a set structure. Then again, it also has significant drawbacks, namely, (1) it does *not* help reduce sexual harassment because all the redundant hurdles discourage people from ever reporting; (2) you may not want or need the harasshole to be formally punished if the harassment is minor and you're simply looking for the behavior to be nipped in the bud; and (3) the sterile formalities of the old-school approach are not conducive to employees raising sensitive and emotionally upsetting issues. Unfortunately, despite these and other known shortcomings, many employers still offer only the old-school approach for reporting sexual harassment.

New-School Approach. The new-school approach offers more options for how employees choose to report sexual harassment and for how their complaint is resolved. Generally, this progressive approach offers informal, formal, anonymous, *and* confidential reporting options. Here are a few examples taken from the *Harvard Business Review* and the 2018 sexual harassment solutions tool kit created by bipartisan think tank New America:

- Instead of zero-tolerance, there's a structured policy with responses that are appropriate for the problematic behavior, whether it be helping the parties maintain a professional working relationship or removing a predatory, serial harasser from the workplace.

- A confidential electronic reporting system that allows employees to request that the report be held until someone else also complains about the same person.
- Employees may report a complaint to any member of management with whom they're comfortable; the manager is then authorized to either informally address the matter with the harasser or to escalate it to designated personnel for investigation.
- Neutral third-party mediators are available to resolve issues between employees where professional and peaceful interaction is the goal, rather than punishment.
- A third-party entity or independent board is retained to investigate complaints, recommend action and punishment, and monitor retaliation in the aftermath.
- Before terminating an employee for sexual harassment, the labor union grievance seven-part test is applied to determine whether it would be appropriate.

The new-school approach helps employers identify and appropriately address harassholes hopefully before they hurt the employer's bottom line. It may require more of a financial investment on the front end, but the benefits employers will reap on the back end are immeasurable. It's all a matter of whether the company wants to invest in eliminating sexual harassment or in ol' boy getting his insecure rocks off.[29]

Other Potential Hurdles

Even if all the best policies and reporting procedures are in place, some employers are still trash. Just ask me. I know. Whether they're HR, supervisors, or colleagues, some individuals will actively try to discourage you from reporting sexual harassment or make you regret it. Here are some of their shady tactics to be on the lookout for, and options for how to handle them.

Disbelief. Many women don't report sexual harassment for fear of not being believed. Decent employers combat this by training report takers on how to show appropriate amounts of compassion and empathy. If the person taking your report lacks those skills or communicates that they don't believe you, do not be deterred. You know the truth, and no one can take that away. While you don't need someone to believe you, you do need someone who is open-minded and impartial. Consider requesting that someone else be assigned to take your report and investigate. If that's not an option, insist that your report be taken nonetheless. You may also have the option of going directly to the EEOC (or analogous state agency) to file a complaint.

⬆ **HEADS-UP!**

It takes a village to cover up sexual misconduct. In a 2016 study, researchers found that sexually harassed women frequently are told three things by managers, coworkers, and HR personnel looking to discourage the woman from reporting or pursing justice. So you can anticipate and avoid them, here's a summary of those reporting barriers and how they work.

1. **Prove the experience is uncommon and significant.** Third parties often try to normalize what a woman experienced by telling her it wasn't harassment and that she'd have to show it was rare and significant in order to file a complaint.
2. **Trust the system to resolve issues.** When a woman files a complaint, third parties often try to encourage her to be patient and allow the process to play out by pushing the "trust the system" rhetoric. It's a dead end.
3. **Suffer the consequences after challenging the system.** Coworkers often suggest a woman not complain about the harassment unless she's willing to face professional repercussions and social isolation.

If you ever hear anything along these lines from your managers, coworkers, or HR personnel, they're trying to shut you down. Stay focused. Persist.[30]

Dismissiveness. Employers summarily dismissing sexual harassment complaints also is a common issue that discourages reporting. When Susan Fowler complained about sexual harassment to Uber's HR department, the whistle-blowing engineer said she was met with indifference that got worse each time she raised an issue. Dismissiveness goes against any policy that promises complaints will be handled promptly and fairly. If your report is being ignored, consider insisting on speaking with someone else, submitting a detailed complaint in narrative letter format, or going to a government agency.

Retaliation. Retaliation is illegal—yet it happens in some three out of four reports of sexual harassment, where employees are demoted, given bad shifts, fired, sexually assaulted, or further harassed.[31] When it comes to handling retaliation, you should consider alerting management if you think it could be helpful, or go to the EEOC (or analogous state agency). Whatever you do, document, document, document any retaliation, just as you would sexual harassment, and definitely check out your legal options.

WHAT TO CONSIDER BEFORE MAKING A FORMAL REPORT

Now that you know the issues surrounding sexual harassment reporting, if you're considering filing a formal complaint, here are several questions you may wish to consider first:

1. Does the behavior violate the company policy, Title VII, or the law?
2. Has the behavior happened more than once? Is it egregious?
3. Unless you're uncomfortable, have you tried to resolve the situation informally?
4. What do you have documented? Is it a he said/she said situation?
5. How well-liked or successful is the harasshole? What about you?
6. Are you willing to leave this job if the behavior doesn't stop?
7. Are you willing to risk being forced out, isolated, or ostracized in order to make the behavior stop?
8. Are there any witnesses, bystanders, or other employees who are willing to take a stand with you?

9. Have other employees also had issues with similar behavior at the company? If yes, did they formally report, and if so, how were they treated?

10. Were you already planning to leave your employer soon?

These questions are important to consider given that employers are not on your side; they're on their own side (and possibly the side of the patriarchy too). Regardless of how you answer any of these questions, do what's best for you. You're entitled to proceed as you wish. You deserve to feel comfortable and safe in your workplace.

REPLAY

* Everyone responds differently to sexual harassment based on individual personality, history, and external circumstances. Never judge or condemn another's response. Never doubt your instincts or think you need to justify your feelings.

* There are three types of responses to sexual harassment: (1) Nonresponse; (2) Informal response; and (3) Formal response. Nonresponses are most common, and the informal response of confronting the accuser is the least.

* When confronted, harassholes typically deny, deny, deny because they're trying to evade accountability, are blatantly ignorant, use moral licensing, and/or are biased by ego.

* While harassed men who come forward face scrutiny, the public reserves much of its condemnation for harassed women who speak out. You can ignore the public outcry. Men receive far more due process when accused of sexual harassment than when accused of other forms of workplace misconduct. Toxic stars often enjoy hefty payouts to bolster their sizable paychecks and are also quick to get second chances.

* If you report sexual harassment to your employer, at the very least you should expect a professional response, appropriate questions geared toward fact gathering, a prompt and fair investigation,

interviews of the harasshole and any relevant witnesses, information about the outcome of the investigation, any appropriate discipline, and a retaliation-free aftermath.

* The old-school complaint-reporting process provides one formal channel of reporting (and maybe a hotline). The new-school approach, however, offers multiple reporting channels at varying levels of formality.

* Management and the HR department are in place to look out for the company's interests—not yours. You may encounter issues with reporting processes and barriers to reporting, but you should not let that stop you from standing up for yourself and your right to work in a harassment-free environment.

CHAPTER 9

The Stress and the Struggle

Understanding the Psychological Impact
of Sexual Harassment

....

Just because you can't see mental illness like you could see a broken
bone, doesn't mean it's not as detrimental or devastating to a family or
an individual.

—*Demi Lovato, empowering singer and devoted fighter*

NO MATTER WHO you are, sexual harassment can be harmful to your psychological well-being. Say that with me one more time: Sexual harassment
can be a mindfuck.

You could be the strongest, most resilient person you know.

It doesn't matter.

You could've saved a baby from a burning building or survived a week
without Wi-Fi.

It. Does. Not. Matter.

You may push through problems like Dwayne "the Rock" Johnson powers through push-ups with the added tenacity of Notorious RBG.

¡No es importa!

没关系

Ça n'a pas d'importance!

это не важно

Translation: Sexual harassment don't give a damn!

But what if you were never fondled, groped, or anything like that? Guess
what . . . It doesn't matter. You need not be touched or targeted to psychologically suffer. Enduring occasional demeaning comments, or even just ob-
serving offensive behavior as a bystander, is enough to adversely impact
your long-term mental health. Hundreds of studies confirm the fact that *no
one* escapes sexual harassment unscathed.

For some seventeen years, I lived by 30 at 9, 3 at 6, and 60, 2, and 1. That's thirty crunches at nine different angles at sunrise and bedtime (totaling 540), supplemented by three sets of six reps of leg lifts at six different angles at least once a day, sixty minutes of cardio at least three days a week—not including the two (three-mile minimum) outdoor runs—plus one day of rest for recovery, of course!

Over nearly two decades of my life, working out felt as good as bathing and as essential as breathing. Then, around the time I left a company under "litigious circumstances," my fanatical interest in fitness fell off. In truth, my interest in everything died. Basic things like washing my hair, changing my clothes, and going to the grocery store all seemed incredibly daunting. Anything but applesauce became impossible to stomach, as all else made me feel ill—like my throat was closing and my body didn't want food. My speech slowed to a stutter, as though my quick-witted, legally trained mind had become inoperable. Sleeping through the night became as rare as leaving the house. Adrienne Lawrence—a woman who was always known for her positivity, smile, and laughter—was now always on edge, triggered at every turn and snapping at everyone.

But *I* was *fine.* "Weak" wasn't a word I knew. How could it be? *I* was always everyone else's rock. *I* was the one with all the answers. All I needed were a few motivational books, some prayer, positivity, and a little enlightenment . . . so I told myself. But *I* didn't need a doctor's help or medication. *I knew me.* I could do this on my own.

I was wrong, very wrong.

Unfortunately, I only realized that after I plummeted from 127 pounds to 114 on a five-foot-seven frame; fought with nearly all of my close friends; fell for a manipulative divorcé with a "mild" drinking problem; jumped from a moving motorcycle; drunk dialed, tweeted, and texted; barfed in a Bank of America parking lot; and tattooed my cat's name on the back of my neck. I was a mess.

Mental health is important, which is why I'm covering the topic in two chapters. In this chapter, we talk about the psychological, emotional, and resulting physical impact that sexual harassment can have on you, and I share with you what to look out for. In chapter 10, I give you the keys to coping in a healthy way. These chapters can be heavy at times. But with a little humor and some unapologetic candor, we can get through it together.

HOW HEAVY IS IT?

Sexual harassment has a heinous impact on one's well-being because it puts stress on the system. It's not just crude, sexist, denigrating comments or unwanted physical contact that can create the stress but also your conscious efforts to avoid harassers, obsessing over the way you look in hopes he won't catcall you, ignoring side-eye and snide remarks, wondering how you'll make rent if you quit now, and so on. To get a sense of the level of stress sexual harassment brings, we look to how mental health professionals and researchers measure stress.

For more than a half century, mental health professionals have been measuring the amount of stress caused by major life events using the Social Readjustment Rating Scale. The scale assigns points to common life-changing events. Some of these milestones seem like causes for joy, like a vacation or personal achievement, but the body doesn't know that. To the body, any major life change—seemingly good or bad—is stress that can harm your health. The scale tells you how likely it is that your health will take a significant hit due to the stressful event.

The scale does have issues though—it isn't the be-all and end-all when it comes to measuring stress. Developed in 1967, when the voices of women were absent from much of clinical research, the scale omits major life events that overwhelmingly impact women, such as sexual harassment. You also won't see stressors that reflect our reality today, like going viral on social media or surviving a mass shooting. Even with its limitations, the scale still provides useful insight that can help us wrap our heads around why sexual harassment is so toxic to the mind and the body. *Ready to take the test?*

♫≡ BONUS POINT

According to the American Institute of Stress, more than 90 percent of your job-related stress comes from your relationships with your coworkers. Researchers have also confirmed that the higher the harasshole is on the food chain, the greater your stress likely will be, given his institutional power.[1]

The Stress Test

Here are the directions: Look at the major life events listed on the following pages. Each time an event has occurred in your life within the past year, or each time the event will occur in the near future, include that impact score in your total stress score. If your employer retaliates against you for reporting sexual harassment by firing you, you may need to relocate to find a new job, tacking on the stress of a move and possibly going into a different line of work. Workplace sexual harassment can cause a ripple effect of stress throughout every area of your life.

Major Life Event	Impact Score	Your Score
Death of spouse	100	
Divorce	73	
Marital separation	65	
Jail term	63	
Death of close family member	63	
Personal injury or illness	53	
Marriage	50	
Fired at work	47	
Marital reconciliation	45	
Retirement	45	
Change in health of family member	44	
Pregnancy	40	
Sex difficulties	39	
Gain of a new family member	39	
Business readjustment	39	
Change in financial state	38	
Death of a close friend	37	
Change to a different line of work	36	
Change in number of arguments with spouse	35	

Major Life Event	Impact Score	Your Score
Mortgage or loan over $151,363[2]	31	
Foreclosure of mortgage or loan	30	
Change in responsibilities at work	29	
Son or daughter leaving home	29	
Trouble with in-laws	29	
Outstanding personal achievement	28	
Spouse begins or stops work	26	
Begin or end school	26	
Change in living conditions	25	
Revisions of personal habits	24	
Trouble with boss	23	
Change in work hours or conditions	20	
Change in residence	20	
Change in schools	20	
Change in recreations	19	
Change in church activities	19	
Change in social activities	19	
Mortgage or loan under $151,363	17	
Change in sleeping habits	16	
Change in number of family get-togethers	15	
Change in eating habits	15	
Vacation	13	
Holidays approaching	12	
Minor violation of the law	11	
Total		

STRESS TEST RESULTS

Now that you have your score, take a look at where you rank on the stress test results chart. A score below 150 means you're less likely to suffer illness in the near future (30 percent or less), a score between 150 and 299 gives you a fifty-fifty chance, and a score of 300 or more means you have a real problem on your hands, as a stress-induced health breakdown is highly likely (80 percent or more).

Life Change Points	Likelihood of Illness in Near Future
300+	About 80%
150–299	About 50%
Less than 150	About 30%

Here's what my mess looked like in the year after I suffered sexual harassment and lost my job: I had "trouble" at work (+23); management "suddenly" screwed up my hours and changed my duties (+20); I was let go from the job (+47); my grandfather's health took a huge decline (+44); I lost my income (+38); I changed to a different line of work by going from salary to freelance (+36); I had to sell my belongings for a dime on the dollar to downsize from a home to an apartment (+25); I moved across the country (+20) and left behind loved ones and friends (+19); I flew across the country twice to receive honors for taking a stand against sexual harassment (+28, +28); and I stopped working out (+24), sleeping (+16), and eating (+15). Without even factoring in the stress brought by being assassinated in the media and losing two colleagues in a mass shooting, my total stress rating was a 383. That put me in the severe meltdown category, making imminent illness all but certain. Still, I was confident that I could handle it alone. I was also wrong, very wrong.

⬆️ **HEADS-UP!**

Experiencing gender harassment—that is, demeaning insults and hostility like those hurled at Lieutenant Franchina in chapter 3—can be just as harmful to your system as enduring sexualized advances. A study of more than ten thousand women working in the law and military found that, compared to women who were not harassed, women who endured gender harassment alone saw a greater decline in their work performance due to both physical and emotional health issues. Additionally, women who dealt with gender harassment suffered nearly as much professionally and psychologically as women who endured unwanted sexual advances.

In sum, never think one form of sexual harassment is necessarily worse than another; each form takes a toll.[3]

Demi Lovato gets it right: Just because you can't see mental illness doesn't mean it's not busy manifesting a toxic mess inside of you, slowly leaking out into your everyday life, affecting you and those around you.

WHAT'S BYSTANDER STRESS?

Many people think sexual harassment isn't their problem so long as they're not directly targeted. Those people really miss the mark on this one. Sexual harassment is so toxic that its mere ambience can erode your mental health when you witness or even hear about it happening to a colleague. Psychologists and researchers call this "bystander stress."

Upon seeing or learning of a peer's harassment, you may experience stress because:

- You're concerned about being targeted
- You feel for your peer's suffering
- You too may feel powerless, or guilty for not doing anything
- You sense injustice due to the organization's failure to prevent or stop the harassment.[4]

Complicating things further, bystander stress arises even when the bystander thinks the behavior is *welcomed*, such as when two colleagues are mutually flirting or bonding by talking shit to each other.[5] Said another way, sexual harassment is bad for everyone no matter how you look at it *and* regardless of the intentions of those involved.

Both men and women who observe female coworkers being sexually harassed are more likely to experience a decline in overall emotional well-being.[6] When the harassed is a man, the experiences differ based on the observer's gender, according to Drs. Angela Dionisi and Julian Barling, who coauthored a 2018 research study on male gender harassment. In this study, they found that men get angry when they see other men get harassed. But when women see men get harassed, they get angry *and* scared; angry because it's wrong and scared because women are more cognizant of the fact that the harassment could happen to them too. In fact, Drs. Dionisi and Barling found the sting went deeper for women who observed men get bullied for deviating from masculine stereotypes or for not being "real men." As they explain, "[E]ven when directed at men, gender harassment communicates implicit and pervasive patriarchal messages that are uniquely damaging to women." The more women observe men engaging in "horseplay" or "hazing" that involves putting down women (for example, calling another man a "bitch"), the more it damages a woman's identity as a woman. Indeed, these insults effectively say that being a woman is bad, which is quite disparaging if you're a woman.[7]

👍 BONUS POINT!

Although there is a social movement among women to reclaim the term "bitch," when men refer to other men as "bitches" in a derogatory sense, the shade to women is quite clear. What may be less clear is the misogyny underlying other commonly used terms in the American language. For example, saying that "sucks" is to say it's bad, right? Well, "sucks" is an implicit reference to fellatio, a sexual act historically performed by women and gay men. That means "sucks" really just shows contempt for a sex act performed by women and gays. Same goes for terms like "cocksucker."

You get to decide what terms you use and with whom and where, but it may be worthwhile to check out their origins before using them at work. #TheMoreYouKnow

Bystander stress leads to workplace withdrawal, causes increased levels of team conflict, lowers the sense of group cohesion, and reduces financial performance.[8] Bystanders who have also been targets of sexual harassment suffer a "double whammy"—adverse occupational, psychological, and health-related effects over and above what's suffered by those who are either bystanders or targets.[9] No matter how it's packaged, the ambience of sexual harassment takes a toll.

HOW THE STRESS MANIFESTS

The psychological consequences of being exposed to sexual harassment can manifest in many ways, all of which are rather shitty. Doctors think it can be psychologically worse for men to be sexually harassed because men as a group are not expected to be harassed and thus are less likely to receive sympathy and tend to lack the social script for how to handle it. For women, who already are more likely than men to perceive behavior as harassing, the issue is different.

Women are more likely to internalize stress accompanying harassment and to do so with greater intensity, making them more susceptible to the psychological injury brought by sexual harassment. This heightened response is completely logical: Women often are more physically and financially vulnerable than men, making the threats women face more real. That's not to discount the psychological stress men suffer as a result of sexual harassment but rather to call attention to the fact that women suffer on more frequent and intense levels that leave a bigger and longer-lasting impact on their lives.

↑ **HEADS-UP!**

When facing sexualized harassment, women often spend time stressing about their appearance, trying to "desexualize" it. These women are playing into the lie that their clothing choices incite uncontrollable sexual arousal in men, which could result in harassment or assault. This myth is used to discourage women from exercising bodily autonomy and to excuse men from being held accountable for sexual misconduct. Don't fall for it.

Remember: Sexual harassment is about maintaining power, not expressing sexual desire, which is why your attire isn't the reason someone may decide to harass you. Women and men from all walks of life are harassed, no matter what they're wearing.

So wear what you want, for you'll likely be harassed anyway.

The rest of this chapter discusses the body's most common responses to sexual harassment based on the current *Diagnostic and Statistical Manual of Mental Disorders* (DSM-5), which medical professionals use for mental health diagnoses. Do keep in mind that this overview is *not* a full medical briefing, nor can it replace the advice of a medical professional. My doctorate is in law, not medicine. On that note, do *not* self-diagnose. Your WebMD game is no match for a *licensed* MD game. See a doctor or mental health provider if you think you may suffer from any of these disorders. There are a range of treatments available—both therapeutic and chemical. The goal is to find what works best for *you*, given your situation and your needs. Remember: You have options. There is hope. You're not alone.

Common Mental Health Side Effects

The three most common mental health side effects of exposure to sexual harassment are depression, post-traumatic stress disorder, and anxiety.

Major Depressive Disorder. Depression is one of the most common mental health diagnoses among those sexually harassed and those exposed to it. This should come as no surprise, as sexual harassment attacks one's self-esteem and sense of self-worth, creating self-doubt, shame, and self-blame that can easily manifest in the form of depression. Symptoms can include feeling sad, empty, or hopeless; crying for no apparent reason; and losing interest in activities that were once enjoyable. The difference between depression and occasional sadness is duration: Depression lasts most of the day, almost every day, for a minimum of two weeks. You also may feel worthless, have trouble concentrating, or contemplate suicide. Depression may be marked by physical symptoms like fatigue, significant weight gain or loss, sleeping too much or too little, and being restless or sluggish.

Depression stemming from sexual harassment has lingering effects, with symptoms often persisting over years and having a cumulative effect over time, making you more vulnerable to harassment in the future. While there's a range of psychotherapy and medication effective in treating depression, being cognizant of the symptoms is key to appropriately addressing the problem.

Post-Traumatic Stress Disorder (PTSD). Another common side effect of sexual harassment is PTSD—a disorder that develops from experiencing a traumatizing event or reoccurring traumas. Approximately 7 to 8 percent of people will experience PTSD at some point in their lives. The likelihood of experiencing it depends on various factors, such as existing mental and physical health, the nature of the traumatic event, emotional response during the trauma, age, gender, support systems, and additional stressors. Some PTSD symptoms include:

1. **Reexperiencing Trauma:** Reliving the events, having nightmares, and experiencing distress triggered by reminders of the trauma.
2. **Active Avoidance:** Avoiding thoughts, people, or things that remind you of the events.
3. **Hyperarousal:** Struggling with sleeping, being on edge, having difficulty concentrating, and being irritable or exhibiting reckless behavior.
4. **Negativity/Loss of Interest:** Trouble recalling key parts of the events, struggling with positive feelings, loss of interest in once-fun activities, and feeling distant from others.

🛑 TIME-OUT

Sexual harassment takes a toll not only on the mind but also on the body. Those exposed to harassment are at an increased risk of suffering headaches, nausea, exhaustion, neck problems, intestinal complications, respiratory issues, weight gain, weight loss, eating disorders, and disordered eating. Compared to those who are not harassed, harassed women are 89 percent more likely to suffer from long-term sleep problems and are twice as likely to have high blood pressure years after the harassment, raising their risk of cardiovascular disease, among other potentially life-threatening problems. Exposure to sexual harassment also makes you more likely than others to abuse substances, such as alcohol, drugs, and nicotine. Men are more likely than women to engage in substance abuse, but rates for all genders may increase due to sexual harassment.

Escapist drinking, pill popping, and chain-smoking are dangerous yet popular forms of self-medication. They dull the senses and lessen the anxieties, allowing you to believe you're coping with your current reality or the lingering effects of a toxic work environment. The illusion of coping is only temporary and is very dangerous, as substance abuse is taxing on your physical health and can severely disrupt your life—if not take it.

PTSD may keep you in an elevated state of fight-or-flight. That's what the doctor said was happening to me when I couldn't eat or sleep for months. While in fight-or-flight mode, adrenaline (a stress hormone) surges through the body so we can be ready to mobilize to stop a threat or run from it. The last thing your body wants to do is eat or sleep, as the mind is convinced there's an existing or imminent threat. Those experiencing PTSD often abuse substances like alcohol and drugs in an attempt to distract from the triggers or to alleviate the anxiety, which can delay discovery of the disorder and affect treatment.

PTSD may manifest immediately after the traumatic event or lie dormant for some time, until awakened by a triggering event. Time doesn't always help when it comes to PTSD, however, as symptoms may last months or years after the initial trauma. The disorder may be alleviated through psychotherapy, medication, MDMA-assisted therapy, virtual reality exposure, and various alternative methods like trauma-sensitive yoga or acupuncture.

Generalized Anxiety Disorder (GAD). From subconsciously fearing for your safety to consciously avoiding a harasser, the chronic stress of GAD can keep you on edge, make you irritable, and turn mundane experiences into taxing endeavors.

The key features of GAD are fear and anxiety. Fear is a response to an existing threat, while anxiety is about fearing a future threat. The combination of the two can be debilitating, even if the threat is not real but imaginary.

GAD can physically manifest itself in a variety of symptoms, including fatigue, sleeplessness, inability to concentrate, muscle tension, and restlessness. It also can appear at any point in one's life, although women are twice as likely as men to develop the anxiety disorder. Treatments range from medication to cognitive therapy. Don't hesitate to seek help.

REPLAY

* No matter how strong you may be, sexual harassment can be harmful to your psychological well-being because it puts significant stress on your system.
* No one escapes sexual harassment unscathed—not even bystanders. It's like secondhand smoke: You need not be the smoker to suffer the adverse health consequences that can take a psychological, emotional, and physical toll.
* Depression, PTSD, and anxiety are the most common mental health issues that arise from sexual harassment. Many experience physical manifestations of stress, such as sleeplessness, headaches, stomach issues, and nausea. Typically, individuals will try to self-medicate through substance abuse.
* Do not try to self-diagnose or self-medicate. Simply recognize when something feels off and don't be afraid to get the help you need. Remember: You have options, there is hope, and you're not alone.

***

This chapter is dedicated to my cat Maverick.
As your love is forever imprinted on the walls of my heart,
your name is forever tattooed on the back of my neck.
I never could've made it through any of the darkness without you
(. . . you and Zoloft).

CHAPTER 10

The Head Game Plan

A Strategy for Surviving the Psychological Impact of Sexual Harassment

Keep your eyes on the finish line and not on the turmoil around you.
—*Rihanna, lyrical artist, businesswoman, and everywoman*

As you read in chapter 9, the mental health consequences of sexual harassment are real. In less than two years, it took me from "Girl, Wash Your Face" to "Gurl, Douse Yo Shit in Kerosene." Sexual harassment is ruthless. But what do you expect from a sadistic power play meant to break your spirit so you play small and drop your professional dreams?

According to a study published by the National Institutes of Health, the adverse psychological effects of sexual harassment may be mitigated by your determination to overcome the effects of the experiences.[1] In English, that means you may have better chances of beating the sexual harassment head game if you're committed to doing so. There's no better way to commit than to have a Head Game Plan! (Or "HGP," as I like to call it.)

In this chapter, I give you the tools to create the ideal HGP, a comprehensive plan that takes you from trauma to transformation with greater ease than without. It helps you to leverage what's within your control and maximizes the supportive resources around you. An HGP was *exactly* what I needed but didn't have during my mental health struggles because I refused to believe that having my job taken away from me impacted more than just my annual income.

To formulate the ideal HGP blueprint for you, I candidly evaluated my many embarrassing and illuminating personal experiences, spoke with a range of people about their own, read up on a considerable amount of research, and sat down with several doctors and mental health professionals.

The HGP blueprint is broken into two parts: Insider Secrets and Outsider Assistance. May they guide you, and Godspeed!

INSIDER SECRETS

You know *you*. You just may not know you *after* sexual harassment. After suffering any type of trauma, mild or severe, you change as a person. That change can be significant or slight, obvious or subconscious. How you navigate the change is the key to whether you ultimately change for the better or for the worse. Here are some stellar mental health tips to guide you through your journey.

Embrace the Struggle. You may be a badass, but you're still human and you can be hurt. It's okay *not* to be okay. Admitting something's wrong is not weakness, but putting on a facade to save face or throwing yourself into meaningless distraction is. We've all seen that person who buries their head in the sand, denying reality as though the situation will change or as if others won't notice. Hell, we've all *been that person* at some point in our lives!

Why do we embrace this ostrich approach as opposed to embracing the struggle? The issue is often twofold. First, some may lie to themselves about what's going on as a coping mechanism, downplaying the events in hopes of escaping the psychological harm. Many busy themselves with distractions, like taking on others' problems or throwing themselves into their work, instead of confronting what's going on inside. During my darkest time, I subconsciously did this, simply trying to delay the inevitable as a storm mounted inside. Acknowledging one's own abuse, or that of another, can be an extremely challenging endeavor that may cause significant internal conflict and stress.

🛑 TIME-OUT

No matter what, some people will not accept that a person is a harasshole simply because it's inconsistent with their view of that person. That's cognitive dissonance—the mental stress someone experiences when they learn new facts that don't jive with their existing beliefs, values, or ideas. For instance, if a client you've known for years suddenly propositions you for sex, you may initially reject the reality that she's a sleaze who doesn't respect you, instead making excuses for her in your mind and continuing to seek her out for business. I've been there. Don't do it. This type of self-preserving cognitive denial is dangerous all around, as it leaves you vulnerable to abuse. In the sage words of gawdess Maya Angelou as summarized via queen Oprah, "When people show you who they are, believe them."

Second, people often pretend to be "okay" because they tend to derive their sense of self-worth from how they're perceived by others. Whether it's family, friends, colleagues, or strangers on social media, society conditions us to look to others for validation and approval. Elevating the opinions of others above your own opinion (especially opinions about yourself) is no way to live. Life is too short to "do you" on someone else's terms, regardless of whether the person is related to you or whether they seem really smart on Reddit.

You should be honest with yourself, respect your feelings, and recognize when things aren't right. No one gets to decide how you should feel about sexual harassment or how you should respond. Whether it bothers you a little bit, leaves you feeling belittled, or becomes all-consuming, you don't have to "let it go" or "drop it," no matter what anyone says. You *are* entitled to your feelings, regardless of whether others feel the same.

If you're dealing with the aftermath of sexual harassment, get the help you want and need. Navigating any type of change (for example, going from a high-powered profession to "passable" circumstances) can be a helluva hit to your psyche. But your mental health comeback tour will begin only once you face and embrace the struggle.

Prepare for the Stages of Grief. You may be mourning the loss of a career or of trust in your employer, but, no matter the loss, take the time you need to mourn. The five stages of grief are denial, anger, bargaining, depression, and acceptance. You won't necessarily go through these stages in this order, however, because grief is nonlinear, explains Therese Mascardo,

PsyD, CEO and founder of Exploring Therapy. One day you might be outright furious; the next, you're denying to yourself that your supervisor was implicitly threatening you. Before you know it, you're spending hours bargaining, telling yourself "if only" you had done this or wishing you could have done that. I went through months of bargaining, blaming myself for foolishly assuming certain people would do the right thing because of their gender, not realizing they were NSFW coworkers. Bargaining was a pointless exercise that kept me up at night and prevented me from living in the moment; but it also was part of the process, part of my journey. It's okay if this and the other stages of grief are a part of yours. You can and will get through it.

Do Not Pull the Triggers. Triggers are the realest unreal events you'll experience after a trauma. Often associated with PTSD, triggers are external things that remind you of the traumatic experience. They can be images, smells, tastes, sounds, words, places, people. Triggers instantly take you back to the trauma. They're stealthy AF too, but you'll know them when you experience them.

Here's the best way I can explain the sensation: Imagine that you've just left the dentist appointment from hell. Your mascara's running, lipstick smudged, half of your face is numb. You've got blood-soaked gauze protruding from your left cheek with drool aggressively dripping from your right. While rushing down the street looking remarkably unattractive (if not utterly revolting), the last thing you want is to be recognized. That's when you run smack-dab into "The One That Got Away" and their new bae, both looking ridiculously radiant and feeling particularly chatty. *That* sudden, visceral shock that ignites within you, making you feel like bolting *and* burning everything down all at once? When something sparks *that* type of intense sensation, it's a trigger.

I remember one trigger very well. It was a month after I left a toxic workplace. I thought I was fine. I was at the gym just doing me when a trigger popped up on the flat-screen TV just a few feet in front of my elliptical. Let me tell you, the speed at which I exited that gym would've earned me a medal in the hundred-meter dash. When I finally mustered the courage to return some weeks later, for months I relegated myself to the cardio equipment in a side room with crummy air circulation but absolutely *no* TVs. Triggers are ruthless, and I'd wish them upon no one. (Although after this book comes out, my name may be a trigger for some harassholes out there, and I'm okay with that.)

Triggers are powerful and may be somewhat unpredictable. Like past lovers, they can appear out of nowhere, disrupting a peaceful moment or destroying an ideal experience. Triggers are heinous, not just because they remind you of the bad stuff but because they remind you of the control the bad stuff has over you. Triggers also can be good, as they're the mind's way of trying to get your attention, telling you there's a problem.

Don't be too hard on yourself if it takes you some time to move past your triggers. They could take months, even years to overcome. More than a year after my trauma, there were emoticons that still induced anxiety for me and places I diligently avoided. I still struggle. But the day will come when they'll no longer be triggers but mere mundane aspects of the world around me. Until then, I respect their existence and use them as a reminder that I still have work to do on my mental health journey.

⭐ PLAYBOOK PRO TIP

Sara Benincasa doesn't just tells funny stories; the stand-up comedian and author of *Real Artists Have Day Jobs*, also speaks to audiences on overcoming mental health issues after trauma. In the realm of surviving sexual harassment, Benincasa offers this advice:

1. **You're not what was done to you.** What you've endured may have shaped parts of you. That's okay. You're still you. Be kind to and patient with yourself.

2. **Shape your own narrative.** You're in control of how you identify yourself—overcomer, survivor, something else. You get to decide how you heal (so long as it doesn't hurt you or anyone else). This is your narrative, and you write this story.

3. **Pay attention to distractions.** When struggling with trauma, some people try to avoid what they're feeling by finding distractions, like throwing themselves into work, traveling, dating, drinking. Some distractions can be healthy, and others simply put a Band-Aid on a bullet wound.

4. **Consider making it a group thing.** Should you be struggling, check out groups like Alcoholics Anonymous, Codependents Anonymous, Overeaters Anonymous, Narcotics Anonymous, Debtors Anonymous, Gamblers Anonymous. You don't have to go through this alone.

5. **The therapy game.** If you opt for therapy, ensure the therapist is properly licensed and try to find a "trauma-informed therapist" who keeps a good balance of respecting your boundaries yet challenging your assumptions.

Be Prepared for More. Mental health issues are wake-up calls. Should you seek therapy or counseling to address those issues, be prepared. You may learn more about yourself and confront some harsh truths you never anticipated. Oftentimes, digging deeper into why you felt or responded a certain way brings up things in your life that have been dormant—and possibly destructive. Wading through earlier work experiences or mulling over memories from childhood may not be easy, but it might be part of your journey toward healing and becoming your best self.

On my journey, for example, I learned that I'm on the autism spectrum, which is awesome in that it explains so much about my life and gave me a greater love of self. Learning that information helps me appreciate my savant-ish abilities, understand my blind spots, and live a fuller life. #Bonus

Map Out a Solid Self-Care Plan. According to Dr. Mascardo, a solid self-care plan (SCP) boosts your chances of successfully overcoming trauma. An SCP is a guide you thoughtfully create, based on your personal needs, to promote your physical, psychological, emotional, and spiritual health. Here are examples of what an SCP may include:

Physical	Psychological
▪ Healthy diet	▪ Morning meditation
▪ Workout regimen	▪ Daily journaling
▪ Regular sleep routine	▪ Creative writing class
▪ Morning yoga stretches	▪ Leave phone at home on Sundays

Emotional	Spiritual
▪ Compliment yourself daily	▪ Attend gatherings
▪ Laugh daily	▪ Listen to spiritual podcasts
▪ Meet with a support group	▪ Reflect on scriptures/principles
▪ Breathing exercises	▪ Engage in prayer/meditation

Whether it's having weekly hot-yoga sessions or enrolling in creative writing classes at a local college, take time out to tend to yourself—it's a significant part of the healing process. The ideal SCP makes a routine out of reserving time for things you relish and activities that refresh you. Map it out and stick with it. Consistency goes a long way.

OUTSIDER ASSISTANCE

Coming back from sexual harassment trauma isn't a solo endeavor or individual sport. It requires a team effort. From recruiting loved ones to picking healthcare providers, you need a solid support network if you intend to successfully go from trauma to transformation. Here are some tips on leveraging outsider assistance.

Leaning on Loved Ones. They may be outside of the workplace, but family and friends can play a significant role in your ability to successfully overcome the psychological effects of sexual harassment by helping reduce stress. Simply being a sounding board can uplift those in harassing environments, for example. In fact, even though a significant number of people remain silent or never report the harassment to management, a solid number do open up to loved ones about the sexual harassment. One-third of employees speak with a family member about what's going on, and some 50 to 70 percent seek support from friends or confidants.[2]

Additionally, having the support of loved ones can make you feel less alone. This is important because just your *perception* of being supported while facing sexual harassment is enough to improve your mental health, especially when coworkers may isolate or mistreat you. My mother and a longtime mentor were a huge source of support on some of my darkest days. While my employer was retaliating against me, I would text them for help in handling a situation or for words of encouragement. They were breaths of fresh of air that I could take in when overwhelmed by my toxic environment. On my last day working at a sexual harassment hotbed, my mother had a dozen red roses delivered to my desk with a card reminding me how talented I am, how proud she was that I stood up for what was right, and how much I am loved. Small showings of support can have a big impact.

To survive the day-to-day madness, consider recruiting a team of amazing loved ones to support you—a designated support network (DSN). A DSN is comprised of people who know you well and who are compassionate, reliable, and respectful. Your DSN should be comprised of good listeners who can be a sounding board and uplift you in your situation. They respect your boundaries, feelings, and decisions, and do not pressure you into doing something that makes you uncomfortable, nor do they blame you for the behavior. Your DSN should be candid with you, however, even if it might hurt your feelings. It does you no good to hear a bunch of lies that could lead you to damage your future, even if it makes you feel better in the moment. Having a DSN with the tact to decipher whether you need blind support or harsh truth is essential.

⭐ **PLAYBOOK PRO TIP**

A DSN is great for getting you through the day-to-day, but an executive team is ideal for helping you achieve long-term goals. Dr. Mascardo, who works with individuals recovering from trauma as well as those simply looking to maintain sound mental health, recommends building a Personal Board of Directors—a team of wise people who can give you high-level advice on specific areas of your life where you're looking for guidance. Here are her steps to getting this done.

1. **Identify.** Identify three to five areas in which you'd like to gain wisdom and knowledge, such as physical, financial, or spiritual health; relationship building; entrepreneurship; or a career change. Outline specific goals you would like to achieve within the next three, six, and twelve months.
2. **Invite.** For each area you identified, find a specific person who has mastered that area and invite them to be your advisor. Explain why you chose them, what you'd like to learn from them over a specified period of time, and how you anticipate their advice would make a positive impact on you and your specific goals. (If they decline, graciously thank them and ask if they can recommend someone else in their specialty.)
3. **Be Open.** Invite your mentor to speak freely and share their insights with complete candor. Let them know you are looking not just for affirmation but for constructive criticism that may help make you better. Ask them to help you identify your blind spots and offer suggestions on how you can improve.
4. **Check In.** Commit to connecting with each member of your executive team at least monthly, offering progress reports on your endeavors and posing meaningful questions you may have for them. Take notes on how they handle themselves and the issues they encounter. Remember to express gratitude and let them know you're learning from them. Executive presence can be a mental health game-changer in your personal life. Go for it!

It's rare that one person in your life meets all the DSN qualifiers. You may want to be selective about who you seek help from based on the issue and their individual strengths and availability. If you don't already have loved ones in your life who can provide this kind of support, consider joining a sexual harassment or trauma support group in your area. There are many good people out there looking to connect as they overcome trauma too. If you're used to flying solo or always being the "strong one," you may feel uncomfortable asking for help or leaning on those who care about you. But you'll be a lot more uncomfortable trying to explain to your new boss why you lost your shit when the FedEx guy leaned in for a signature. Altogether, we need each other. Do yourself a favor and focus on getting mentally healthy with the help of those here to support you.

Coping with Coworker Shade. Over a lifetime, the average American spends more than ninety thousand hours at work. With that much time at the office, it's only natural that coworkers can become closer than friends, even more intimate than family. Then again, coworkers also can become gaslighting guerrillas and trash-talking terrorists who make your everyday work life an absolute living hell.

It may be hard to stomach, but it's best that you know now: If you're in a sexual harassment situation, colleagues who you may consider "friends" are more likely to distance themselves from you than to help you.[3] The reason for that is because people are terrible. Just kidding . . . sort of. As explained in the American Psychological Association's *Journal of Occupational Health Psychology*, fellow workers tend to avoid those entangled in sexual harassment situations because they too fear mistreatment and retaliation by employers.[4] Basically, even if they claim to be good people, say they love you, and know that what's happening to you is ethically wrong and incredibly illegal, most people are still unwilling to jeopardize their paychecks. You should be prepared for this harsh reality. I wasn't.

Watching colleagues distance themselves from me as though *I* had done something wrong by standing up for what was right was one of the most devastating things I experienced during my ordeal. Many of them stopped inviting me to events, isolated me at work, unfollowed me on social media. The ostracism—especially from those I supported and stuck my neck out for— was a painful reminder of how disappointing some people can be. Then again, there were a handful of folks who wouldn't leave my side. They offered to be references, checked in on me, and continued to have my back, making it easy for me to be a resource for them when my situation improved.

Just because research reveals that coworkers are more inclined to turn their backs on you doesn't mean that they *all* will look the other way or sit in silence. Try to find those who will offer some support, as it can be essential to your psychological survival. Symptoms of depression and anxiety lessen for individuals when they believe they have social support in dealing with the effects of sexual harassment. There are strong people out there who *will* uplift you and join you on the picket line—they're just few and far between.

Beware of Psychological Warfare. One of the most common forms of psychological warfare, often used against women who fight against sexual harassment, is gaslighting. This manipulative tactic occurs when someone makes you question your reality and stop trusting your reasoning and emotional responses. Gaslighting is most likely to occur in relationships where there is an unequal power dynamic, like boss/subordinate or mentor/mentee.

⭐ PLAYBOOK PRO TIP

Gaslighting can be heinous on your head game. Dr. Robin Stern, associate director of the Yale Center for Emotional Intelligence and author of *The Gaslight Effect*, offers solid tips to help you identify when gaslighting is going down.

According to Stern, in addition to denying that something happened and accusing you of misremembering, gaslighters may respond to confrontation or observations by saying you're being sensitive, hysterical, insecure, crazy, paranoid, making it up, imagining things, overreacting, dramatic, getting worked up, or ungrateful. Gaslighters also may respond by telling you they were joking or accusing you of trying to throw them off track.

Stern indicates that someone may be gaslighting you if interacting with them often leaves you apologizing, wondering why you're not happier, unsure if you're good enough, making excuses for the person's behavior, unable to make simple decisions, lying about your perception so that it aligns with their statements, and asking yourself several times a day, "Am I too sensitive?"

Sexual harassment situations are prime for gaslighting—not just because men typically use the tactic against women who, as a gender, are socialized to doubt themselves. Rather, gaslighting is common in sexual harassment because it's often a he said/she said situation that can be emotionally charged, and harassholes nearly always deny your version of the events, undermining your reality from the start. Supervisors and colleagues also may try to make you question yourself by suggesting you're overreacting, misinterpreting, or misremembering. This is one of the go-to techniques used by the Handler.

Do not let them gaslight you! Continuing to think independently and standing by your instincts are imperative. Seeking validation from others makes you more likely to fall victim to gaslighting. You need self-reliance and self-confidence in your own reality despite their attempted distortion. You know what you experienced. It's not okay. Stick with your gut.

Getting Pros Who Know. A great game plan involves having good doctors waiting in the wings for you. Whether they be counselors, therapists, or psychiatrists, make sure you connect with them and feel like more than just another name on file.

Good doctors listen well, look you in the eye, and make decisions *with* you—not *for* you. They make time for questions, have a solid number of other patients but are still accessible, and respond within a reasonable time. Although they're continually gaining knowledge about their area of practice and your needs, good doctors also acknowledge when something is not in their wheelhouse, offering either to look into the matter further or to recommend you to a specialist who may better meet your needs. If you happen to be well informed or WebMD savvy, good doctors are not threatened by your knowledge or by respectful challenges to their conclusions. They're grateful that you are dedicated to your health and committed to getting good care because that's what they want for you too.

🛑 TIME-OUT

When it comes to overcoming the mental health effects of sexual harassment, the most common professionals sought out are counselors, psychiatrists, and psychologists. Each professional usually pushes a different type of treatment based on their specialty. Typically, counselors want you to talk, psychiatrists want you to medicate, and psychologists may be anywhere in between. But only you can decide what the right treatment path is for you. Regardless of who you see for help, ensure the provider knows that your concerns arise from workplace issues. It's important that your doctors keep that in mind for paperwork, should you pursue your legal options.

Speaking of options . . . If you're unsure of whether medication is right for you, make your decision notwithstanding any social stigma. People all but inject caffeine when they're hazy, get hopped up on NyQuil on a moment's sneeze, and pop Advil at the first inkling of an ache. The mind can get sick just like the rest of the body. Medication may or may not be a good option for you on your journey, but do what you need to do to get to where you need to be, regardless of any social ignorance.

As you may know, not all doctors are good. Some have biases, poor bedside manner, and issues—BIG ISSUES. On my journey back from sexual harassment trauma, I'll never forget one psychiatrist who I couldn't get away from fast enough. When I arrived at his office, the only place for me to sit was on a brightly colored, child-size couch surrounded by stuffed animals facing a collection of *adolescent* psychiatric manuals. Naturally, the room's décor raised a few questions for me. In response to my inquiry, the man tried to convince me that he specialized in *adult* care and that *only* he could help me. This was just the start of his hustle, mind you. From his strategically hoisted seat peering down at me, this small-time charlatan claimed that the two written psychiatric tests I'd read extensively about—*and had completed on my screening visit the week before*—did not exist. Not that there was no record of these tests or that the results were lost, but that there were *no tests whatsoever*. But for the Botox in my forehead, a look of astonishment would've been all over my face. This man must've had a BS in psychiatry and a PhD in gaslighting. I did not have time for it and quickly found another doctor.

If your relationship with a doctor doesn't work for you or doesn't feel right, it's okay not to see that doctor again. You should not have to psychoanalyze a psych. It's okay to ask a respected medical provider or trusted friend to recommend someone else. And do not hesitate to report an inappropriate or incompetent medical provider to the powers that be. You may not recoup your copay or that thousand-dollar deductible, but you will have paid it forward by helping prevent others from having your same lackluster experience, making their mental health journey a little bit easier.

Get Your Legal Team on Board. If you've opted for the legal route (which you can read more about in the next few chapters), you want counsel who is considerate of what you're going through. The attorney-client relationship is an important and intimate one that can fall apart if communication fails. You should speak candidly with your attorney about your struggles, what your limits are, and what you need from your legal team.

A good attorney will be supportive, try to alleviate any unnecessary emotional and mental hurdles for you, and look to protect you from needless exposure to matters that are upsetting. But keep in mind that they're doctors of law, not medicine. Attorneys can't be expected to identify the mental health issues you may be experiencing as a result of sexual harassment, or to fully appreciate your mental health journey. As with all other significant relationships, patience and communication go a long way.

Sideline Social Media. Online platforms meant to connect you with the world can also leave you feeling like you're failing in it or everyone is out there living a better life. I'll let you in on a little secret: Chloe from college doesn't have it all together despite how gorge she looks on the Gram.

You can't let the imagery you see online impact your view of yourself. For a quick fix, if certain profiles conjure anger or envy, mute or unfollow their account, suspend your account, or delete the app altogether. You don't need it in your life. For long-term happiness, figure out what's going on inside. What's keeping you from being a sincere cheerleader for others? Nothing that anyone has or does not have should induce fury or impact your sense of self-worth. Be the best version of you.

⚑ BONUS POINT

The journey to good mental health has numerous stops. One stop that is less than awesome—but incredibly eye-opening—is getting a look at the true hearts and priorities of those around you as you learn who will make sacrifices and who will sacrifice you.

At the height of my PTSD, for example, I uncharacteristically screamed at two close girlfriends, then skipped one's birthday party that night. The next day, I apologized, explaining to both of them that I needed to step away to take care of my mental health. Their respective responses were telling. One used my mental illness against me while issuing me an expletive-fueled stream of insults. The other (the birthday girl) told me that she loved me, wanted me to get better, and would be there waiting for me on the other side. Can you guess which friend remains a fixture in my life today?

As you work to overcome your mental health challenges, you'll need people to give you space *and* grace. Some people will struggle with the fact that you need help and can no longer make them a priority. There's a very good chance that *those* people are not *your* people. While you can't expect everyone to understand your journey if they've never walked it, you should expect loved ones to support you rather than compound the trauma.

In short, hold on to the givers and have the takers see their way out!

SELF-CHECK-INS

The head game can be the worst part of dealing with sexual harassment. If you *think* about it, the mind is a big player when it comes to navigating life. (See what I did there?) To stay on top of your mental health, consider calendaring weekly (if not daily) self-check-ins to sincerely evaluate how you're feeling and interacting with the world around you. Create a check-in process that resonates with you. The approach I take, for example, draws on pop culture and makes me smile. Here it is!

There's a theory that each of the Winnie-the-Pooh characters represents a different mental health issue (although this may not have been author A. A. Milne's intent when he wrote the children's books back in the 1920s—even if he was struggling with PTSD after returning from World War I).[5] Medical minds have nonetheless attached each fictional character to the following disorders:

Pooh—Impulsivity
Piglet—Anxiety
Roo—Autism
Tigger—ADHD
Eeyore—Depression
Rabbit—OCD
Kanga—Social Anxiety
Owl—Dyslexia
Milne—PTSD

With this in mind, each week I ask myself aloud, *Do I have a Pooh problem?* After I stop giggling like an idiot, I proceed to go through each character's traits to see if there's any overlap with my feelings and behavior from that week. If there is overlap, I consider the circumstances that invoked the feelings or behavior, whether my response was an isolated incident or may continue, and if I should reach out to a mental health provider to explore the matter further. During this weekly self-assessment, I reflect on the words that character Christopher Robin said to Pooh:

Promise me you'll always remember: You're braver than you believe, and stronger than you seem, and smarter than you think.

REPLAY

* To beat the psychological impact of sexual harassment, you need a Head Game Plan that draws from the resources you have within (Insider Secrets) and those resources around you (Outsider Assistance).
* Being prepared in advance can make all the difference between going from trauma to transformation with relative ease and spending the rest of your life concealing a tattoo of your cat's name on your neck.
* The key Insider Secrets are to embrace the struggle, prepare for the stages of grief, respect traumatic triggers, expect that more issues may come out, and map out a solid self-care plan.
* To take advantage of Outsider Assistance, you'll want to lean on loved ones, be ready to cope with coworker shade, beware of psychological warfare such as gaslighting, have an arsenal of ideal medical health providers, get your legal team on board, and consider sidelining social media until you're in a healthier place.
* Stay on top of your mental health by calendaring regular self-check-ins. You can devise a cute Q&A based on pop culture references (for example, *Do I have a Pooh problem?*) or outline a list of self-evaluation questions that fit your needs. Either way, in between appointments with your medical team, stay actively involved in monitoring your mental health so you can keep the upper hand in the head game.

***

This chapter is specially dedicated to
Donna Johnson Delegeane, NP, and Dr. Kimberly R. Petrick, MD.

CHAPTER 11

�111111111111111111111111111111111111111111111

Legal Claims and Defenses

An Overview of Sexual Harassment Law

....

Just because something is legally prohibited doesn't mean it stops.
—*Catharine A. MacKinnon, feminist legal scholar to behold*

IN THE SUMMER of 2018, a Manhattan jury of four men and four women heard conflicting stories about Dr. Enrichetta Ravina's experience as an assistant economics professor at Columbia Business School. According to Ravina, finance guru Geert Bekaert had spent more time pursuing her sexually than supervising the research she needed to make tenure. During their years working together at Columbia, Bekaert would stare at her breasts, try to kiss her lips, boast of sexual exploits. Given his clout, she tried to manage him. Ravina would send a thoughtful card when he'd withdraw, or suggest they meet in a group when he'd push for dinner. After years of Ravina refusing to reciprocate, in 2016 he threatened to jeopardize her tenure application by slowing their research—*unless* she were "nicer" to him.

According to Bekaert, none of this happened. He basically told the jury that Ravina was making it all up or reading too much into things. Unfortunately, Ravina didn't keep workplace logs, send SFUs, record any conversations. She had little to no evidence to back up her sexual harassment claim against a prominent married man who was eleven years her senior. Her case was all he said/she said—except for one thing that came courtesy of Bekaert: emails he sent industrywide calling Ravina everything from an "evil bitch" to "schizophrenic" in an attempt to smear her name after she complained about him to Columbia.

After nearly three weeks of trial, the jury said there wasn't enough evidence to support Ravina's sexual harassment claim, but there was sufficient evidence of retaliation based on Bekaert's emails. The jury awarded her $1.25 million for damages and more than $5 million for legal fees and expenses.[1]

All sexual harassment may be abhorrent, but not all sexual harassment is illegal. As we touched upon in chapter 2, only certain misconduct will get you a day in court, as the law is written to favor men, inconsistently applied, and quite convoluted. It also doesn't help that our society has been slow to value women's contributions to the workplace. While I can't singlehandedly amend the law or erase the patriarchy, I can tell you what you need to know about the legal aspects of sexual harassment.

This chapter and the next make the complicated legal stuff clearer and palatable. Here you'll get the skinny on federal sexual harassment law (aka Title VII), the two types of claims, defenses your employer may use, and insight on sharing a coworker's experience. In chapter 12, we talk retaliation, remedies available to you, and how to land a good lawyer. But before you dive in, a word of warning: Just because you read a couple of chapters on the legal aspects of sexual harassment does *not* make you a legal expert, no matter how strong your Google game may be. These chapters are *not* intended to be legal advice and cannot fully capture the breadth of the law as it applies to the nuances of your particular situation. Consult an attorney or two to get a better read on whether the harassment you're experiencing has become a legal issue. To get nuggets of solid information and killer insight to keep in your arsenal should a harasshole or employer act up, read on!

THE LAW

Workplace sexual harassment is banned under both federal law (Title VII) and state laws. Some laws are broader than others, depending on what jurisdiction you're in. Given that state laws vary and are limited to each state, we focus our attention on federal law, which is largely a benchmark that applies across the country.

The reigning federal law is Title VII of the Civil Rights Act of 1964, which makes it illegal for employers to discriminate based on "sex." This law applies to U.S. employers (also including labor unions, governments, and employment agencies) with at least fifteen employees. If you work for a small company with fewer than fifteen employees, you may be covered by state sexual harassment laws. Title VII also protects regular and part-time employees, and job applicants—but it does not apply to temporary part-time employees and independent contractors.

↥ HEADS-UP!

Bear in mind that everything has a special meaning under the law. Even if an employer says you or your harasshole is an "employee" or "independent contractor," that does not make it so under Title VII. Employment status is a legal determination based on numerous factors. The same goes for who is a "supervisor." Under Title VII, this person does not have to be in your chain of command, oversee your day-to-day work, or have an official title. They simply must have authority to significantly change your job status (such as hiring, firing, promoting, reassigning, or changing benefits), or your boss defers to their recommendations.

Consult an attorney if you're unsure whether Title VII applies. And even if it doesn't, there may be state laws that can help.

The Equal Employment Opportunity Commission (EEOC) is the federal agency in charge of enforcing Title VII. (Most states also have analogous agencies that enforce their anti–sexual harassment laws.) The EEOC accepts and monitors complaints, creates rules and regulations, and sues and fines employers. Typically, if Title VII applies to you and you want your day in court, you'll likely interact with the EEOC (or its analogous state agency) at some point.

Although employment discrimination based on sex has been outlawed since Title VII became law in 1964, the ban on sexual harassment is still pretty new. It wasn't outlawed until 1986. The case was *Meritor Savings Bank v. Vinson*, which we touched upon in chapter 2. In that case, the Supreme

Court clearly said sexual harassment could be a form of sex discrimination in the workplace. Since then, the law on the matter has evolved slowly yet surely with the help of court opinions and EEOC guidance. There are still unanswered questions, but we now know what's necessary to bring a sexual harassment case to court *and win.* This brings us to the two types of sexual harassment claims you can make under Title VII and the defenses employers often use.

SEXUAL HARASSMENT CLAIMS AND DEFENSES

Title VII allows you to sue for sexual harassment based on quid pro quo and a hostile work environment. Both claims reflect the ways in which sexual harassment can legally occur, and they can have some overlap.

	Quid Pro Quo (QPQ)	Hostile Work Environment (HWE)
Legal Definition	Quid pro quo harassment occurs when "submission to [sexual] conduct is made either explicitly or implicitly a term or condition of an individual's employment" or "submission to or rejection of such conduct by an individual is used as the basis for employment decisions affecting such individual[.]"[2]	A hostile work environment is created when unwelcome "conduct has the purpose or effect of unreasonably interfering with an individual's work performance or creating an intimidating, hostile, or offensive working environment."[3]

	Quid Pro Quo (QPQ)	Hostile Work Environment (HWE)
Rough Translation	You have to give head to get ahead or to avoid punishment, or others are benefitting from play-for-pay.	The workplace is dripping in offensive sexual and/or sexist commentary, conduct, and nonsense, to the point where it's hard to do your job.
Overlap	QPQ and HWE claims may have some overlap depending on the circumstances. When sexual favoritism in a workplace is widespread, for example, you will have QPQ and maybe HWE.	

Both QPQ and HWE claims address unfair changes in the employment agreement. For QPQ, something sexual becomes a new condition of your employment. For HWE, the put-downs or come-ons are so frequent or severe that it creates a whole new employment experience. Regardless, it's not what you signed up for!

QUID PRO QUO

Quid pro quo, which translates to "this for that" in Latin, is the most common scenario that comes to mind when people think of sexual harassment. In the context of Title VII, QPQ occurs when a person in a position of power promises benefits if you perform sexual favors or threatens punishment if you decline.

The Basics of QPQ

QPQ isn't very complicated. Basically, it's play-for-pay—an abuse of power. The person in power doesn't have to be a supervisor or have a fancy title; he simply controls something that you'd like to have or something you'd like to avoid and barters it in exchange for something sexual. A perfect example of this is Mechelle Vinson's case. The teenage bank teller said her boss threatened to ruin her career if she didn't sleep with him. Disgraced producer Harvey Weinstein reportedly used this explicit sex-for-work tactic to pressure actresses to sexually submit to him.

The threat of punishment or promise of benefit doesn't have to be explicit. It can be implied by words and conduct. In fact, most QPQ tends to be subtle, such as an HR official commenting about your body and its possible sexual uses. When Kevin Tsujihara stepped down as Warner Bros. chairman and CEO in 2019, for instance, the married exec reportedly was having a three-year affair with a young aspiring actress. Although he may not have openly promised her job opportunities in exchange for sex, per the alleged text messages between them, he was initiating intimate encounters with the young woman *while* promising to help her obtain roles. This type of relationship reeks of QPQ.[4]

Not all sexual relationships in a work environment are problematic, however. For example, a consensual relationship between two colleagues that has no effect on employment decisions or an exchange that doesn't involve anything sexual wouldn't support a QPQ claim for sex discrimination.

⬆ **HEADS-UP!**

Sexual favoritism in the workplace is the worst. While an isolated incident of a boss elevating her lover may not be enough to support bringing a QPQ claim, widespread sexual favoritism certainly can. When it's nearly a business practice, it communicates to employees that they're "sexual playthings" or that sexual favors are a prerequisite to better treatment. That's illegal. Both women and men offended by the behavior may sue under Title VII.

QPQ can be tough to weed out. Most employees won't report it if they're receiving a benefit or fear losing their job. Nonetheless, if you give in and provide the sexual favor, you still may be able to hold your employer accountable. Said another way, your employer isn't off the hook simply because you gave in.

HOSTILE WORK ENVIRONMENT

A hostile work environment occurs when unwelcome, offensive behavior is so severe or pervasive that it changes the conditions of your job and creates an abusive work environment.

The Basics of HWE

HWE is more complicated than QPQ. There are no bright-line tests for HWE, which is why it's tough to bring a claim and win. Nonetheless, the courts have outlined some basic concepts that can help you better understand what it takes to make an HWE claim. I cover many of these concepts on the following pages, but for greater nuance and legal detail, consult counsel in your area.

Unwelcome. First and foremost, HWE requires that the behavior under consideration be unwelcome, which means that you did not solicit or incite it. Courts determine if you welcomed the behavior by looking at your actions and responses. Did you ask your coworker about his sex life first? Did you tell him the behavior was inappropriate or smack her hand away? How did you communicate disapproval? All of the circumstances are relevant to the issue.

 TIME-OUT

When determining whether sexual harassment was "unwelcome," courts do look at *all* of the circumstances—but within limits!

Back in the day, an employer could use evidence of a woman's sexual history, sexual preference, dress, vulgarity, and past "unladylike" behavior to try to prove that she welcomed the harasser's advances or would not have been offended by the environment. In other words, employers could slut-shame employees in court. Can you guess what impact that had on women who were deciding whether to sue? Exactly. Thankfully, things have changed.

Under today's rule, your sexual history, sophistication, dress, speech, STD status, private sexual preferences, and all other extraneous matters are *not* admissible in sexual harassment cases. For there to be an exception to this rule, an employer faces significant hurdles, and the exception is insanely rare.

So, worry not—what happens in Miami Beach stays in Miami Beach!

Courts don't conflate welcome with voluntary, however. For example, just because a woman was not physically forced against her will to stay in the conference room while her coworkers told sexist jokes doesn't mean she "welcomed" the behavior.

Fortunately, courts also recognize that speaking up as a woman is not always easy. As author and essayist Margaret Atwood famously said, "Men are afraid that women will laugh at them. Women are afraid that men will kill them." Although Atwood's insight may not have been the impetus, courts do recognize that there are situations when a woman's silence *can* communicate that behavior is unwelcome, such as when she consistently doesn't respond to suggestive gestures.[5]

Said another way, no response can be a response, and it's not necessarily your fault if ol' boy doesn't get the message. It all just depends on the totality of the circumstances. (You'll hear that a lot when it comes to how courts make decisions.)

Severe or Pervasive. In addition to being unwelcome, the harassing behavior must be severe or pervasive, more than just teasing or offhand comments. That determination is made on a case-by-case basis, considering all of the circumstances—not just isolated incidents. It's a fact-intensive test that considers things like the type of behavior, its frequency and severity, whether it was physically threatening or interfered with you performing your work. No one factor is decisive. Not all behavior is treated alike.

Offensive comments alone usually must be harsh and frequent to support an HWE claim—that is, *unless* a comment is combined with more serious behavior like unwanted touching or threats of physical harm. For example, a former female FedEx driver was able to state an HWE claim by alleging that her supervisor and coworkers said annoying things to her like women should be "barefoot and pregnant" and that she "looked like a porn star," *and* tried to intimidate her by sabotaging the brakes on her truck five times. Instances of trying to physically harm you can bolster the legal significance of offhand, offensive comments. It's rare that a single incident, such as a supervisor groping an employee's breasts, would be enough to establish HWE (even though it could support a criminal complaint). *But* a lone incident may establish HWE if it's severe enough. A flight attendant who said she was raped by a coworker during a layover abroad, for example, did *not* need to be raped more than once to establish an HWE claim.[6] The act of rape was severe enough.

There's no set list of behaviors that constitute HWE—it all runs on a spectrum. At the less severe end of the spectrum is problematic behavior that must create more than just an unpleasant workplace. A female school counselor failed to do this, however, despite evidence that a male science teacher often visited her office, always ending their conversations by touching her arm, and called her at home to discuss his failed relationships and intimate details of his personal life, ending each call by telling her he loved her and that she was very special. The court thought his behavior was that of someone in search of a friend more than that of a sexual predator.[7] The bar can be high.

Objectively and Subjectively Bad. Lastly, HWE must be both objectively *and* subjectively hostile. The objective part asks whether the average reasonable woman (or man) in your situation would find the environment offensive. The court determines this by looking at all of the circumstances. For instance, in her lawsuit against General Motors, Marilyn Williams said she'd endured behavior during her thirty years at the automotive company that would offend *any* reasonable person. According to Williams, her super-

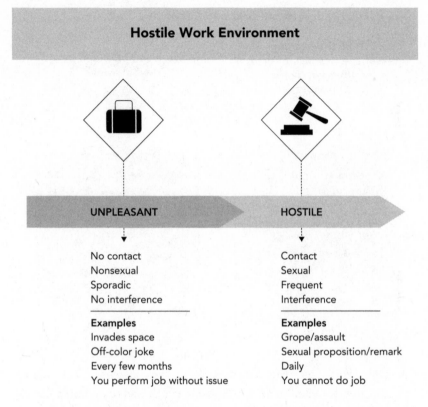

visor ogled her breasts and said, "You can rub up against me anytime," and told her, "You left the dick out of the hand" as she was writing "Handcock Furniture Company" on a document. In the predominantly male environment, Williams was the only one denied breaks, overtime, and keys to the office. Her male coworkers threw things at her and yelled, "Hey, slut!" and "I'm sick and tired of these fucking women." They also locked Williams inside of a storage unit and glued her office supplies to her desk. This behavior indeed would offend the reasonable person.[8]

For the subjective part of HWE, you must show that *you* were actually offended by the behavior, perceiving the environment to be hostile. This can be apparent by looking at (you guessed it!) *all* the circumstances. For example, in some workplaces, I started wearing a wedding ring, put up a picture of myself and a faux SO, brought my lunch from home, changed my work

Objective Test and Subjective Test

Would the average
reasonable woman (or man)
be offended by the
behavior?

Were you offended by
the behavior?

A reasonable person in
your circumstances must
be able to find the work
environment hostile or
abusive.

This is the objective
component that helps
ensure the work
environment is more than
just unpleasant.

You must have been
offended by the behavior.

This is the subjective
component that helps
distinguish between
flirtation or rudeness and
illegal sexual harassment.

schedule to avoid interacting with harassholes, messaged friends and family about the problems, and so on. My behavior confirmed that I found the environments hostile.

Of course, an employer may try to show that you were fine, as you didn't miss or mess up any work during the alleged harassment, or that you continued to enjoy the harasser's company without objection or complaint. Harassholes and employers will reach for just about anything to undermine you. Don't take it personally.

EMPLOYER LIABILITY AND DEFENSES

Employers rarely—if ever—admit error and accept responsibility for sexual misconduct that goes down on their watch. They typically try to fight back, even if they know you're telling the truth and they should be held liable. Don't take it personally. Also, don't assume the employer will automatically be held liable. It all depends on the standards set by the courts in the jurisdiction you're in, unfortunately.

Although employer liability may be fluid, it's safe to say that employer knowledge is less so. For the most part, there must be evidence that the employer knew or should've known of the harassment. In some jurisdictions, a supervisor harassing you is enough and is imputed to the employer. In other jurisdictions, it's not. This is why you should seek counsel to check the standards in your area.

⬆️ HEADS-UP!

You don't have to wait until you're fired, demoted, suspended, or in a dangerous situation to have an HWE or QPQ claim. If the harassment is so bad that you have to resign, it may be considered a constructive discharge that is the legal equivalent of being fired.

As it concerns defenses, employers have numerous options for defending against QPQ and HWE claims. Typically, they claim that you're lying, which is why you keep receipts. They also may feign ignorance if you didn't report the harasshole. Fortunately, where the court expected you to report the harassment to give your employer a chance to fix the situation, there are limited exceptions that may excuse your reason for not following company protocol. These exceptions, which are not fail-safe, include (1) a legitimate belief that the employer wouldn't take the harassment seriously; (2) credible fear of retaliation; and (3) real obstacles to reporting the harassment or cooperating with your employer's protocol.

If you were fired, not hired, suspended, or otherwise retaliated against (which we'll cover more in chapter 12), the most common defense employers use is to claim it was for a legitimate nondiscriminatory reason. This is what Meritor Bank tried to do in Vinson's case, claiming she was fired for taking too much unauthorized leave rather than for getting a serious boyfriend and rejecting her boss's demands for sex. You may be able to refute your employer's defense by showing it's just a cover-up. These pretextual setups happen *all the time* and frequently involve attacks on your work performance, which is why it's imperative to maintain the sexual harassment and workplace performance logs we discussed in chapter 7.

SHARING A COWORKER'S EXPERIENCE

If you file a lawsuit, you may end up having to speak about your coworker's experiences because it may be necessary to establish a claim, it may be a part of the facts of your case, or in the discovery process you'll be forced to turn over all of the evidence you have of sexual harassment in the workplace. This may be difficult—not just because you'd be breaking your coworker's trust but also because your employer may retaliate against your coworker for sharing that information with you. This predicament is a by-product of the system courts have created for those seeking justice under Title VII, unfortunately.

 TIME-OUT

Bear in mind that what happened to your coworker played a role in what happened to you by contributing to the environment in which you suffered, the stress you endured, and possibly even your rationale for not using your employer's reporting system. Regardless, the harasshole-enabling employer is the one at fault— *not you.*

Fortunately, all is not lost. If you have to share a coworker's experience and your employer has a reputation for retaliation, there's a way you may be able to protect her. I'll explain by way of hypothetical: A coworker shares with you her harassment experience, which is documented in text messages that your employer *will* obtain in discovery—putting a big target on *her* back. She could be mistreated, demoted, fired, or blacklisted without her or anyone other than your retaliation-happy employer knowing why. What should you do? Consider including her story in the complaint that you file in court. It's a public document for all to see—including the media. Now that *everyone* knows what happened to her, your retaliation-happy employer has two options:

(A) retaliate against her while everyone is watching, risking public backlash and the possibility that she may end up telling the truth and/or supporting your case;

OR

(B) treat her well by allowing her to professionally advance, negotiate a lucrative exit package or settlement, or otherwise remain steadily employed without issue, in exchange for her silence and/or support for your employer.

Although the employer's arrogance coupled with the coworker's rank can impact their decision, nearly all employers with something to hide go with Option B—which effectively takes the target off your coworker's back and puts the power in her hands (which she'll hopefully recognize). The same goes for any of your colleagues whose stories you tell, or who you otherwise put in a position where your employer would need them to lie or conveniently not recall. This strategy can be effective because it stokes your employer's fear of being exposed as a sexual harassment hotbed by someone in addition to you. (Did someone say "class action"?) There's power in numbers.

That's not to say there aren't downsides, such as your coworker feeling betrayed or siding with your employer to conceal the misconduct. But I'll let you in on a little secret: Just like coworkers will distance themselves from you if you're in a sexual harassment situation, it's extremely common for them to lie under oath to protect themselves and their employment prospects. Of course, any employee who risks perjury for an employer is already a fool—but she's a damn fool if she doesn't get something out of it. On that note . . . Whatever leverage your coworker has won't last forever, as she may become vulnerable to retaliation once she testifies in your employer's favor or once your lawsuit ends.

This may be the unsavory world we live in, but that doesn't mean we too should lie or that we shouldn't all be working together to make this world a better place for those who come after us.

REPLAY

* Title VII of the Civil Rights Act of 1964 is the federal law that bans workplace sexual harassment. It applies to U.S. employers with fifteen or more employees and protects certain employees and applicants. State laws differ and may be broader than Title VII.

* The two sexual harassment claims under Title VII are quid pro quo (QPQ) and hostile work environment (HWE). QPQ arises when professional opportunities are conditioned on how you or others respond to sexual advances that are explicit or implicit. HWE is a work environment that is dripping with so much unwelcomed intimidation, ridicule, sexual conduct, or offensive imagery that it changes your job.

* The law is always evolving, with new court decisions coming out every day that reflect changes in our society and how it views certain behavior. Whether you can establish a sexual harassment claim may depend on the court decisions relevant to your case. Seek counsel should you have any questions.

* In a sexual harassment lawsuit, your coworker's sexual harassment experience may come into the mix. If your employer is known for retaliation, you may be able to give your coworker leverage by publicly sharing her experience in your complaint. Remember, the harasshole-enabling employer is the one at fault—not you!

CHAPTER 12

Legal Ratchet and Lawyering Up

Insight into Retaliation, Remedies, and Great Counsel

....

If we want to stop discrimination, harassment, and unethical decision-making, we need to end retaliation against the people who speak honestly about these problems.

—*Meredith Whittaker and Claire Stapleton,*
tech gawdesses and Google Walkout leaders

ALL SALES REPRESENTATIVES hired at PMT, a Minnesota-based medical device manufacturer, were men under the age of forty. Company president Alfred Iversen apparently had a policy of refusing to hire women and anyone over forty as sales representatives. Patricia Lebens was unaware of this when she signed on to work in PMT's HR department. When Lebens learned of this unwritten policy, she tried to encourage the president to change. But her efforts were to no avail. So, like any ethical bad bitch, she anonymously tipped off the EEOC. After the agency came knocking on PMT's door, the president purportedly threatened to "go after" whoever reported him. Lebens quit shortly thereafter.

Two years later, the president reportedly discovered that Lebens was the one to tip off the EEOC about his discriminatory policies. So, like any twisted whack-job, he contacted the local sheriff and claimed that Lebens stole some $2,000 from his company. After an investigation, the sheriff realized the president's claim was shenanigans. The EEOC sued the company on Lebens's behalf. PMT paid more than $1 million as part of a settlement.[1]

Claire Stapleton was among thousands of Google employees fed up with how the company handled (or mishandled) sexual harassment complaints.

In November 2018, the twelve-year company woman was among seven Google employees to lead a historic protest that resulted in twenty thousand employees walking out of the job. Stapleton & Co. collected some 350 co-workers' stories about sexual harassment at Google, reading them aloud and demanding change from the tech giant. Google ultimately agreed to end forced arbitration of discrimination complaints and to address its sexual harassment issues. A win that Stapleton didn't savor long.

Two months later, Stapleton said she was demoted, and her projects as well as half of her staff were taken away. She escalated the matter to HR and an executive, per Google protocol. Then things got worse. Stapleton's superiors allegedly tried to force her to go on medical leave, despite the fact that she wasn't sick. Only after she hired an attorney to get involved did Google "investigate" her retaliation complaint and walk back the demotion, she said. In an April 2019 letter publicizing her experience in the aftermath of the walkout, Stapleton said, "While my work has been restored, the environment remains hostile and I consider quitting nearly every day."[2]

As these women's experiences suggest, retaliation and remedies come in many forms, and sometimes companies won't act right unless you have legal counsel. This chapter explores what retaliation looks like, what you can do about it, the compensation available, and how you can land a good lawyer by your side. You got this!

RETALIATION

Retaliation occurs when an employer or someone in a position of power mistreats you or others for reporting or opposing harassment, participating in an investigation or lawsuit, or otherwise engaging in an activity protected by Title VII. Simply put, retaliation is just petty revenge—but it does real damage.

Remember Dr. Ravina, who was at Columbia University? After Bekaert sent those heinous emails about her to their colleagues, she had to leave her tenure-track teaching position at the New York City Ivy League school, moving to the Midwest for a temporary teaching job. Recall Lieutenant Franchina at the Providence Fire Department? Not only did she suffer years of appalling mistreatment but also the female coworker who testified at

Franchina's trial about the hostile workplace was suddenly demoted by the department three weeks after her testimony.[3]

Retaliation is very real and very illegal, yet *extremely* common. As we've discussed, some 75 percent of employees who file sex discrimination complaints with the EEOC also allege to have suffered retaliation.[4] In addition to being common, retaliation claims also happen to be the most *successful* claims in sexual harassment cases because it's easier to prove than HWE or QPQ. Think about it: Sexual harassment often involves a he said/she said situation, whereas retaliation typically entails sudden termination, abrupt demotion, or unexplained professional turmoil. One moment you're a talented rising star; the next, an underperforming ingrate. Juries have an easier time believing your career suddenly took a hard left *because* you complained about a harasshole, especially if your employer's explanation is trash. Bottom line: Retaliation is a helluva claim.

The Basics of Retaliation

First, retaliation comes into play only when you've engaged in Title VII protected activity, which can include reporting harassment, filing an EEOC complaint, or participating in an investigation or legal proceeding about a harassment claim. Your employer cannot legally punish you so long as you had a reasonable and good-faith belief that what you shared with your employer, the EEOC, court, or other entity was true. That reasonable and good-faith belief element is essential because even if it turns out that you weren't being sexually harassed (by legal standards), it's *still* illegal for your employer to punish you, just like in Dr. Ravina's case.

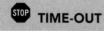 **TIME-OUT**

You can file an EEOC complaint and sue your employer for violating Title VII while you're still actively working for your employer— and you still have the right *not* to be punished for anything you do involving your case.

Suing an employer while still working there is a bawse move. But hey, why pass on a paycheck simply because your employer wants to break the law?

Second, retaliation can come in many forms. But no matter its form, the action must be "materially adverse." According to the Supreme Court, this means that the retaliation must be so harmful that it would dissuade a reasonable employee from making or supporting a sexual harassment complaint. While that sounds reasonable, courts have *not* consistently been as reasonable in interpreting it. Here's what the landscape looks like on what actions federal courts have considered materially adverse enough to support a retaliation claim:

Almost Never Sufficient	Could Go Either Way	Nearly Always Sufficient
Shunning	Discipline	Termination
Ostracism	Reprimand	Demotion
Isolation	Negative review	Denied a promotion
	Work schedule changes	Pretextual layoff
	Paid suspensions	
	Administrative leave	

This may seem crazy to you. Oh, it *is*. Wouldn't you be dissuaded from reporting sexual harassment if you knew you'd be disciplined, given a bad review, or put on leave as a result? You're not alone! Studies have confirmed that more than 50 percent of college-educated people wouldn't stand up for themselves if it resulted in a paid weeklong suspension.[5] Clearly, the courts have a poor read on what retaliation would dissuade a reasonable person from reporting sexual harassment.

⬆️ **HEADS-UP!**

The EEOC provides a long list of employer actions that are retalia-
tory and are much more reflective of what would dissuade a living,
breathing reasonable person from complaining about sexual harassment. Unfortunately, the courts have not been 100 percent
persuaded by the EEOC.

Lastly, a retaliation claim requires that you prove there's a connection
between your protected activity (for example, reporting a harasshole) and
your employer's actions against you (for example, terminating your job).
Rarely does an employer who fires or demotes you *ever* admit that it was because they wanted to punish you for standing up to sexual harassment.
Ninety-nine percent of the time employers lie, offering some seemingly
innocuous reason for suddenly derailing your career, like citing layoffs or
claiming you were a low performer. Without a copy of that proverbial "smoking email" asking to get rid of you for complaining about Shameless Dude,
you'll want to fight your employer's lie with circumstantial evidence that
undermines their reasoning and shows that they wouldn't have taken the
action against you but for your report. Answers to these questions may do
just that:

- **Timing.** How long after you complained about sexual harassment did
  your employer start acting up? Did the employer seize the first opportunity to drop you, such as waiting until there were mass layoffs?
- **Process.** Did your employer follow the proper protocol before sending
  your career into a downward spiral? For example, if you were fired
  without warning, but the company policy requires that employees receive a warning first, that suggests something's off.
- **Performance.** Did you suddenly receive your first bad review or
  start getting criticized by the boss after you complained about sexual
  harassment?
- **Mistreatment.** Did your boss or colleagues stop inviting you to meetings or social gatherings, mess with your schedule, ice you out of

opportunities, or otherwise treat you differently after you reported the harasshole?

- **Bad Guy.** Is the harasser the same person who controls your fate? Is he good friends with management?
- **Bad Excuse.** Is the reason for the adverse action airtight (company closing), convenient (layoffs), or pathetic (no reason given)? Is your employer suddenly claiming your work's lousy despite the fact that your clients are raving about you?
- **Colleagues.** How are your similarly situated or lower-ranking colleagues being treated? Are they getting promoted over you or given opportunities you applied for but they didn't? Did they get bonuses or were their contracts renewed despite performance issues or lack of experience?
- **Similar Situations.** How is the company treating other employees who reported sexual harassment or discrimination? Were they demoted or forced out too? Were their contracts terminated? Does the company have a history of acting up when employees report sexual harassment?

Employer Defense

When facing a clear retaliation claim, an employer can defend itself by attacking any of the elements we just discussed. Typically, employers will argue that they had a legitimate, nondiscriminatory reason for the action against you. For example, if you were laid off because *everyone* at the company was laid off and the company was closing, the employer has a leg to stand on in court. But if you were the only person "laid off" during a corporate expansion and hiring frenzy, your employer probably doesn't have a strong defense. As always, it boils down to the totality of the circumstances.

REMEDIES

Let's talk remedies—that's the compensation available to you for fighting sexual harassment. Although we're discussing only federal law here, you want to keep in mind that there may be more remedies available to you under state laws. Here are the remedies under Title VII:

- **Compensatory Damages.** Money to compensate you for pain and suffering, job search expenses, reputational damages, therapy costs, and so on.
- **Punitive Damages (aka Exemplary Damages).** Money you receive that is meant to punish your employer, to make an example of them, for violating Title VII.
- **Injunctive Relief.** A court order telling your employer to stop whatever discrimination it engages in or to adopt a new practice.
- **Reinstatement.** Reinstatement means you get your job back (if it is available *and* you want it). But, if the court orders reinstatement, you can't get front pay.
- **Front Pay.** Money you get for losses you suffer from the date of a court decision in your favor until a specified time in the future. The amount of front pay often depends on how old you are, how long you were in the job, how many years you likely would have stayed in that job, among other things.
- **Back Pay.** Money you would have earned from the time you suffered at the job to the time a court ruled in your favor. This includes anticipated lost wages, raises, bonuses, tips, commissions, vacation and sick pay, benefits, stock options, and so on. Federal law may limit back pay to two years from the date you filed your lawsuit. Your back pay also may be reduced by any wages you earned at new jobs or if you didn't try to minimize your losses by sincerely looking for other jobs.
- **Attorneys' Fees and Costs.** If you win on your claims, the employer must pay your attorneys' fees and the administrative costs incurred in your lawsuit.

STOP TIME-OUT

Prevailing on federal sexual harassment claims are unlikely to make you a legend at the bank. As we touched on in chapter 6, Congress has set limits on the amount of compensatory *and* punitive damages *combined* that you can receive under Title VII, based on your employer's number of employees.

Number of Employees	Award Limit
15–100	$50,000
101–200	$100,000
201–500	$200,000
500+	$300,000

SMH. Just remember: If these numbers look small to you, you also may be able to collect the other remedies we discuss, in addition to larger awards, under state anti–sexual harassment laws. On a positive note, the #MeToo movement may be moving juries toward more generous awards for punitive damages under state laws. In Massachusetts, for instance, juries were giving out just *one* punitive damage award over $600,000 per year before #MeToo popped off in October 2017. By October 2018, Massachusetts juries had given out *six* such awards, including one for $25 million in punitive damages. If that's a signal as to where things are going, more sexual harassment plaintiffs could be going to the bank in the future.[6]

LAWYERING UP 101

If you were looking to have open-heart surgery, you likely wouldn't try to do it without a licensed professional, right? The same principle goes for handling legal issues. You should have an attorney help you navigate a sexual harassment case, before you ever set foot in court.

Before you jump to any conclusions about lawyers, please consider a few things. First, I'm a lawyer. So please be kind. Second, our rights and privileges as citizens are the product of centuries of hard work performed by diligent lawyers, many of whom fought for a more egalitarian future for little, no, or less pay than they could've commanded (such as Ruth Bader Ginsburg). And third, there is no third. It just seems neater to list things in threes. On that note, this section focuses on three things: understanding the typical legal path for a sexual harassment case, learning when to lawyer up, and knowing how to get good counsel. Let's do this!

THE TYPICAL LEGAL PROCESS

The legal process is pretty predictable in most sexual harassment cases. Of course, there are always exceptions. There could be things specific to your case that could change the process, such as mandatory arbitration. You also could enter voluntary mediation or settle the case at any point along the journey. Outside of any exceptions or binding arbitration, here's a brief description of the eight typical stages of a sexual harassment case.

Stage 1: Private Mediation. You may participate in private mediation with your employer before you file a complaint with the EEOC or a court. Mediation is an informal way to resolve a dispute, and it's usually voluntary. A neutral third party (perhaps a retired judge or professional mediator) helps you and your employer come to an agreeable resolution. It can be a low-cost way to gain perspective on your entire case and an expeditious way to resolve a dispute before entering the legal system. It also can be a complete and utter waste of time if your employer isn't sincere and is simply trying to figure out what evidence you have because they're shady. (Believe me. I know.)

Stage 2: EEOC Filing. After the discrimination, you'll have a certain window of time to file a complaint (also known as a "charge") with the EEOC or its analogous state agency, which may cross-file your complaint with the EEOC. Essentially, your complaint outlines the allegations and provides the EEOC with facts to investigate. Once your complaint is filed, the EEOC will review it to ensure the facts you provided amount to a discrimination claim. The EEOC will then notify the employer.

⚖ BONUS POINT

In some states, you may be able to bypass the investigation stage by requesting a Notice of Right to Sue letter after you filed your complaint, which would allow you to go straight to federal court!

Stage 3: EEOC Investigation. At the start of an investigation, the EEOC will tell you and the employer whether the case is eligible for voluntary mediation through the EEOC, if you wish to mediate for the first time or again if you've already done it. The employer will then be asked to respond to your complaint and to any EEOC requests—for additional information, interviews, or on-site visits, for example. You may have an opportunity to respond to the employer's statement.

Stage 4: EEOC Findings and Right to Sue Notice. After all necessary information is submitted, the EEOC reviews the file and issues one of three decisions:

(i) If the EEOC can't confirm that you were discriminated against, it will send you a Dismissal and Notice of Right to Sue letter, which gives you ninety days to file a lawsuit in court.

(ii) If the EEOC thinks you were discriminated against, it will send you and the employer a Letter of Determination, inviting both sides to try to resolve the complaint through an informal EEOC process known as conciliation.

(iii) If that's unsuccessful, the EEOC has the authority to sue your employer in court on your behalf. If the EEOC opts not to, it will send you a Notice of Right to Sue letter, which gives you ninety days to file a lawsuit in court.

Stage 5: Lawsuit. If you choose to go forward with a lawsuit, you must file a complaint in the appropriate court within the ninety-day window. An attorney can help you with this and see that the correct paperwork is served on your employer. Remember that the complaint is a public document, so anyone can read it.

⬆ HEADS-UP!

Arbitration is an alternative option for resolving a dispute. The process is somewhat similar to litigating in court, but there's no judge or jury; instead you and your employer select up to three arbitrators to review the evidence and make a decision. Although arbitration often is binding, whether the parties are bound by the arbitrators' decision depends on their agreement.

Arbitration has the benefit of being quicker and cheaper than fighting in court. But it has so many detriments for employees. For example, the arbitrators' decision is nearly impossible to reverse, unlike the appeal process in court. Arbitration awards also are typically lower than what you can get in court. The American Arbitration Association (AAA), which handles half of all employment cases in the country, awarded employees money in a meager 1.8 percent of 8,209 complaints filed between 2013 and 2017.[7]

Arbitration agreements have been hot topics in sexual harassment cases because they're private, there's no government oversight, and harassholes are often shielded from exposure and public accountability. Due to employee protests and some public pressure, several companies have stopped forcing employees into arbitration agreements, including internet giant Google. Additionally, some states are now passing laws to ban employers from forcing mandatory arbitration agreements. Even so, about 60 million American workers at more than half of U.S. companies are still forced to settle their disputes through private arbitration, keeping the misconduct behind closed doors and the employees practically powerless.

Stage 6: Dispositive Motions. After your complaint is filed, your employer may try to have the case dismissed by filing various dispositive motions, most likely a motion to dismiss, which the court will rule on and decide whether your case can move forward.

Stage 7: Discovery. In the discovery process, you and the employer show your cards. You exchange documentation, evidence, supporting materials, just about everything you have that supports your case, including any medical records. You may sit for a deposition where you're asked to answer questions under oath about your case, and possibly a psychological exam. At the end of discovery, there's a second round of dispositive motions (motions

The Process

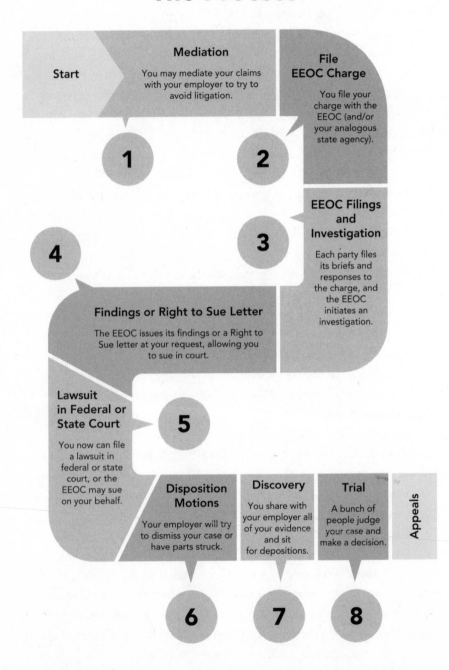

Start

Mediation
You may mediate your claims with your employer to try to avoid litigation.

1

File EEOC Charge
You file your charge with the EEOC (and/or your analogous state agency).

2

EEOC Filings and Investigation
Each party files its briefs and responses to the charge, and the EEOC initiates an investigation.

3

4

Findings or Right to Sue Letter
The EEOC issues its findings or a Right to Sue letter at your request, allowing you to sue in court.

Lawsuit in Federal or State Court
You now can file a lawsuit in federal or state court, or the EEOC may sue on your behalf.

5

Disposition Motions
Your employer will try to dismiss your case or have parts struck.

Discovery
You share with your employer all of your evidence and sit for depositions.

Trial
A bunch of people judge your case and make a decision.

Appeals

6

7

8

for summary judgment) to determine whether the case goes to trial and, if so, what issues.

Stage 8: Trial. In the trial stage, the witnesses and evidence are determined in advance so there are no surprises. (No, it's nothing like *Legally Blonde* or *Law & Order.*) A jury is selected, unless you've decided to have the judge make the ultimate decision (bench trial). Both sides present their evidence, calling witnesses and making arguments. The jury issues a decision (verdict) on each one of your claims and how much money you should receive for each claim. (After a verdict is rendered, the next phase would be the appeal process, which can go on for years.)

Sexual harassment cases, like almost all cases in the legal system, can take years to resolve. On average, it takes the EEOC approximately 295 days just to process your complaint, which may be before you can even go to court.[8] Indeed, the legal process isn't for the faint of heart or the impatient. Nor is it something you should ever go through alone.

LAWYERING UP

Despite your newfound knowledge of sexual harassment law, there is *no* suitable substitute for good legal counsel. That's why you lawyer up!

Most of us can't afford to keep an attorney waiting in the wings, which is why it's important to know *when* to lawyer up. If you're uncertain about that, using what you've learned about sexual harassment and retaliation claims, there are a few nifty flowcharts on the following pages that may help guide you. Take note that these charts aren't the end-all and be-all. Go with your instincts!

HOW TO GET A GOOD LAWYER

Like it or not, lawyers are necessities. The good ones know the law, how to make the right arguments, and how to navigate the legal system. The bad ones know how to make you hate lawyers. The goal is to get a good one. You likely don't want to just go with the lawyer whose photo you saw plastered on a freeway sign or that your cousin's sister-in-law's stylist recommended. A lawyer-client relationship is sacred. It's like a marriage—and a divorce can

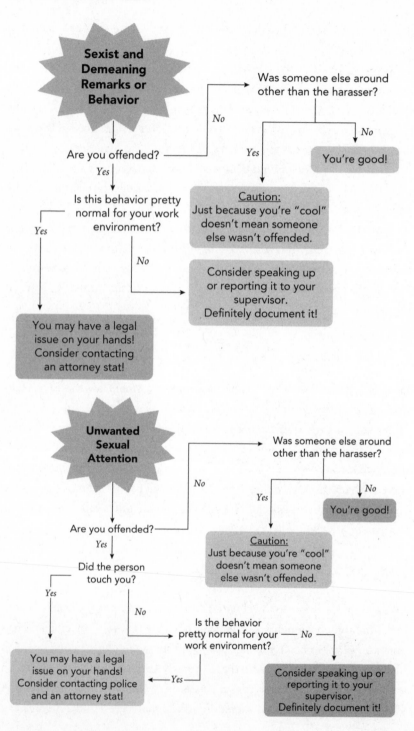

Sexist and Demeaning Remarks or Behavior

Are you offended? — *No* →

Was someone else around other than the harasser?

Yes |

No → You're good!

Yes

Is this behavior pretty normal for your work environment?

Yes

Caution: Just because you're "cool" doesn't mean someone else wasn't offended.

No

Consider speaking up or reporting it to your supervisor. Definitely document it!

You may have a legal issue on your hands! Consider contacting an attorney stat!

Unwanted Sexual Attention

Are you offended? — *No* →

Was someone else around other than the harasser?

Yes |

No → You're good!

Yes

Did the person touch you?

Yes

Caution: Just because you're "cool" doesn't mean someone else wasn't offended.

No

Is the behavior pretty normal for your work environment? — *No* →

Yes →

You may have a legal issue on your hands! Consider contacting police and an attorney stat!

Consider speaking up or reporting it to your supervisor. Definitely document it!

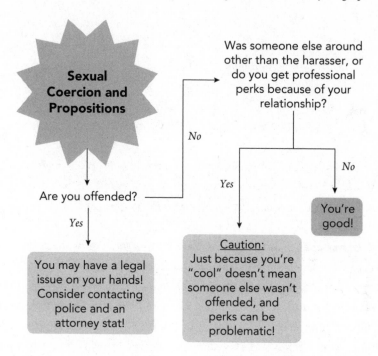

be costly and emotionally draining. As an attorney who has hired and fired sexual harassment attorneys, and worked on the cases herself, I know the score. These pro tips can help you find the right counsel for *you*:

- **Sexual Harassment Specialists.** You want an attorney who specializes in sexual harassment cases because she has a head start on everything. From the research to the case law, she will be intimately familiar with what you faced and what can be done about it. The last thing you want is a patent attorney navigating through decades of sexual harassment case law, reinventing the wheel, and racking up ridiculous legal bills.

BONUS POINT

There are thousands of attorneys out there. Finding the right one can feel overwhelming. To help alleviate the stress, here are three good ways to start your attorney search:

1. **High-Profile Cases.** Do an online search of recent high-profile sexual harassment cases that ended well and look to see who the attorney was who represented the harassed.
2. **Check with Organizations.** Reach out to BetterBrave or the Time's Up Legal Defense Fund to get contact information for attorneys.
3. **Ask the Bad Guys.** Do an online search for top sexual harassment *defense* firms and ask an attorney in their office which *plaintiff's* law firms they do *not* want to go up against.

- **Experience Going Against *Your* Employer.** You want an attorney who has experience representing other former employees of your employer because, once again, they'll have a leg up. They'll know how your employer litigates and may have some secret information about things your employer has done to others at your company. This factor is especially important if your employer is a big company, as big corporations are very powerful and few attorneys are willing and equipped to go against them. You do not want to be in a situation where your attorney is actually playing for the other team . . .

- **Has No Ties to Your Employer.** Look out for attorneys who have ties to your employer. The legal and business communities can be very incestuous, but a true plaintiff's attorney should not have direct ties to your employer. It's best if the attorney has never worked, golfed, or slept with your employer, as this could blur the lines of loyalty—despite the ethical rules that require attorneys to be all in for *you*. One attorney I hired turned out to have had a chummy relationship with the CEO of my former employer, which was revealed to me around the time my attorney started acting up. Let's just say our attorney-client relationship imploded not long after that.

- **On-Point Approach and Personality.** You need counsel who is a good fit for *you*. Ensure that the attorney's approach aligns with your own. Maybe she likes to use press conferences to leverage, à la Gloria Allred? Does he like to go full-on Michael Avenatti messy? Or does she keep things quiet like that attorney you've likely never heard of? Regardless of their approach, make sure it suits you. Your attorney is an extension of you, and you should be represented in a way that jives with you. Also, you want to feel secure in your counsel's hands. Attorneys who scream and yell at you, or get indignant when you ask questions, may not be your speed. Find one who fits you.

■ **Communicates Well by Phone and in Writing.** Communication is key! Some lawyers struggle with it. But that's no excuse. Lawyers have an ethical duty to communicate with you. They should be responding to your emails or phone calls in a timely fashion, or at least communicating when you can expect a response. It's basic professionalism. You also deserve communication that *is* professional. That means words are spelled correctly in correspondence and court filings, and there are no glaring grammatical issues, emojis, or hashtags. You want to be represented well and taken seriously. Your attorney must have these basic skills.

■ **Time and Resources Ready.** The size of your case is key. You do not want a small law firm with limited resources running a major class action with hundreds of witnesses. Your attorney should have the resources to successfully see your case through, no matter what direction it takes. Do you want your attorney trying the judge's patience by seeking numerous extensions because she has too many cases to handle and too little time? No. Before hiring counsel, don't hesitate to ask for an outline of their game plan. You also should confirm in writing who will be staffed on your case. Some attorneys will try to reduce their own costs by staffing your case with inexperienced attorneys or people you're not comfortable working with, which will lead to big problems down the road. #HardPass

■ **Geographically Relevant.** Although it's not necessary, hiring an attorney who practices in the state where your case will be heard is extremely helpful. She's more likely to have rapport with local judges, be familiar with the court rules, and know what jury pools look like, among other things. Plus, you don't want to get "hometowned" because you hired an attorney who comes off as an "outsider" to the judge or jury. I saw a client lose a billion-dollar case by putting a Texas lawyer who dressed like Yankee Doodle and sounded like Matthew McConaughey in front of a Baltimore jury. Let's just say he wasn't all right, all right, all right!

🛑 TIME-OUT

If you're an heiress and money is of no concern, this little info block is not for you. For the rest of us, shelling out $500 an hour for legal fees is *not* an option. But there are other ways of getting good counsel without liquidating your entire IRA or renting out your womb as a surrogate for hire. Here they are:

- **Contingency Fee Agreement.** A contingency fee agreement (CFA) is a popular way of paying attorneys in sexual harassment cases. In a CFA, you agree to let your attorneys take a certain percentage of whatever money your employer may give you at the end of your case. If you don't get anything, your lawyer does not get paid. The standard contingency percentage for lawyers is about 33 percent, but that number can change depending on your situation. Just remember: Everything is negotiable!
- **Pro Bono.** When an attorney takes your case pro bono, she takes your case for free. As you may guess, pro bono cases are less common than CFA cases, and they most often occur when the harassed person has no resources, the case is high-profile, or the attorney is part of a university or nonprofit org. Additionally, because attorneys' fees are awarded under Title VII, the attorney still may get paid by the employer if your case is a winner. Wahoo!

WHEN YOUR LAWYER BECOMES A PROBLEM

It is not uncommon to distrust lawyers. But you should trust *your* lawyer. They're *your* confidant, and they act on *your* behalf. Unfortunately, there are times when your lawyer becomes a problem. Here are three common issues you could run into and some solid solutions:

Relationship Breakdown. Just like any relationship, the attorney-client relationship can break down. It may be a difference in outlook or style—

either way, it's okay to move on. Either of you can call it quits. If you two break up after a breakdown, your attorney should give you your case file, and refund any unused fees you paid in advance. Do check your legal agreement, as your attorney may be entitled to a portion of whatever you recover at the end of your case. To avoid having to give your now-former attorney a cut, upon parting ways you may want to ask for a lien release—that is, a signed statement from the attorney that says she won't try to claim rights to any money you may recover in the case. Whether she agrees to the release is her decision, although she may be more inclined to do so if you're parting ways because she violated ethical rules.

Ethical Issues. All lawyers are governed by ethical rules. While each state's bar rules may differ slightly, they are uniform in that they all require your attorney to be a trusted advisor, advocate, negotiator, and evaluator. Your lawyer should take those rules very seriously and abide by them—that includes not sharing confidential information, hiding money from you, or acting in a way that violates ethical rules or the law. If your lawyer breaks ethical rules or engages in criminal activity, they risk being sanctioned, suspended from the practice of law, or even disbarred. If you have any issues with your lawyer or are concerned about their conduct, consider contacting the appropriate law enforcement authorities and going to the American Bar Association (ABA) website, where you can find information on the state bar rules that govern your attorney's conduct and gather information on how to file a complaint, if need be. You also have the option to put them on blast via the media, which we talk about in chapter 13. You're entitled to quality representation and professionalism by a trained, law-abiding advocate. Never tolerate less.

Beware of BOAs. The attorney who represents you should be invested in your case and committed to the cause—namely, ending sexual misconduct. Many of the best sexual harassment attorneys have *always* represented the underdog against the employer or have been plaintiffs' attorneys for decades. Then again, no matter how much an attorney may tout #MeToo, there's always a chance they could be a turncoat. Beware of the BOA—the Bought-Out Attorney.

Basically, a BOA plays for both teams and is neither here for you nor committed to the cause. Most BOAs are motivated by money alone. They may represent you yet take cash from your employer or harasshole to mess up your case, to unnecessarily push you toward settlement, or to engage in other shady tactics that undermine your case and the cause. Before you ask . . . Yes, BOAs *may* be in breach of the ethical rules that govern licensed attorneys; but they also may be acting within those rules and are just showing you their true colors, which happen to be shades of green.

Actress-turned-activist and author Rose McGowan has seen her fair share of BOAs since exposing producer Harvey Weinstein in 2017. For example, before hiring her counsel Jose Baez and Ronald S. Sullivan Jr., McGowan told them she was concerned that they would be "bought-off" by Weinstein while representing her. According to McGowen, Baez responded by saying, "I don't like to lose." About a year later, Baez and Sullivan signed on to represent her accused rapist, Weinstein, claiming there was no conflict of interest and wishing McGowan well. Rightly so, the author of *BRAVE* felt betrayed.[9] Baez and Sullivan's decision to represent the disgraced movie mogul may not have violated ethical rules, but it still was pretty damn shady. Of course, karma may have caught up with both men as Harvard forced Sullivan to step down as a faculty dean once it was publicly announced that he would represent Weinstein, only for both Baez and Sullivan to bow out of the case six months later apparently because it was too difficult to work with Weinstein. (As it turns out, a man who's been publicly accused of verbally and/or sexually abusing more than one hundred women isn't easy to get along with. #Shocker)

Just a few months before Baez and Sullivan flipped on McGowan, a prominent women's rights attorney was reportedly doing McGowan dirty by calling around Hollywood, offering info to damage her and other women who boldly spoke out against Weinstein. That attorney was Lisa Bloom—who had just been lauded for bringing down Fox News's Bill O'Reilly and standing beside accusers of America's Dad and convicted rapist Bill Cosby. The daughter of attorney Gloria Allred and longtime defender of women had gone to the dark side, agreeing to be retained by Weinstein, which meant that none of his accusers could hire Bloom because it would be a conflict of interest—something she knew. In public, Bloom defended Weinstein as being respectful. In private, the Weinstein Company optioned the rights to her book, promising to develop it into a miniseries. Yay! If that wasn't bad enough, Bloom also agreed to represent the head of Amazon Studios, Roy Price, who resigned in October 2017 shortly after journalist Kim Masters published a story about him sexually harassing a coworker. Bloom allegedly tried to kill that story by spreading rumors about Masters. Although Bloom has since apologized, as said in the *Los Angeles Times*, "not only was she a hypocrite, but she was a sellout."[10]

You don't want to have to question alliances when your employer or the harasshole happens to have deeper pockets than you. Be wary of attorneys who play both sides, as they could turn out to be BOAs, secretly backing the highest bidder even when they're supposed to be behind you or the cause.

REPLAY

* Retaliation, a claim frequently filed in sexual harassment lawsuits, includes any punishment, heat, or shade from your employer because you complained about sexual harassment, participated in an investigation or lawsuit, or otherwise engaged in activity protected under Title VII.
* If you prevail on your Title VII claims, you have a number of remedies available to you, but your compensatory and punitive damages could be capped based on the employer's number of employees.
* The legal process in most sexual harassment cases involves eight stages: mediation, EEOC filing, EEOC investigation, EEOC findings and Right to Sue notice, filing a lawsuit, filing dispositive motions, discovery, and trial. If you signed an arbitration agreement, the process will not be in court, but it will be somewhat similar— although arbitration tends to end less favorably for employees than litigating in court.
* Choose your legal counsel wisely, like you would choose a significant other. It's an important relationship that could cost you your case and your sanity.
* Go with an attorney who specializes in sexual harassment cases, has experience going against your employer, has no ties to your employer, has an on-point approach and personality, communicates

well by phone and in writing, has the time and resources to handle your case, is willing to negotiate a contingency fee (if need be), and has the right ties to the court (or arbitration panel) and community.

* Your lawyer may become a problem if there's a breakdown in the attorney-client relationship, if the attorney breaks the law or violates ethical rules, or if the attorney is not committed to your cause, consider getting new counsel and, if need be, contacting the appropriate authorities.

* Beware of BOAs! The Bought-Out Attorney is not loyal to your case or the cause. They may be difficult to spot, but trust your instincts.

CHAPTER 13

Keeping Up Appearances

Managing Your Public Persona and Leveraging the Media

....

You don't want to have this become you or your brand. . . . In some ways, the higher the profile of the person you're accusing is, the more likely that is to happen.

—*Anita Hill, anti–sexual harassment OG, attorney, and law professor*

WHOEVER SAID "All publicity is good publicity" has never been attacked in the media. Anita Hill knows a thing or two about surviving a media attack. Her Congressional testimony made newspaper headlines across the nation and led nightly news stories in the fall of 1991. Upon sharing her experience about being sexually harassed by then Supreme Court nominee Clarence Thomas, Hill was not only despised by many but also publicly lied about in the media. Fortunately for her, it was 1991—the badass whistleblower spoke out in a time before online media was as expansive as it is today and before social media even existed. Hill was spared the harrowing experience of a digital dragging.

In the decades since her testimony, much has changed in media and the public response to women standing up to sexual harassment. Still, coming forward is nearly always crucifying for women and most certainly life-changing. And, as Hill indicated, taking a stand could become your brand when you go against a powerful man. Regardless of the harasser's social status, publicly exposing sexual misconduct is not for the faint of heart. I'm still surprised I survived my ordeal.

On December 14, 2017, when Jenn Abelson of the *Boston Globe* published a report that included my sexual harassment complaint against my former employer ESPN, I thought I was prepared.[1] I had already alerted loved ones and close colleagues, notified my then employer, archived any photos on so-cial media that could be taken out of context. I was ready for a news-cycle charade—or so I thought. *Nothing* could have prepared me for what hap-pened next.

Without diving into too much triggering detail, let's just say the World-wide Leader in Sports responded to the *Globe* report by creating its own fiction. With the creative efforts of their all-male outside legal team, ESPN shared with the world a strategically *altered* string of the text messages an Ulterior Motive Mentor sent to me that omitted his creepy comments and half-naked photos, only to tell a story different from the *Globe* report.[2] ESPN's manufactured story made *me* out to be the aggressor of the older, high-profile broadcaster I complained about.[3] It made me out to be a liar, a jezebel. To say my social media "detonated" would be an understatement.

Sports fans around the world hurled insults, issued threats, waged at-tacks. Talk radio shows blasted my name. Fox News and other major outlets plastered my face across the screen. Public figures in sports fanned the flames from their verified accounts. I'd later learn that ESPN was feeding media outlets and high-profile people the manufactured texts. What better way to discourage other women from coming forward and to distract the public from the rest of the *Globe* report—namely, parts where my former coworkers talk about being touched without their consent and being mis-treated because they were pregnant?

You could say ESPN had a lot to hide. Of course, its distraction campaign gave me nowhere to hide. The noise on Twitter, Instagram, Reddit, and Facebook all branded me a liar, accusing me of undermining the #MeToo movement, making a money grab. The short statement I posted on Twitter did nothing to stop the heat.[4] "Friends" distanced themselves. Colleagues unfollowed me on social media. Confidants who said they'd stand by me stood at a distance, silent. The handful of folks who tried to defend me on-line were attacked and drowned out by trolls, a few of whom found my phone number and repeatedly called. The abuse lasted months; the trauma, well over a year.

Information can travel at lightning speed. The media and online mobs can be relentless. The outcome can be life-changing. Going public with a sexual harassment claim often brings far more harm than what was inflicted by the harassment itself. Does that mean you stay silent and opt not to stand up for yourself? Fuck no. You get a gangsta-level game plan—one that harnesses the power of the media while recognizing the scarcity of secrets in our overexposed TMZ-type world. Luckily, I've got the game plan for you!

In this chapter, I give you game-changing advice on how to leverage the media and handle social media should your sexual harassment experience become news. In addition to drawing on my own experience, I offer the insight of experts in their field and real-world experiences. Herein lie the things I wish I'd known before, during, and after the mind-numbing months of my online assassination. What happened to me hopefully will *never* happen to you. But should media mayhem ever come your way, you'll know what to do and that you're not alone.

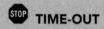 **TIME-OUT**

If you want to tell your story, you can choose the court of law or the court of public opinion or both. People who want you to stay silent, or solely fight in a courthouse, are trying to enable the culture of silence as they know staying quiet enables misconduct and the legal system works against you. Ignore those people. Do what you need to accomplish your goals. Plus, if change is what you seek, fighting in the media is likely your best bet, as we know employers won't take action unless the public learns of the misconduct. Speaking of action . . . With the bar so high, a legal action may not be an option, especially if you made a procedural misstep along the way.

All said, they tried to rob you of your dignity; never let them take your voice too.

MEDIA STRATEGY

When it comes to surviving a sexual harassment story on the public stage, a successful game plan starts with a strategy. Your strategy should be a reflection of you—your goals, your personality, and your circumstances. While you can never be completely prepared for media attention, you do not want to be completely unprepared. Here are several things to consider when formulating your strategy:

1. **Who are *you*?** Are you a brassy bitch, a classy professional, a dynamic diva—or are you unsure of who you are? Surviving sexual harassment changes you. Do your best to figure out who *you* are post–sexual harassment and who *you* want to be moving forward. It's easier to navigate the public space if there's no variance between who you are and who you present yourself to be. Trust me on this.

2. **What are your social identifiers?** Are you white, Asian, Black, mixed? Are you curvy, thin, short, tall? Do you come from affluence, poverty, the middle class? Did you get your education on the streets or in the books? Consider your social identifiers, the stereotypes attached to them, and how the world interacts with people like you. For example, if you're a Black woman accusing a prominent white man of sexual harassment, you will face more of an uphill battle in the media as a result of the racial stereotypes we discussed in chapter 3, which members of the media may try to leverage, like ESPN did to me. That should not stop you from taking a stand, but it is something to bear in mind.

3. **Who do you want to speak for you?** Should the public hear from you directly, a spokesperson, your attorney, or no one? If you're in a state of crisis, you may not have the mental and emotional bandwidth to articulate yourself in an eloquent fashion devoid of four-letter words. That's okay. That's also good reason to remain silent or to let your spokesperson or attorney speak on your behalf. Having someone speak for you also reduces the chances of having your words used against you later in the court of law or public opinion. Choose your spokesperson wisely.

🖒 BONUS POINT

Defamation is a problem. It occurs when someone makes a false, damaging statement about you that concerns something important. Truth is always a defense, however, as are fair comments, statements that are clearly identified as mere opinion, and unimportant nonsense such as obvious hyperbole. Also protected are statements made to law enforcement, the courts, the EEOC, and other government bodies.

While you don't want others' comments to become your focal point in life, you also don't want powerful media outlets ruining your good name. Stay mindful of defamation—and stay away from it too by using qualifying language when making statements in the media that you can't prove. While truth is always a defense, you do not want to expose yourself to being sued for some speculative comment you made about your harasser on a talk show or in an interview.

4. **How do you want to appear to the public?** Do you want to appear an activist, survivor, game-changer, person of mystery? You probably don't want to look like an opportunist, thirsty, jilted, or untrustworthy. Even when the employer goes low, do like Michelle Obama suggests, and go high. Keep public perception in mind, especially when considering your tone in social media posts and public statements. Check to ensure it matches your overall strategy and doesn't limit your future opportunities.

⬆ HEADS-UP!

Some members of the media (and trolls) will latch on to anything that makes you look bad and spin it to suit a narrative. Don't give them fodder. That sultry bikini pic from spring break 2019 may be the last thing you want making the rounds on CNN. You should do you, yes. But realize that appearances are powerful and social stigma can be hard to overcome. Here are some things you may want to consider *removing* from social media before a scandal:

- **Questionable Photos.** Reconsider any highly sexualized or intoxicated-looking photos of yourself online, including those pics of you holding alcohol or a red Solo cup, with half-open eyes, or baring skin. If you're a bikini model, alcohol distributor, or the like, you have less cause for concern, as people would expect certain photos of you. But if you're an accountant or academic, these can easily be used against you to the benefit of a harasshole or heinous employer.

- **Hate Speech.** If you've made any comments or "jokes" that are racist, sexist, homophobic, transphobic, ethnocentric, and so on, and you're comfortable with those remarks, by all means leave them on social media, as people should know who *you* are. But if they do not reflect the person you are today, take them down stat and consider issuing a sincere apology *now*. We all grow. Owning our mistakes can mean the difference between getting dragged in the media and getting sympathy.

Setting your account to "private" is *not* enough when it comes to shielding questionable posts. The best practice is simply to take them down, and to refrain from posting similar material again. This world is trifling, as are the trolls in it.

5. **What media channels are best for you?** You may be invited on talk shows, morning shows, radio shows. You can release a video on social media or sit down with a reporter. You can post a message on social media. Use the channels that will give you the opportunity to share the message *you* want to share in a way that best suits your personality and circumstances. For example, after I was attacked on social media, I passed on invitations to appear on shows, in part because I was not in a good place mentally and didn't want to say something I'd regret. I would've done more harm than good by publicly appearing at that time. Make the right decision for you.

6. **What resources are available to you?** Take a comprehensive look at your resources, such as social media pages, personal websites, media contacts, and connected friends. You have more available to you than you know. Do not be afraid to reach out and ask for help. When I was under siege, my most powerful ally was a woman I had known for a mere six months and had

hung out with just twice. Miko Grimes had a big social media following and an even bigger heart. On a moment's notice, the spicy sports commentator and devoted wife of NFL cornerback Brent Grimes used her online presence to go to bat for me. She became my unofficial and unapologetic spokeswoman, doing all that I couldn't do without harming my future case and coming off salty in the public eye. In my weakest hour, Mrs. Grimes was my greatest strength. Good people can be great resources. Discover yours.

7. **Do you need professional help?** If you're in over your head, public relations professionals can be lifesavers—especially the Olivia Popes of the world who focus on crisis management. They have established media contacts, experience, and a wealth of knowledge. Did you know there are companies that can have negative press about you scrubbed from the internet so as not to impair your employment prospects? PR professionals know this stuff. They can cost a pretty penny, but they can also deliver big-time. If you have the means, consider hiring one.

MAKING SENSE OF THE MEDIA

The media is not the enemy. Free media is essential to a free democracy. That's why the right to free press is memorialized in the First Amendment to the U.S. Constitution. The media is intended to be *the* independent check on government corruption and to keep the people informed. James Madison and his ol' boys' club probably never thought about the media playing a major role in exposing sexual harassment. Yet hundreds of years later, here we are!

The Media and Sexual Harassment

When it comes to exposing sexual harassment, historically the media has been heinous to whistle-blowers, especially women. Case in point: Anita Hill. She was dragged through the media to the point of defamation. David Brock, author of a bestselling book in which he labeled Hill "a little bit nutty and a little bit slutty," later said he did everything in his power to "ruin Hill's credibility" in the media, using "virtually every derogatory and often contradictory allegation" against her.[5] In 2001, Brock fessed up to being part of a coordinated campaign of lies to shut down Hill in a larger bid to put Clarence Thomas on the Supreme Court.[6] It worked.

More than fifteen years after Hill's testimony, it still works—the coordinated campaign of lies to silence sexual misconduct, that is. My experience in December 2017 is evidence of that fact, as are the many experiences of other women who bravely came forward and journalists like Ronan Farrow and Rich McHugh who boldly exposed it all. The fact remains that some members of the media are still giving journalists a bad name when it comes to reporting on sexual harassment.

Journalists were among the army of spies producer Harvey Weinstein reportedly hired to monitor his exposure. They would interview women about their allegations and then report back to the media mogul.[7] Remember when NBC tried to tell us that it passed on Ronan Farrow's Weinstein exposé because it didn't meet the network's "editorial standards," even though Farrow was an NBC correspondent at the time, an experienced journalist, and his exposé went on to win a Pulitzer Prize?[8] Let's not even get into the *National Enquirer* finally admitting in 2018 to killing stories of Donald Trump's sexual misconduct during his 2016 presidential bid.[9] You get the point.

🛑 TIME-OUT

Catch and kill (C&K) is a ploy media outlets use to keep your story from becoming public because it could damage a powerful person. Here's how it works: A media outlet offers to pay you for the exclusive rights to tell your story, the outlet has you sign an NDA, you tell the outlet your story, the outlet never publishes your story, but you can't tell another outlet because you're legally bound by the NDA. Shady, aye?

C&K is nothing new. Numerous high-profile men over the years have reportedly been the beneficiaries of the ploy—from actor Arnold Schwarzenegger to golfer Tiger Woods.

C&K is a trash tactic that needs to be killed and that also underscores why you cannot trust every reporter out there. In fact, a good rule of thumb is to avoid any outlet that offers you cash in exchange for exclusivity.

Although there are many trustworthy journalists out there, the media can be complicit when it comes to protecting powerful men accused of sexual misconduct. Why? There are several possible reasons, but three stand out. First, because of the blue-face Benjamins. Many of the exposed harassholes were cash cows and their respective employers didn't want to lose them, even if keeping them costs millions and kills women's careers. Don't forget that the largest broadcast news outlets—ABC, CBS, and NBC—are *not* wholly independent of other powerful entities. In fact, they're parents and subsidiaries and siblings of large, influential companies that do big deals with other large companies, some of which happen to be sexual harassment hotbeds. Disney, which owns ABC and ESPN, for example, also owned Weinstein's now-former company Miramax for more than a decade. Both Disney and Miramax were sued in 2018 for allegedly turning a blind eye to Weinstein's sexual misconduct, which was an open secret.[10] Do you think ABC would've put Weinstein on blast? Exactly. The incestuous nature of media outlets and big business can indeed interfere with reporting truth if it'd mean less income or exposing in-house trash.

Second, the media tends to condemn women accusers and protect harassholes because news is still a man's game. In 2018, the Pew Research Center revealed that U.S. newsrooms are 61 percent male and 77 percent white, making the percentage of white males working in newsrooms higher than that of the overall U.S. workforce.[11] This lack of gender and racial diversity impacts who tells stories and how they're told. Check out these disturbing facts from the Women's Media Center, a gender-focused media watchdog:[12]

- 63 percent of TV primetime news broadcasts feature male anchors and correspondents; 37 percent feature women.
- 69 percent of newswire bylines (AP and Reuters) are snagged by men, 31 percent by women—by far the biggest gender gap in news media.
- 60 percent of online news is written by men, 40 percent by women.
- 59 percent of print news is written by men, 41 percent by women.

According to the Women's Media Center, men report evening news twice as much as women do on the four largest news networks.

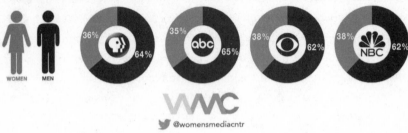

ANCHORS/CORRESPONDENTS/REPORTERS (EVENING BROADCASTS)

Those percentages are post-#MeToo. In 2017, before women pushed for change, ABC nightly news was at an abysmal 12 percent women, and all of the other networks were at least 32 percent.[14] Yes, well into the twenty-first century, women are still being boxed out of the media. That's a big problem, especially when it comes to reporting on sexual harassment. Female journalists interview women and write about how the misconduct impacted them more often than male journalists, who as a group tend to focus on the *woman's* behavior, as though she were responsible for the harassment or assault.[15] If men are the key storytellers of sexual harassment and, as we discussed, men are less likely to find certain behavior harassing, more likely to victim-blame, and more likely to benefit from the status quo than women, the American people are more likely to get slanted coverage on an important social ill that overwhelmingly harms women.

Fortunately, with organizations like the Women's Media Center calling out gender inequality in media, news coverage on sexual misconduct is improving slowly yet surely. Since #MeToo ignited in October 2017, more sexual misconduct stories are being told in major publications, bringing these issues to the forefront of the public conscience.

That brings us to the third and final reason sexual harassment likely receives less-than-stellar media coverage: Sexual harassment is rampant in the media. *Before* #MeToo made it easier to speak out, nearly two-thirds of female journalists told the International Women's Media Foundation in 2013 that they had experienced some form of sexual harassment, intimidation, or sexualized or physical violence while on the job.[16] Since #MeToo, many familiar faces who deliver or report our news have been accused of misconduct: Charlie Rose, Tom Brokaw, Ryan Seacrest, Glenn Thrush, Matt Lauer, Alex Jones, Tavis Smiley, Michael Oreskes, John Buccigross, Jann Wenner, Daniel Zwerdling, James Rosen, Adrian Carrasquillo, Mark Halperin, Mike Rosenberg, George "Tyrus" Murdoch, Dylan Howard, Kevin Braun, and so on. The news coverage on sexual misconduct will continue to suffer so long as women working in media suffer as well.

⬆ HEADS-UP!

If a reporter contacts you and starts asking questions, it may catch you off guard. Pause, take a breath, and remember these four tips:

1. **Never Say "No Comment."** "No comment" can make you look shady. If you're not prepared to speak, consider saying something like this: "Thank you for your call. If you could please call me back and leave a message with your contact information, your questions, and the deadline to get back to you, that would be best. Take care." Then hang up. Be polite yet firm.

2. **Never Delay.** If you plan to speak to the media, do it in a timely fashion. The news cycle changes quickly, and you may not have a chance to get in your say if you unnecessarily delay.

3. **Never Attack.** Take the high road. Avoid appearing angry, jilted, or emotional. Even if you have good reason to be ticked, you want to appear calm and reasoned, rather than incensed and possibly defamatory.

4. **Never Lie.** You're not obligated to answer every question asked of you, but never lie. Lies create more issues than they resolve. Also, more than thirty states allow for one-party phone recordings, so the reporter may not necessarily have to tell you whether she's recording the conversation. Don't play yourself.

WORKING WITH REPORTERS

Despite the factors that impair sexual harassment media coverage and feed the catch-and-kill culture, there are plenty of reporters who are passionate about journalism and committed to keeping We The People informed. Here are some nuggets of solid information that can guide you when it comes to working with a good reporter.

Getting a Good Reporter

Like attorneys, not all reporters are created equal. Some are more skilled and devoted than others. With the range of options, here are some tips to help you locate a good one:

- **Experience Telling Sexual Harassment Stories.** Your ideal journalist is experienced in reporting on sexual harassment. She's sympathetic to your situation yet won't shy away from asking you tough questions and telling the truth. The last thing you want is for a reporter to advance harmful stereotypes, such as focusing on what *you* were wearing during the harassment or using loaded language like "purportedly" when describing your account. You want and need someone who *gets it.*

- **Strong Communication Skills.** Your ideal reporter has strong communication skills when interacting with you and others. She's patient with you, given that there are a lot of emotions in play when it comes to surviving sexual harassment. She also appreciates that your story is sensitive, so she's open to using encrypted channels, such as the Signal app and ProtonMail.

- **Selective and Prepared.** Your reporter is selective with her stories. She doesn't accept anything and everything but recognizes her strengths and limitations. She also has the time to dedicate to investigating your story and doing it justice. For example, if there are racial components to your story, a good reporter will consult or partner with a journalist who has expertise in this area and can appropriately share them with audiences. You don't want the public to overlook what happened to you because the reporter's insensitive statements in your story become *the story.*

- **Independent Yet Connected.** A good reporter stands on her own yet has plenty of backup. She adheres to the ethics of journalism and will not compromise her integrity. She does not succumb to bribes or catch-and-kill opportunities even if they would fill her coffers. That's a big deal because journalists rarely secure the bag, so turning down cash can be a tough call—but it's one that good reporters will certainly make. Speaking of calls . . . Good reporters have a strong contact list of editors at publications to whom they can pitch. While not every editor is great for every story, a good reporter has a reputation that can open doors.

- **Checks and Balances.** A good reporter checks up on your story and makes sure everything balances out. She doesn't just accept what you say as gospel but asks for supporting documentation and corroborating witnesses. She'll ensure that everything matches up because she values fairness and accurately presenting the truth.

 PLAYBOOK PRO TIP

In addition to being the first woman to speak out during the #Me Too movement about her experience with actor Steven Seagal, investigative journalist Lisa Guerrero tells her fair share of sexual misconduct stories on camera for *Inside Edition*, the number one syndicated news magazine, which draws in some five million viewers a night. Guerrero offers this advice should you want to share your story on camera:

1. **Shoot for National Media.** Sharing your story on camera can be an emotionally taxing event that most people do not wish to do more than once. When selecting outlets, consider the one with the largest audience and biggest platform, so there will be no need to share your story again and again.
2. **Multiple Platforms.** Consider whether the reporter would use multiple platforms to tell your story. Stories on TV are often limited by time slot and audience reach. TV reporters who

also use online platforms like YouTube, Instagram, and podcasts reach more people and more diverse demographics. For example, *Inside Edition* has built a loyal TV audience over thirty-five years, but it also reaches new demographics on YouTube, where Guerrero's investigative stories alone received more than 120 million views in 2018.

3. **Review the Reporter's Previous Work.** Did the reporter give the person time to tell her story, take anything out of context, confront the accused, or use unprofessional graphics? Given the limits of our legal system, sometimes sharing your story in the media is the only reckoning you may get. The reporter for you should handle sexual harassment stories in a way that you respect and that gives you justice. Choose your reporter wisely!

Pitching Stories to Reporters

Generally, reporters are very intelligent people. They also tend to be very busy people who cannot be expected to mind read or piece together minute details. When reaching out to a reporter, the right approach can make a world of difference between getting your story told and getting ghosted. Here are some tips on how to tee up a story:

- **Start with the "Why."** Ask yourself, "Why will my story be of interest to audiences?" With the ever-changing news cycle in the clickbait world in which we live, all stories are not created equal. A celebrity can drive a story about adopting a new hamster because people are fascinated with the celebrity and their everyday activities. If you're Everyday Jane, however, your name may not carry that kind of weight. When approaching a reporter, you should know what your driver is: Is there something unique about your story? Is your harasshole high profile? Was the harassment particularly egregious? Did your employer respond horribly? Figure out the power your story wields when it comes to getting an audience's attention.

- **Be Clear and Succinct yet Detailed.** After you've identified a good motivator for *why* audiences would pay attention to your story, move on to the who, what, when, and where of the events—and keep it tight. No one—especially a busy reporter—has time to read a dissertation or weed through insignificant details. Some facts may be meaningful to you but irrelevant to readers. Do not take it personally. It's all about time.

- **Keep the "How" Open.** How your story gets told is a negotiation point. It's something you and the reporter should talk about. You may prefer that your story come out in *Marie Claire* rather than *Maxim*. A good reporter will discuss options with you before pitching to certain publications. Just remember that the reporter does not control whether editors at certain publications want your story.

- **Offer an Exclusive.** A reporter doesn't want to invest time interviewing you if everyone else will have the same access. Ensure the reporter knows that she'll have the exclusive story, which she'll appreciate, as it gives her more leverage when shopping your story to publications. This is different from catch-and-kill situations where you'd sign an NDA in exchange for exclusivity and cash. A good reporter won't ask you to sign anything but will rely on your word.

- **Don't Be a Nuisance.** Reporters are people too. No one wants to be hounded, insulted, or pushed around. You're going through a tough time, yes. But being testy or pushy will not improve your situation or how your story is told. It'll just make you look like an asshole, and the reporter may portray you as such.

Levels of Attribution

Levels of attribution refer to how the reporter may or may not use the information you provide. This is important because you may want information to become public, but you may *not* always want the public to know that *you* were the source of that information. Here are the four levels and their common meanings:[17]

1. **On the Record.** You're all in! Everything you say can and may be used and attributed to you by name and title. Unless you and the reporter agree otherwise, this is the default.

2. **On Background.** On your terms! This means the information can be published only on the terms you agree to with the reporter. Typically, a source doesn't want their name used but doesn't mind being identified generally ("a professional athlete" or "a former employee").

3. **Deep Background.** You're incognito! That means the information can be used as background to help the reporter find another source, but the material cannot be attributed to you, even on condition of anonymity.

4. **Off the Record.** You never said it! The information you give cannot be published.

Before you speak to a reporter, you should specify the level of attribution and make sure you both agree on what that level means. Also, bear in mind that this is all based on an honor code. There's nothing legally binding the reporter to a level of attribution, which is why you want to use your best judgment when deciding whether to share the information with a reporter. Also, no matter the level, a reporter is free to verify the information with another source and to publish it. The best rule is to share nothing you couldn't bear to see in print.

🔖 BONUS POINT

Should you wish to get information to the media without putting your name in the mix, there are anonymous and untraceable ways to leak information—namely, use fully encrypted services such as the Signal app, ProtonMail email, and the Tor browser. Check out chapter 14 for details. #TheMoreYouKnow

---

Reporter Privilege

Reporter privilege legally protects reporters from being forced to reveal their anonymous sources or confidential information. The federal courts, thirty-nine of the fifty states, and the District of Columbia all have some type of reporter privilege law. The scope and detail of each law varies depending on the jurisdiction.[18]

The goal of reporter privilege is to keep the press independent, so that citizens feel comfortable anonymously speaking with reporters. Think about it: If law enforcement could force reporters to reveal their sources and disclose confidential information, no one would talk to the media. Reporter privilege is like a poor man's attorney-client privilege. What do I mean by that? Just because a reporter can't be forced to disclose information or sources in certain jurisdictions does *not* mean that the reporter *will not* do so under threat of prosecution or under actual persecution or when faced with a big check (à la reporters working for Weinstein). While these types of breaches are rather rare, they also underscore the importance of getting with a good journalist.

REPLAY

* When it comes to surviving a sexual harassment story on the public stage, a successful game plan starts with taking into account who you are, your social identifiers, who you want to speak for you, how you want to appear in the public, what media channels are best for you, the resources available to you, and whether you should get professional PR help. Appearances are everything when you're under the media microscope.

* Although it has historically done a heinous job of reporting sexual harassment, the media is not the enemy. Things are improving as more women, people of color, and diverse voices are becoming storytellers at media outlets. There's still much work to be done.

* There are plenty of reporters who are committed to keeping We The People informed of the truth. A good working relationship with the media can make the difference between being vilified and vindicated in the eyes of the public.

* Invest in finding a reporter who has experience telling sexual harassment stories, has strong communication skills, and is selective, prepared, independent yet connected, and objective.

* Pitch stories to reporters by showcasing why it matters to the public, be clear and succinct yet detailed, stay open-minded about how your story gets told, offer an exclusive, and don't be a nuisance.

* Mind and leverage the levels of attribution: on the record, on background, deep background, and off the record. Remember that these are part of an honor code and cannot stop a reporter from publishing the information.

* Reporter privilege protects reporters from being forced to reveal their anonymous sources or confidential information. Leverage it to the best of your abilities!

CHAPTER 14

Surviving Cyber Scandal

Overcoming Online Harassment
and Digital Warfare

....

This scandal was brought to you by the digital revolution.
—*Monica Lewinsky, anti-bullying advocate and scandal survivor*

WHAT CAN BE SUPER fun *and* utterly fucking terrifying at the same time? Social media, of course! It's where online harassment happens the most.[1] Nearly half of Americans have felt unsafe online, and some 90 percent of the nation believes online attackers are enabled by anonymity.[2] Add that to the speed with which information travels online and the threat of digital mobs, and social media can be an all-out nightmare—especially for women who use their voice. Just ask Ana Kasparian, cohost of *The Young Turks*, a progressive political news program that generates more than fifty million views online each month.[3]

In 2008, during a live broadcast, Kasparian condemned those on social media who were mocking the victim of a hate crime. In response to her call for kindness, trolls on 4chan—an anonymous online board notorious for hosting hate—sprang into action. Within hours, the trolls were plotting assaults on the then twenty-one-year-old commentator and circulating her parents' home address and phone number—a tactic known as "doxing." The trolls stormed Kasparian's social media and flooded her home phone with vitriol. They also waged a ground attack, ordering thousands of dollars' worth of escorts and Chinese takeout that arrived at her family's home at all hours of the night and for which *no one* had paid. (As you may imagine, neither the escorts nor the restaurants took it well.) The personal attacks and online abuse were relentless, including rape threats and ethnic slurs.

Kasparian, a proud Armenian American and devoted social justice advocate, did her best to keep her loved ones and herself safe. For her own well-being, she stepped away from social media for a time. But online terrorists could not keep her away for long.

Kasparian has no backdown when it comes to fighting the nefarious. She continues to use her voice on social media and across media platforms to empower women and girls around the globe. In spring 2019, despite online threats, she spoke before the United Nations about increased efforts online to silence women journalists, a topic she's passionate about addressing.

Like Kasparian, you too should use your voice online to advocate for issues important to you—notwithstanding online harassment. Also, should your sexual harassment experience hit the media, you should be prepared to navigate the virtual space where seedy employers and harassholes incite mobs and leverage trolls to fix the narrative in their favor, in addition to using their resources to gain access to your emails, hard drive, and other online accounts.

To help keep your voice elevated and your data protected, in this chapter I share with you proactive tactics and reactive tips for surviving cyberattacks and digital warfare. You get insight based on proven research and personal experience, as well as recommendations from activists groups, cybersecurity expert Satnam Singh Narang, and digital anti-dox advocate Brianna Wu. Prepare yourself for what I like to call the "Snowden Deluxe."

SURVIVING THE DIGITAL SPACE

Social media is an essential part of most people's professional and personal lives, but if it feels like it's getting to be too much, do what's best for you. You're not unduly sensitive. Even supermodel and everywoman Chrissy Teigen has locked her Twitter account at times when the negativity became too much. You're not alone—nor are you without help. Here are some keys to surviving online mayhem.

Trolls

Online trolls are the worst. We're talking about lowlifes on the internet who get their jollies from unfairly criticizing others and hurling hate. Women are more likely than men to be targeted by trolls for severe online abuse, such as sexual harassment and physical threats.[4] Online abuse can take a toll. A Pew Research Center study found that women are far more likely than men to suffer emotional stress from online harassment and to see it as a major problem that authorities don't make a priority to stop.[5] Unfortunately, until there's social change and social media platforms consistently enforce their rules, trolls are gonna troll—and they'll evade accountability using the shield of anonymity. So, let's talk about productive ways you can deal with it.

■ **Do Not Engage.** Trolls feed off of thinking they're getting a rise out of you. Starve them with silence. Disengage. They'll get the message. If you feel you *must* respond to trolls, show class and kindness. You don't want your comments to be taken out of context or used to condemn *your* character.

■ **Shut Off/Filter/Delete Comments.** With the one exception provided in the next HEADS-UP!, consider shutting off, filtering, or deleting negative comments. Do not wade through the online trash even if you are curious. The negative energy is *not* worth your time. Protect your peace.

⬆ HEADS-UP!

If your story hits the media and there's a chance you'll be involved in litigation, do NOT shut off, filter, or delete social media comments from trolls. Depending on the circumstances of your situation, you may want to use those comments in your case to show how the public responded to the allegations and how it impacted you. Not erasing the comments may be difficult because they can be hurtful, and trolls can be cruel. But you got this!

Once things settle down (which is typically about forty-eight hours after the news breaks), protect your future interests and your mental health by having a team of trusted friends or loved ones go through your social media to screenshot comments—including the URL. After the comments are documented, consider reporting those that violate the platform's terms of service, and block the sender.

Preserving evidence *and* your mental bandwidth are bawse moves!

- **Do Not Hesitate to Report.** If a troll is threatening you or making you feel unsafe, consider reporting the troll following the social media platform's protocol and contacting law enforcement. Even with the shortcomings of social media platforms and law enforcement agencies, threats of violence are illegal and you shouldn't have to deal with them.

Doxers

As Kasparian experienced, doxing is heinous. It's when someone shares your personal information online (such as your home address, phone number, or Social Security number) with the sadistic goal of giving crazies fodder to harass you to the point where your life is unbearable.

Doxing is unethical and universally despised. But it's not illegal, unfortunately. It also isn't difficult. Doxers can find your information pretty easily by searching publicly available databases and social media platforms. That's what happened to Dr. Christine Blasey Ford, when she was publicly identified as the woman accusing then Supreme Court nominee Brett Kavanaugh of sexual assault. The harassment was so bad that Dr. Ford and her family had to hire private security and move out of their home, relocating at least four times in the months surrounding her Congressional testimony. Dr. Ford even scrubbed her social media profiles before coming forward, but that wasn't enough.

Although it's nearly impossible to erase your entire digital footprint, you can still shut down what personal information is available about you online. There are two ways to accomplish this: (1) Open a search engine that specializes in protecting user information (for example, www.duckduckgo .com), search for your name, review what personal information is publicly available for doxers to grab, and go to each site individually to opt out of having your content appear. (2) Pay one of the many data-cleaning companies to perform the task for you, such as DeleteMe or PrivacyDuck. No matter your choice, protect yourself.

Lastly, know that just because doxing isn't illegal does not mean you have no legal recourse. Those who harass or stalk you using doxed info may be held accountable under state or federal laws, depending on the circumstances. You are neither alone nor without options.

DEALING WITH DIGITAL WARFARE

There are measures you can take to prevent or reduce the damage of being doxed or hacked. The following is a CliffsNotes version of what you should do *before* and *after* an attack; although you may want to take advantage of some of the post-attack recommendations to bolster your security before an attack. Added security is never a bad thing, especially when it's at no cost to you.[6] Yes, about 85 percent of these recommendations are fabulously free! #Bonus

Preempt an Attack

- **Virtual Private Network (VPN).** Get a VPN for yourself. It's very affordable and one of the best investments you can make. In addition to allowing you to browse anonymously, a VPN shields your IP address and protects you from eavesdropping, data monitoring, unwanted exposure, and much more. Private Internet Access and VyprVPN come highly recommended.

- **Financial and Credit Solicitations.** Consider opting out of receiving financial and credit solicitations. The Network Advertising Initiative website has solid recommendations on resources available online for mass opt-out, so you don't have to individually address each soliciting entity. Also www.optoutprescreen.com lets you opt out of solicitations sent by email, phone, and mail.

- **Mail and Package Delivery Alerts.** To keep mail from going missing, consider signing up for Informed Delivery from the U.S. Postal Service, alerts from UPS My Choice, and notifications from other delivery sources to receive free email/SMS/text notifications when letters and packages are sent to you. That way nothing goes missing without you knowing!

■ **Online Monitoring Alerts.** Take advantage of free resources that monitor use of your name online so you can track what is being said about you. This keeps you in the know when it comes to your online brand. Talk-walker and Google Alerts are good resources.

■ **Fully Encrypted Email.** Because many well-known email providers, such as Gmail, have limitations and are penetrable, it is best to use fully encrypted email providers like Tutanota or ProtonMail (free). For group conversations, check out Zoom and turn on the encrypted feature.

■ **Aliases and Dummy Accounts.** Use aliases for signing online petitions, check-in sheets, and other noncritical matters. Also open a dummy email account to use for all your online shenanigans that aren't essential, like list serves and free offers.

■ **Virtual Phone Number.** Use a virtual phone number for interactions with people and companies who are not established fixtures in your life, such as delivery people, online dating prospects, etc. This added barrier brings a level of protection and allows you to ditch the number should things get crazy. A Google Voice number linked to a dummy Gmail account is a solid move.

■ **Exercise Digital Hygiene.** Just like you care for your personal hygiene, you should be exercising digital hygiene. We're talking about regularly changing passwords and backing up your hardware on a regular basis so you have copies of everything should your system ever get hacked.

■ **Unique Passwords and Two-Step Authentication.** Passwords should be like dating after your twenties: complicated. Ensure all of your passwords are unique and not linked to any of your personal information, such as your birthdate or pet's name. Consider getting a password manager like 1Password or LastPass. Also, enable two-step authentication where it's available, but try to avoid using text/SMS as your authentication source because text messages can be intercepted. The Google Authenticator app or the Authy app are options.

After an Attack

■ **Notify Financial Institutions and Utility Service Providers.** Call your credit card companies, mobile phone provider, utility companies, and banks to let them know you have been targeted. They may be able to add an extra layer of security to your account. Also, consider freezing your credit so no one can open any lines of credit in your name. It's a simple step you can take online that requires contacting the nationwide credit reporting agencies (Equifax, Experian, and TransUnion), who will freeze your credit within one business day.

■ **Encrypted Messaging.** As we've discussed, use fully encrypted, untraceable messaging apps, like Signal, through which you can send free calls and texts, which can be set to completely disappear. WhatsApp and Telegram are decent alternatives. Whichever app you use, ensure your data is not being saved on the cloud by turning off the app's cloud backup. (Former Trump campaign manager Paul Manafort forgot to change this setting before using WhatsApp, which is how the FBI caught him.[7] Oops!)

■ **Use an Anonymous Browser.** Surf the internet on an anonymous browser, such as Tor, to prevent anyone from tracking you and collecting your data and online searches. Anonymous browsers, especially when coupled with a VPN, help you stay untraceable, which is also helpful should you need to leak information to the media.

■ **Log the Incidents.** Keep an organized log of the attacks, detailing the source of the attack, nature, date, and any other relevant information. A log can help you identify patterns and can be useful for detecting the source of the harassment should law enforcement get involved. Keep the log in an encrypted place.

■ **Breathe and Know You Got This.** It may seem like your world is caving in and that you're all alone. That is not the case. You *will* get past this, and you *will* be stronger than ever. During the tough times, make time for yourself.

TAKING CARE OF YOU OFFLINE

A support system is essential for surviving cyberharassment and digital warfare. Brianna Wu stresses this because she's lived it. In October 2014, the online game developer turned Congressional candidate was doxed by members of #Gamergate, a digital campaign that sought to silence outspoken women working in gaming. The online group spread Wu's mobile number and home address, encouraging several members, including a popular You-Tube personality, to make detailed death threats that forced Wu and her husband to flee from their New England home. She faced incessant hack attempts. Masturbating incels called her at all hours of the day, sent pictures of slaughtered dogs, and wrote think pieces about her demise. The FBI ultimately apprehended several of the men, one of whom admitted to calling Wu at least forty to fifty times to threaten her, intentionally ramping up the harassment when he could hear she was upset. But authorities opted not to prosecute them, leaving Wu without redress.

Although Wu still regularly receives violent threats when she uses her voice online, the gender-equity advocate continues to champion for safer digital spaces for women, in addition to informally counseling those seeking to overcome the traumatic effects of doxing. Wu's primary recommendation is to protect yourself psychologically and emotionally, as doxing can do damage to your entire life. In addition to seeking out therapy, Wu recommends openly talking about your experiences with loved ones who can validate your feelings and support you. She offers these sage words to women working, living, or just existing in the digital world:

> There's no magical way to *not* make yourself a target. You can stay away from controversy, steer away from politics, be careful in what you say—and yet you still may be targeted; so don't let these digital mobs scare you from being who you are. There's an army of women who have had quite enough of this bullshit, and we will be standing right beside you.

REPLAY

* Women are more likely to be targeted for online harassment and abuse than men. Law enforcement authorities have yet to consistently make prosecuting virtual threats and harassment a priority, and social media platforms have not consistently enforced their rules.
* Trolls and doxers are heinous. The former follows you around online to criticize and harass you, and the latter spreads your personal

information in hopes of others using it to harass you. By and large, both trolls and doxers aren't doing anything illegal, but they can nonetheless do considerable damage to your public and private life. Stay ready with a proactive offense and a structured defense.

* To ward off a cyberattack, you may want to use a virtual private network (VPN); opt out of receiving financial and credit solicitations; sign up for mail and package delivery alerts; monitor mentions of your name online; fully encrypt your email; use aliases, dummy email accounts, and virtual phone numbers for noncritical matters; exercise digital hygiene; and use unique passwords and two-factor authentication.

* After being doxed or suffering a cyberattack, notify your financial institutions and utility service providers, use encrypted messaging platforms and an anonymous web browser, log the incidents, and remember to breathe. You also always can take advantage of these cybersecurity features before an attack to boost your security.

* It may seem like your world is caving in and that you're all alone. Please know that's not the case. During the tough time, make time to take care of yourself and take full advantage of a support network of loved ones and mental health providers. You *will* get through this, and you *will* be stronger than ever.

CHAPTER 15

##

Leveling Up

Embracing the New You, Always Doing You, and Making a Badass Comeback

....

I just took a DNA test. Turns out I'm 100 percent that bitch.
—*Lizzo, emboldened artist and badass uplifter*

TWO YEARS AFTER giving up my established life and lucrative legal career to pursue a dream of sports broadcast, that dream was dead. It was destroyed by sexual harassment, and I was told I would never work in media again. The network I'd left reportedly had a well-documented history of destroying women who dared to challenge its toxic culture. They wielded that kind of power, making and breaking names at will. I, on the other hand, wielded nothing more than fanciful dreams and unapologetic determination. Blacklisting me would've been easy for them, but they had no idea that I *am* 100 percent that bitch.

I was, am, and always will be Adrienne Lawrence—a warm and intelligent woman who's been through her fair share of bullshit yet still truly believes there's good in people, remains passionate about uplifting others, and is convinced she can do anything she puts her mind to. I never was nor will I ever be the person they wanted me to be or wanted the world to believe I was. Even in the midst of the storm, when my name was slandered across the media, my social media was inundated with disdain, and many of my supposed friends were nowhere to be found, I knew who I was and would never forget it. This bitch was set on making her comeback.

Within nine months of being kicked off ESPN's airwaves and having my good name kicked through the dirt, I was back on its network broadcasting sports through a third-party outlet that happened to sign a deal with them after signing with me. That was a memorable moment, yes. But that was *not* my comeback. My comeback manifested months later—the day I woke up and realized that I was no longer bothered, enraged, or insulted by any of it, that I'd risen above their bullshit, flicked my light back on, shined it brighter than ever, and fell so deeply in love with my life that anyone who tried to wrong me became a laughable, ridiculous, distant memory.[1]

In this chapter, I give you the tools to level up after surviving sexual harassment, to decide what a comeback looks like for *you*, and to make it happen. You'll learn how to grow from the experience and dream another dream, get practical tips for creating and navigating new professional endeavors, and gather insight on reshaping your professional image and keeping your mind right. As we've already established, you are a bawse. Now we're about to confirm that you're also that bitch.

GROWING AND GLOWING

Growth is a key part of overcoming a traumatic experience. It requires reflection and reflects maturity. Growth moves you past assigning blame and holding on to hurts, drawing you toward peace and helping you own your power. Growth doesn't just involve change; it requires adapting while preserving who you are.

Although I'm still *me*, I've had to adapt and I've completely changed as a result of all that comes with sexual harassment. I've taken from the lessons and learned from the hardships, finding new ways to thrive that are true to the core aspects of me, yet reflective of the woman I am today and the gawdess I aspire to be. For the first time, I accept full and complete responsibility for my life and for those I keep in it—and I unequivocally, unapologetically fucking love it. Like Lizzo covered in MAC bronzer, I am glowing!

Of course, this state of being didn't just appear overnight and, as you know, it didn't come to pass without a number of missteps and at least one neck tattoo. But I did start to grow—once I put myself first, ignored everyone's expectations, and invested in me. It took me well over a year from the date I finally admitted *and* accepted that everything wasn't fine *and* that I did not have to go through it alone.

You too are not alone. You may be in a difficult place right now. Or you may be far enough away from the trauma but still struggling to find peace.

Regardless of where you are in your journey, here are some nuggets of wisdom to help you go through it, grow through it, and get your glow up:

■ **Adjust Your Outlook.** Sexual harassment can throw your life out of order and rob you of your dignity, self-confidence, and career. But you have two choices: You can accept the experience for what it was or you can continue to hold on to what it was supposed to be. It means the difference between growing forward and going back. Life is all a matter of how you see it.

⬆ HEADS-UP!

If you were burned by a sexual harassment hotbed, take solace in knowing that you're not the only one with wounds. There's likely a network of individuals who survived the toxic employer too. Ask around. Check the internet. Try to locate others who left the employer disgruntled. Find the person on LinkedIn, reach out, and build a relationship. It can be cathartic. Plus, you never know: They may open doors for you, as they know what you've endured behind closed doors.

■ **Look for the Lesson.** You may have been out of school for a while, but lessons will never end. Everything that happens to you has a lesson behind it. When there's enough distance between you and the trauma, be open to figuring out the lesson you can learn from the experience. Without placing any blame, ask yourself what you can take away from what happened and the aftermath. Perhaps you found your voice along the way. Maybe you realized your instincts were trying to get your attention. That was it for me: I learned to trust my instincts. I also learned to focus within for my happiness and to know I'm stronger than I ever imagined. In my future endeavors, I've committed to taking those lessons with me and applying them wisely. Find the lessons, commit to them, and use them to make your future brighter than ever.

■ **Figure Out the New You.** Who are you? What do you stand for? What moves you? Forget what others may think or who your parents raised you to be. *Who are you?* The answer to that question requires honesty, vulnerability, introspection. Be still. Drop everyone's expectations and follow your instincts in defining yourself for yourself. Road test a persona, if need be. Give yourself permission to explore every corner of the woman you've become and the gawdess you aim to be.

▪ **Own the New You.** Embrace yourself. Be unapologetic about your fabulousness. Let out your inner Laverne Cox. Channel your Alexandria Ocasio-Cortez. Werk the Oprah Winfrey within. Do you! Love you! Cherish every single inch of you and your exquisite self. Have fun, laugh hard, live big! You are a bawse and that bitch.

FINDING A NEW WAY

You may be in a bad situation or have just left one. Either way, do not let some harasshole, toxic employer, or fear scare you out of the field of your dreams or make you think that you're finished in your industry of choice. You've worked too damn hard. And even if you are new to your industry, like I was, you're still entitled to live your best life. Before you even consider dreaming another dream, consider another way to make your dream come true.

Here are my top five recommendations for locating a position you love with an employer you deserve:

▪ **Get Your Head Straight.** If you're at a point where you're willing to drop your dreams and play small because of a toxic workplace experience, you may want to consider talking to a professional. There are career/life coaches with cognitive behavioral backgrounds and experience in helping women return from traumatic professional experiences. They can help you sort through the trauma so you're in a healthy mind-set when selecting your next professional path.

TIME-OUT

To share or not to share: Should you tell a prospective or new employer or colleagues that you left your last position because of sexual harassment?

The short answer: It's your call. But here are a few things you may want to consider:

1. **What Defines You?** Sexual harassment doesn't define you. You're a skilled individual who your former employer couldn't appreciate. That's not your problem—so long as you're not letting it become your mental or emotional baggage.
2. **Is It Still Taboo?** Some industries and companies are more progressive than others. On the other hand, there are small minds who may be reluctant to hire a woman who spoke out for fear that she'll not stay silent if they harass her too. You've probably guessed it—those are not your people.
3. **What's the Purpose?** Is there a legitimate reason why these people need to know about your past employment experience (for example, they're looking into hiring your harasshole)? If there's no justifiable reason, perhaps wait until you know them better and there's a legitimate reason to make your past relevant.

■ **Consider a Headhunter.** Recruiters know a lot about open opportunities and ideal work environments. They also can be very resourceful when it comes to navigating references (or lack thereof) from a bad past workplace experience. Build a good relationship with a headhunter you trust. If you're comfortable with her, explain your situation and your needs, and let her work her magic!

■ **Leverage Your References.** Just over one-third of people found their current position through a professional reference.[2] It's time to start asking those you trust about their knowledge of available opportunities. See if they can put feelers out for you. A good reference can go a long way.

■ **Maximize Your Time and Network.** If you're still with your toxic employer and it happens to offer subsidized educational or training programs, take it all in! Also use your free time away from the office wisely by signing up for conferences, freelancing gigs, job forums, professional associations, alumni events, and other opportunities that either expand your contact list or make you more marketable. Make sure potential employers can find you online, your profile information is current, and your settings indicate you're accepting inquiries.

- **Consider Entrepreneurship or Freelancing.** If you're over the overseer game, consider going out on your own! Perhaps you could become a consultant, start your own business, forge your own path on your own terms. There's a wealth of opportunities for women business owners out there. The freedom to make your own schedule and to play by your own rules could be exactly what you need! Stay positive and keep calm. You have options.

 PLAYBOOK PRO TIP

Redefining your public or professional image can feel like a chore after a career change or sexual harassment scandal. But you're always in control. Attorney-turned-branding-expert Brittany Hoffman, who leverages LinkedIn and other social media outlets, has five Cs for reestablishing your public persona online after chaos:

1. **Clarity.** Get clear on who you are and what you want to happen. Take personal inventory and ownership of how you define yourself. Who do you want to be serving and why? What are the skills and experiences that you bring to the table and that make you unique? When people hear your name, what do you want them to say?
2. **Consistency.** Appearing consistently online with a reliable message has very real-world effects offline. Influence is based on trust, and consistency is one of the best ways to build credibility. All online profiles, platforms, and content that you create should reflect the position you've decided on and the message you want to communicate.
3. **Community.** Don't wait for a community to come to you. Go out and find it! The easiest way to do that is by engaging with

people online who you want in your world. Add value and join relevant conversations.

4. **Candor.** Authenticity is key! Your brand should reflect who you are in real life, how you speak, and your voice. People are going to buy into you and your message because they like *you*.

5. **Changeable.** Your brand is never set in stone. Even the biggest scandals with the biggest names don't live long in a news cycle anymore. People will move on, but you need to make sure you move forward in the best way for you.

DREAMING ANOTHER DREAM

You may be at a point where your time in an industry is over. Maybe you're inspired to do something different, or you simply have no love for this game anymore and the harasshole helped you realize that. Either way, your conscious choice to dream another dream is a bawse move. You deserve a career that challenges you and speaks to your many professional talents. As someone who's had numerous careers over her life, including going straight from a big law office to an international anchor desk to becoming an author and speaker. I can tell you how fulfilling it is to do what you damn well please. Here are my top five recommendations for switching careers:

■ **Take Your Time and the Limits Off.** If money, time, and access weren't a factor, what would you do? What brings out the best in you? What did you love doing as a child? Open your mind to all of the incredible things you can do. Don't rush into another position. Spend time exploring your options and yourself. You're coming out of a traumatic experience. If you're feeling overwhelmed, pull together a support team of loved ones to help you organize your thoughts. Take your time to find the right path for you. Also, don't hesitate to use the advice in chapter 4 to gather a strong reconnaissance on prospective employers, so you don't rush into the arms of the wrong one and end up right back where you are now.

★ PLAYBOOK PRO TIP

Many people who survive trauma make their mess their message. I did. If you decide to take the public speaking path, preparation can mean the difference between being revered or vilified. Here are some tips from Christine K. Jahnke, professional speaking coach and author of *The Well-Spoken Woman Speaks Out*:

1. **Choose your message.** Decide what you want to say, how you wish to be perceived, and how you are going to say it. Preparing in advance will ensure you avoid rambling or getting overly emotional in front of a reporter or the audience.
2. **Write out your words.** Good storytelling seems effortless, but it requires considerable work. Begin the process by writing out what you want to say in full. Bullet points won't help you decide how to share information that may be sensitive or painful; written text, however, will help you clarify why you are speaking and why the audience should care.
3. **Practice by recording yourself.** Once you have a draft, practice aloud and record yourself. Then play back the video and listen. Words on paper often sound different when spoken aloud, so you will likely need to do some editing. You may want to seek out candid loved ones or colleagues who will provide constructive feedback. Practice builds confidence and stories improve with each telling.
4. **Be prepared for feedback.** After you've shared your story, be ready for feedback from people who will applaud you and from those who will feel threatened by you. Focus on those who are receptive to your message and who want to help you bring positive change.

■ **Don't Be Afraid to Dabble.** When I was practicing law and wanting to explore journalism, I signed up for a ten-week course at the UCLA Extension school. Getting back into the academic environment excited me, and I dabbled in various subjects until I found something that spoke to me. You can get insight and inspiration from similar programs in your area or online. Also consider taking a community college course or emailing a university professor to explain your interests and inquire about auditing one of her classes and possibly chatting afterward.

- **Build Relationships and Ask Questions.** Networking is an ideal way to get insight into your potential career path. Find individuals in the field you're interested in and see if you can buy them lunch to pick their brain. Ask about the good and the bad, and listen to what they have to say. Get opinions from a range of people in that field, so you have a well-rounded look at life in that industry.

- **Volunteer to Get Experience.** Yes, I said what I said. I'm a huge proponent of getting experience by giving your time. It opens doors that you otherwise may not have access to and puts you in front of people you otherwise may not have met. For example, when entering broadcast, I needed on-air experience and footage to assemble a reel. A small digital media outlet allowed me to produce and host a weekly show in their studios. I didn't get paid, but I did get material for a reel! So long as you're not being used or taken advantage of, get the experience you need before committing to the field.

- **Commit to What Brings Out Your Best.** This isn't 1940. Americans don't stay in one industry with one employer for their entire lives. This is the twenty-first century: You make your own destiny! If today you want to be in marketing, and tomorrow in technology, you do you. Live your best professional life by having a career that lets you be the best version of your beautifully evolving self. Remember, you are that bitch.

REPLAY

* Just because sexual harassment holds you down doesn't mean your professional comeback can't raise you up. You will come back. When you do, you get to decide what your comeback looks like, what it means to you, and who you are in the aftermath of your experience.

* Sexual harassment can change you. In your evolution, you can grow and glow by staying positive, looking for the lesson to be learned, figuring out the new you, and owning every aspect of her.
* Never let a harasshole or toxic employer force you out of the industry you're passionate about. Make another way to stay in your field by getting your head straight, considering a headhunter, leveraging your references, making the most of your time and network, and considering entrepreneurship or freelance options.
* If you're ready to change careers, independent of your toxic experience and after careful consideration, dream another dream. Take your time in exploring possible new careers and take the limits off of yourself. Do not be afraid to dabble in programs where you can learn more about your interests, build relationships with and ask questions of those already in the field, consider volunteering to get experience, and commit to what brings out your best.

Taking the Lead

We need to shape our own perception of how we view ourselves. We have to step up as women and take the lead.

—*Beyoncé, queen*

YOU MADE IT. Congrats! You're now equipped to beat sexual harassment! You know the score and have a leg up on harassholes and sexual harassment hotbeds. No matter how horrible the harasshole or heinous the employer, you can overcome anything and unapologetically thrive in the next chapter of your life. That's huge for your professional game and personal well-being. It's also just the beginning . . .

While a lot has been done to advance women in the workplace over the past half century, a great deal of work still awaits. At the organizational level, you can challenge your employer to do better and be better. Push for education on effective sexual harassment and bystander training, encourage greater accountability, and inspire impactful change. Perhaps advocate for a gender-equity speaker to hold a seminar at your workplace or ask your employer to promote awareness about the lesser-known forms of sexual harassment. Package your recommendation as a proactive loss-prevention effort aimed at preserving your employer's bottom line.

At the societal level, you can further equality by uplifting women and members of marginalized groups in the workplace and across your industry. No matter our differences, it doesn't take much to make a difference. For example, in July 2019 when journalist Yashar Ali (*HuffPost*) broke news of the lewd text messages Fox News host George "Tyrus" Murdoch reportedly sent his now-former cohost Britt McHenry, I had no issue publicly supporting her and her decision to challenge the way Fox handled the harassment.

McHenry, a conservative voice with whom I have little in common, may be opposite me in political discourse—but sexual harassment isn't an issue of politics, and it will *never* end if we remain divided. Practice empathy, show solidarity.

At the individual level, let your words match your actions. Drop the "I'm lucky to work here" bullshit and recognize your worth. Speak life to yourself and to other women and members of marginalized groups who are vulnerable to harassment. Stay mindful of the limiting and hypersexualized racial stereotypes oppressing your colleagues of color, interject when you hear others bashing someone who has bravely spoken out against a harasshole, befriend the LGBTQ+ colleague being ostracized for exercising her rights. Be a good bystander. When you see sexual harassment go down, use the four Ds we discussed in chapter 8. Likewise, given that women have higher standards for acceptable behavior than men, you can encourage men to do better and hold them accountable for their misconduct. Speak up. Men must understand that their identities are not dependent upon women's oppression and that the workplace isn't a zero-sum game.

Finally, remember that you're empowered to make change beyond your office or industry. Think about how you can help fight sexual harassment on a larger scale. Perhaps start a grassroots movement as *Fight Like a Mother* author Shannon Watts did in 2012 when she founded Moms Demand Action, or rally support online through organizations like Coworker.org, which lets you create a digital campaign to raise awareness and collect signatures. Have you considered running for office à la Alexandria Ocasio-Cortez, pressuring your Congressperson to change the law, or drafting legislation yourself? We know sexual harassment law is problematic. In fact, here are two issues where your campaign for change could start:

First, the $300,000 cap for compensatory and punitive damages in Title VII cases is limiting and too low. The cap was implemented in 1991, some thirty years ago, when the average new home cost $147,000 and a gallon of gas was $1.14. Keeping this damages cap in place today does nothing to stop harassment. Employees shouldn't be discouraged from fighting for their rights, and large companies must be deterred from enabling or ignoring harassholes.

And second, you could advocate to change the unwelcomeness requirement in hostile work environment claims. You may have noticed that the law is set up so that *you* have to show the harassment was unwelcome. Said another way, the law presumes that a woman *welcomes* sexual harassment in her *workplace* unless she can sufficiently prove otherwise. WTF is that? This twisted legal setup effectively eliminates the element of consent, placing the onus on *you* to object to sexualized or degrading messages in order for the law to even consider doing something about it. Wouldn't it make more sense to presume that you were *not* interested in fielding sexualized or degrading remarks while working on a budget report, placing the onus on the harasshole to seek *your* consent before engaging in such non-work behavior in the workplace? Indeed, the latter would make more sense in an egalitarian society where genders are treated equally. But that's not our society—unless we make change.

The fact that the law refuses to adequately compensate women for harassment *and* forces women to prove they did not welcome it is simply another powerful reminder of the unequal status between men and women in our society—an unequal status that must end.

Join me. Take your seat at the table, and take the lead in making change.

Acknowledgments

My Family

Adnan Virk

Alexis Rios

Alyssa Mannis

Amy Trask

Ana Kasparian

Andrea Kaufman

Andrew Echenique

Andrew W. Schilling

Anita Kabaei

Anna Marie Davidson

Ari Luxenberg

Ashlee Buchanan

Barbara Travis

Bärí Williams

BlogHer

Bob Hunter

Bobbie L. King Jr.

Britni de la Cretaz

Carmen Rios

Cary Greenberg

Chief Judge Eric T.
  Washington

Chisa Tolbertson

Chris "Dubby" McFarland

Christine Jahnke

Christine Kan

Cora Brumley

Cpt. Abigail Sutton

Cristal Williams Chancellor

Craig Engle

Danielle Turner

Dave Grunfeld

David S. Jonas

David W. Satterfield

Debbie Spander

Dr. Brenda Russell

Dr. Debra Oswald

Dr. Heather McLaughlin

Dr. Shardé Davis

Dress for Success of
  Hartford, CT

Eric V. Rowen

Ernest Tuckett III

Frantz M. Paul

Ian Ballon

Jade McCarthy

James Conolly

Jamie Stein

Jay Hulme

Jay Scott Smith

Jayar Jackson

Jen Rottenberg

Jenilee Borek

Jennifer & Edgar
  Montesdeoca

Jennifer Herrera

Joanna Hewitt

Joanna Ng

John Duke

Joseph Lynch

Josh Goldman

Juanita Figueroa

Juanita Wallace

Judith Benezra

Julie Burton

Julissa Garcia Zambrano

Justin Barton

Justin McWhirter

Kalinca Escamilla

Kara Flanagan

Kate McCarthy

Kathy & Rick Cooke

Katessa Davis

Kayla Ward

Kelsey Miller

Kristin Marguerite Doidge

Larry Lawson

Linda Makings

Lindsay Gibbs

Lindsay Spadoni

Linh Le

Maya Raghu

Megan Alsop

Megan Newman

Merle Vaughn

Michelle Lipkowitz Stevens

Mike Burks

Mya G

Mike Yam

Miko Grimes

Mona Leung

Nadia Kachwaha

Nathan Ikon Crumpton

Nelbà Marquez-Greene

Nicole Lawrence

Nicole Watson

Nina Hernandez Farmer

Nuria Santamaria Wolfe

Princell O'Hare

Rev. Joseph Bryant

Rico Williams

Rosalind Jones

Ryan Alvarez

Ryan Cook

Saeed Jones

Sara Avatapalli

Satnam Naram Sarang

Scott Bertzyk

Scotty Riggs

Shannon Watts

Soraya Chemaly

Stephane Ariot

Talia Levin

Dr. Therese Mascardo

Thomas Chow

Women's Media Center

And to all those who I cannot name without putting them at risk of suffering retaliation.

I forever remain grateful to you all.

Notes

Introduction

1. "Ending Sexual Assault and Harassment in the Workplace," National Sexual Violence Resource Center, 2018, https://www.nsvrc.org/sites/default/files /publications/2018-03/Publications_NSVRC_Tip-sheet_Ending_Sexual _Assault_Harassment_in_Workplace.pdf.
2. Carly McCann, Donald Tomaskovic-Devey, and M. V. Lee Badgett, "Employer's Responses to Sexual Harassment," Center for Employment Equity, University of Massachusetts Amherst, December 2018, https://www.umass.edu /employmentequity/employers-responses-sexual-harassment.
3. Louise F. Fitzgerald and Lilia M. Cortina, "Sexual Harassment in Work Organizations: A View from the 21st Century," in *APA Handbook of the Psychology of Women: Perspectives on Women's Private and Public Lives*, eds. Cheryl B. Travis et al. (Washington, DC: American Psychological Association, 2018), 215–234, http:// dx.doi.org/10.1037/0000060-012.

Chapter 1: Knowing the Score

1. Sundance Institute, "Cinema Café with Ruth Bader Ginsburg and Nina Totenberg," streamed live on January 21, 2018, at the Sundance Film Festival (Park City, UT), YouTube 1:07:16, https://youtu.be/pDXxsRB4s7Y?t=1045.

Chapter 2: The Truth We'd Rather Not See

1. Talia Jane, "Creepy Men Slide into Women's DMs All the Time, but They Can Be Shut Down," *The Guardian*, May 7, 2019, https://www.theguardian.com /commentisfree/2019/may/07/creepy-men-dm-online-harassment.
2. Elena Dall'Ara and Anne Maass, "Studying Sexual Harassment in the Laboratory: Are Egalitarian Women at Higher Risk?," *Sex Roles* 41, no. 9–10 (November 1999): 681–704, https://doi.org/10.1023/A:1018816025988.

3. Schultz, Vicki, "Reconceptualizing Sexual Harassment, Again," Yale Law School, Public Law Research Paper No. 647 (April 19, 2018), http://dx.doi.org/10.2139 /ssrn.3165561.

4. Heather McLaughlin, Christopher Uggen, and Amy Blackstone, "Sexual Harassment, Workplace Authority, and the Paradox of Power," *American Sociological Review* 77, no. 4 (July 2012): 625–647, https://doi.org/10.1177/0003122412451728.

5. Brenda L. Russell and Debra Oswald, "When Sexism Cuts Both Ways: Predictors of Tolerance of Sexual Harassment of Men," *Men and Masculinities* 19, no. 5 (December 2016): 524–544, http://doi.org/10.1177/1097184X15602745.

6. Fitzgerald and Cortina, "Sexual Harassment in Work Organizations," 2018.

7. Lilia M. Cortina and Jennifer L. Berdahl, "Sexual Harassment in Organizations: A Decade of Research in Review," in *The SAGE Handbook of Organizational Behavior, Volume 1: Micro Approaches*, eds. Julian Barling and Cary L. Cooper (Newbury Park, CA: SAGE Publications, 2008): 469–496, http://dx.doi.org/10.4135 /9781849200448.n26.

8. Jennifer L. Berdahl, "Harassment Based on Sex: Protecting Social Status in the Context of Gender Hierarchy," *The Academy of Management Review* 32, no. 2 (April 2007): 641–658, http://www.jstor.org/stable/20159319.

9. Russell and Oswald, "When Sexism Cuts Both Ways," 2016.

10. Christopher F. Karpowitz et al., "The American Family Survey 2018 Summary Report: Identities, Opportunities and Challenges," Utah: *Deseret News* and the Center for the Study of Elections and Democracy at Brigham Young University, 2018, http://deseretnews.com/american-family-survey.

11. Frank J. Till, "Sexual Harassment: A Report on the Sexual Harassment of Students," National Advisory Council on Women's Educational Programs, 1980.

12. Louise F. Fitzgerald et al., "The Incidence and Dimensions of Sexual Harassment in Academia and the Workplace," *Journal of Vocational Behavior* 32, no. 2 (April 1988), 152–175, http://dx.doi.org/10.1016/0001-8791(88)90012-7.

13. Fitzgerald and Cortina, "Sexual Harassment in Work Organizations," 2018.

14. Emily Longeretta, "Harvey Weinstein's Ex Assistant Opens Up About Working for 'Repulsive Monster,'" *Us Weekly*, December 20, 2017, https://www.usmagazine .com/celebrity-news/news/harvey-weinsteins-ex-assistant-talks-working-for -repulsive-monster.

15. James Campbell Quick and M. Ann McFadyen, "Sexual Harassment: Have We Made Any Progress?," *Journal of Occupational Health Psychology* 22, no. 3 (July 2017): 286–298, http://dx.doi.org/10.1037/ocp0000054.

16. Fitzgerald and Cortina, "Sexual Harassment in Work Organizations," 2018.

17. Chadwick v. Wellpoint, Inc., 561 F.3d 38 (1st Cir. 2009).

18. Price Waterhouse v. Hopkins, 490 U.S. 228 (1989).

19. Fitzgerald and Cortina, "Sexual Harassment in Work Organizations," 2018.

20. Russell and Oswald, "When Sexism Cuts Both Ways," 2016.

21. Fitzgerald and Cortina, "Sexual Harassment in Work Organizations," 2018.

22. Oncale v. Sundowner Offshore Services, 523 U.S. 75 (1998).

23. Fitzgerald and Cortina, "Sexual Harassment in Work Organizations," 2018.

24. Ashley Judd v. Harvey Weinstein, 2:18-cv-05724 (C.D. Cal. filed June 28, 2018).

25. Meritor Savings Bank v. Vinson, 477 U.S. 57 (1986).

26. McLaughlin, Uggen, and Blackstone, "Sexual Harassment, Workplace Authority, and the Paradox of Power," 2012.

27. Fitzgerald and Cortina, "Sexual Harassment in Work Organizations," 2018.

Chapter 3: Harassholes and Targets

1. Franchina v. City of Providence, 881 F.3d 32, 43-44 (1st Cir. 2018); transcript of Jury Trial Volumes I and II in *Franchina v. City of Providence*, No. 12-517M (D.R.I. Nov. 7, 2016).

2. Fitzgerald and Cortina, "Sexual Harassment in Work Organizations," 2018.

3. McLaughlin, Uggen, and Blackstone, "Sexual Harassment, Workplace Authority, and the Paradox of Power," 2012.

4. Heather McLaughlin, phone interview with author, February 15, 2019.

5. Russell and Oswald, "When Sexism Cuts Both Ways," 2016.

6. Berdahl, "Harassment Based on Sex," 2007.

7. Jin X. Goh and Judith A. Hall, "Nonverbal and Verbal Expressions" of Men's Sexism in Mixed-Gender Interactions." *Sex Roles* 72, no. 5–6 (March 2015), 252–261, doi:10.1007/s11199-015-0451-7.

8. Goh and Hall, "Nonverbal and Verbal Expressions," 2015.

9. Goh and Hall, "Nonverbal and Verbal Expressions," 2015.

10. Russell and Oswald, "When Sexism Cuts Both Ways," 2016.

11. Russell and Oswald, "When Sexism Cuts Both Ways," 2016.

12. Heather McLaughlin, Christopher Uggen, and Amy Blackstone, "The Economic and Career Effects of Sexual Harassment on Working Women," *Gender & Society* 31, no. 3 (June 2017): 333–358, doi:10.1177/0891243217704631; Heather McLaughlin, email exchange with author, February 21, 2019.

13. Amy Blackstone, Heather McLaughlin, and Christopher Uggen, "State of the Union 2018: Workplace Sexual Harassment," Stanford Center on Poverty and Inequality, March 2018, https://inequality.stanford.edu/sites/default/files/Pathways_SOTU _2018_harassment.pdf.

14. Blackstone, McLaughlin, and Uggen, "State of the Union," 2018.

15. Jason N. Houle et al., "The Impact of Sexual Harassment on Depressive Symptoms During the Early Occupational Career," *Society and Mental Health* 1, no. 2 (July 2011): 89–105, doi:10.1177/2156869311416827.

16. Berdahl, "Harassment Based on Sex," 2007.

17. Berdahl, "Harassment Based on Sex," 2007.

18. Berdahl, "Harassment Based on Sex," 2007.

19. McLaughlin, Uggen, and Blackstone, "Sexual Harassment, Workplace Authority, and the Paradox of Power," 2012.

20. Nikki Graf, "Sexual Harassment at Work in the Era of #MeToo," Pew Research Center, April 4, 2018, https://www.pewsocialtrends.org/2018/04/04/sexual -harassment-at-work-in-the-era-of-metoo.

21. McLaughlin, Uggen, and Blackstone, "Sexual Harassment, Workplace Authority, and the Paradox of Power," 2012.

22. McLaughlin, Uggen, and Blackstone, "Sexual Harassment, Workplace Authority, and the Paradox of Power," 2012.

23. Blackstone, McLaughlin, and Uggen, "State of the Union," 2018.
24. Russell and Oswald, "When Sexism Cuts Both Ways," 2016.
25. Karpowitz et al., "The American Family Survey 2018 Summary Report."
26. Angela M. Dionisi and Julian Barling, "It Hurts Me Too: Examining the Relationship Between Male Gender Harassment and Observers' Well-Being, Attitudes, and Behaviors," *Journal of Occupational Health Psychology* 23, no. 3 (July 2018): 303–319, doi:10.1037/ocp0000124.
27. Blackstone, McLaughlin, and Uggen, "State of the Union," 2018.
28. Hively v. Ivy Tech Cmty. Coll. of Ind., 830 F.3d 698, 706 (7th Cir. 2016), *rev'd en banc*, 853 F.3d 339 (7th Cir. 2017).
29. Rosalind Jones, email exchange with author, July 14, 2019.
30. Dían Juarez, in-person interview with author, December 14, 2018.
31. Saeed Jones, phone interview with author, March 21, 2019.
32. Dían Juarez, in-person interview with author, December 14, 2018.
33. Blackstone, McLaughlin, and Uggen, "State of the Union," 2018.
34. McLaughlin, Uggen, and Blackstone, "Sexual Harassment, Workplace Authority, and the Paradox of Power," 2012.
35. Amanda Rossie, Jasmine Tucker, and Kayla Patrick, "Out of the Shadows: An Analysis of Sexual Harassment Charges Filed by Working Women," National Women's Law Center, 2018, https://nwlc-ciw49tixgw5lbab.stackpathdns.com/wp-content/uploads/2018/08/SexualHarassmentReport.pdf.
36. Rossie, Tucker, and Patrick, "Out of the Shadows," 2018.
37. NiCole T. Buchanan, Isis H. Settles, Ivan H. C. Wu, and Diane S. Hayashino, "Sexual Harassment, Racial Harassment, and Well-Being Among Asian American Women: An Intersectional Approach," *Women & Therapy* 41, no. 3–4 (2018): 261–280, https://doi.org/10.1080/02703149.2018.1425030.
38. Buck Gee, Denise Peck, and Janet Wong, "Hidden in Plain Sight: Asian American Leaders in Silicon Valley," Ascend Foundation, May 2015, http://cdn.ymaws.com/www.ascendleadership.org/resource/resmgr/Research/HiddenIn PlainSight_OnePager_.pdf.
39. "What #MeToo Means for Corporate America: Key Findings," Center for Talent Innovation, 2018, https://www.talentinnovation.org/_private/assets/WhatMeTooMeans_KeyFindings-CTI.pdf.
40. Mary Annette Pember, "#MeToo in Indian Country; 'We Don't Talk About This Enough,'" *Indian Country Today*, May 28, 2019, https://newsmaven.io/indiancountrytoday/news/metoo-in-indian-country-we-don-t-talk-about-this-enough-oXkstdPmDk2-zSXoDXZSZQ.
41. Waleska Suero, "'We Don't Think of It as Sexual Harassment': The Intersection of Gender and Ethnicity on Latinas' Workplace Sexual Harassment Claims," *Chicana/o Latina/o Law Review* 33, no. 1 (2015), https://escholarship.org/uc/item/0x57d7tc.
42. Elise Gould and Adriana Kugler, "Latina Workers Have to Work 10 Months into 2017 to Be Paid the Same as White Non-Hispanic Men in 2016," Economic Policy Institute, November 1, 2017.
43. Dr. Maytha Alhassen, in-person conversation with author, March 19, 2019.
44. Suero, "'We Don't Think of It as Sexual Harassment,'" 2015.

45. NiCole T. Buchanan and Alayne J. Ormerod, "Racialized Sexual Harassment in the Lives of African American Women," *Women & Therapy* 25, no. 3–4 (2002): 107–124, https://doi.org/10.1300/J015v25n03_08.

46. Blackstone, McLaughlin, and Uggen, "State of the Union," 2018.

47. Buchanan and Ormerod, "Racialized Sexual Harassment in the Lives of African American Women," 2002.

48. Vicki Schultz, "Open Statement on Sexual Harassment from Employment Discrimination Law Scholars," *Stanford Law Review* 71, no. 17 (June 19, 2018), http://dx.doi.org/10.2139/ssrn.3198727.

49. Rossie, Tucker, and Patrick, "Out of the Shadows," 2018.

50. Isis H. Settles, NiCole T. Buchanan, and Brian K. Colar, "The Impact of Race and Rank on the Sexual Harassment of Black and White Men in the U.S. Military," *Psychology of Men & Masculinity* 13, no. 3 (July 2012): 256–263, doi: 10.1037/a0024606.

51. "What #MeToo Means for Corporate America," 2018.

52. Settles, Buchanan, and Colar, "The Impact of Race and Rank," 2012.

53. Pennsylvania State University professor Brenda L. Russell, phone interview with author, July 29, 2019.

54. Marquette University professor Debra L. Oswald, email exchange with author, July 29, 2019.

Chapter 4: Recon Like Ronan

1. Graf, "Sexual Harassment at Work in the Era of #MeToo," 2018.

2. "The Corporate Pipeline" in "Women in the Workplace 2018," Lean In and McKinsey & Co., 2018, https://womenintheworkplace.com.

3. Fitzgerald and Cortina, "Sexual Harassment in Work Organizations," 2018.

4. Jocelyn Frye, "Not Just the Rich and Famous: The Pervasiveness of Sexual Harassment Across Industries Affects All Workers," Center for American Progress, November 20, 2017, https://www.americanprogress.org/issues/women/news/2017/11/20/443139/not-just-rich-famous.

5. Chai R. Feldblum and Victoria A. Lipnic, "Report of the Co-Chairs of the EEOC Select Task Force on the Study of Harassment in the Workplace," U.S. Equal Employment Opportunity Commission, June 2016, https://www.eeoc.gov/eeoc/task_force/harassment/report.cfm.

6. Jason Whitely, "Sexual Harassment from Surgeons Has Gone Unchecked for Too Long, Saleswoman Says," WFAA (Dallas, Texas), June 19, 2019, https://www.wfaa.com/article/news/sexual-harassment-in-medical-sales-has-gone-unchecked-for-too-long-victim-said/287-ed989008-8c9f-46b2-bae0-261a51624791; Boston v. Orthofix Medical, Inc., et al., 4:19-cv-00438 (E.D. Tex. Filed June 14, 2019).

7. Frye, "Not Just the Rich and Famous," 2017.

8. Feldblum and Lipnic, "Report of the Co-Chairs of the EEOC," 2016.

9. James Campbell Quick and M. Ann McFadyen. "Sexual Harassment: Have We Made Any Progress?," *Journal of Occupational Health Psychology* 22, no. 3 (July 2017): 286–298, http://dx.doi.org/10.1037/ocp0000054.

10. Chelsea R. Willness, Piers Steel, and Kibeom Lee, "A Meta-Analysis of the Antecedents and Consequences of Workplace Sexual Harassment," *Personnel Psychology* 60, no. 1 (Spring 2007): 127–162, http://dx.doi.org/10.1111/j.1744-6570 .2007.00067.x.

11. Feldblum and Lipnic, "Report of the Co-Chairs of the EEOC," 2016.

12. Susan Fowler, "Reflecting on One Very, Very Strange Year at Uber," February 19, 2017, https://perma.cc/T4KM-HQGZ.

13. Schultz, "Open Statement on Sexual Harassment from Employment Discrimination Law Scholars," 2018.

14. Schultz, "Open Statement on Sexual Harassment from Employment Discrimination Law Scholars," 2018.

15. Feldblum and Lipnic, "Report of the Co-Chairs of the EEOC," 2016.

16. Feldblum and Lipnic, "Report of the Co-Chairs of the EEOC," 2016.

17. Elyse Shaw, Ariane Hegewisch, and Cynthia Hess, "Sexual Harassment and Assault at Work: Understanding the Costs," *Institute for Women's Policy Research*, IWPR #B376, October 2018.

18. Feldblum and Lipnic, "Report of the Co-Chairs of the EEOC," 2016.

19. Feldblum and Lipnic, "Report of the Co-Chairs of the EEOC," 2016.

20. Feldblum and Lipnic, "Report of the Co-Chairs of the EEOC," 2016.

21. Amy Blackstone, Christopher Uggen, and Heather McLaughlin, "Legal Consciousness and Responses to Sexual Harassment," *Law & Society Review* 43, no. 3 (September 2009): 631–668, https://doi.org/10.1111/j.1540-5893.2009.00384.x.

22. Sunyoung Lee, Marko Pitesa, Madan Pillutla, and Stefan Thau, "When Beauty Helps and When It Hurts: An Organizational Context Model of Attractiveness Discrimination in Selection Decisions," *Organizational Behavior and Human Decision Processes* 128 (May 2015): 15–28, https://doi.org/10.1016/j.obhdp .2015.02.003.

23. Paul Farhi, "'I Don't Want to Sit on Your Lap,' She Thought. But, She Alleges, Mark Halperin Insisted," *Washington Post*, October 26, 2017, https://www .washingtonpost.com/lifestyle/style/i-dont-want-to-sit-on-your-lap-she-said-but -mark-halperin-insisted/2017/10/26/0baa883c-ba64-11e7-9e58-e6288544af98 _story.html.

24. Justine Tinkler, Skylar Gremillion, and Kira Arthurs, "Perceptions of Legitimacy: The Sex of the Legal Messenger and Reactions to Sexual Harassment Training," *Law & Social Inquiry* 40, no. 1 (Winter 2015): 152–174, https://doi.org/10.1111 /lsi.12065.

25. Frank Dobbin and Alexandra Kalev, "Why Diversity Programs Fail," *Harvard Business Review*, July–August 2016, https://hbr.org/2016/07/why-diversity -programs-fail.

26. Dobbin and Kalev, "Why Diversity Programs Fail," 2016.

27. Elena Greguletz, Marjo-Riitta Diehl, and Karin Kreutzer, "Why Women Build Less Effective Networks Than Men: The Role of Structural Exclusion and Personal Hesitation," *Human Relations* 72, no. 7 (July 2019): 1234–1261, https://doi.org /10.1177/0018726718804303.

28. "The Corporate Pipeline," 2018.

29. Drew DeSilver, "Women Scarce at Top of US Business—and in the Jobs That Lead There," Pew Resource Center, April 30, 2018, https://www.pewresearch.org/fact

-tank/2018/04/30/women-scarce-at-top-of-u-s-business-and-in-the-jobs-that-lead
-there.

30. DeSilver, "Women Scarce at Top of US Business," 2018.
31. "The Corporate Pipeline," 2018.
32. Oliver Staley, "Read It and Weep: There Are 624 Public Companies with No Women on Their Boards. Here's the List," *Quartz at Work*, December 15, 2017, https://qz.com/work/1130589/there-are-624-public-companies-with-no-women-on-their-boards-heres-the-list/.
33. McLaughlin, Uggen, and Blackstone, "Sexual Harassment, Workplace Authority, and the Paradox of Power," 2012.
34. Frank Dobbin and Alexandra Kalev, "Training Programs and Reporting Systems Won't End Sexual Harassment. Promoting More Women Will," *Harvard Business Review*, November 15, 2017, https://hbr.org/2017/11/training-programs-and-reporting-systems-wont-end-sexual-harassment-promoting-more-women-will.
35. Dobbin and Kalev, "Training Programs and Reporting Systems Won't End Sexual Harassment," 2017.
36. NiCole T. Buchanan, Isis H. Settles, Angela T. Hall, and Rachel C. O'Connor, "A Review of Organizational Strategies for Reducing Sexual Harassment: Insights from the U.S. Military," *Journal of Social Issues* 70, no. 4 (December 2014): 687–702, https://doi.org/10.1111/josi.12086.
37. Lynn Parramore, "$MeToo: The Economic Cost of Sexual Harassment," Institute for New Economic Thinking, January 2018, https://www.ineteconomics.org/research/research-papers/metoo-the-economic-cost-of-sexual-harassment.

Chapter 5: NSFW Coworkers

1. Laura McGann, "Exclusive: *NYT* White House Correspondent Glenn Thrush's History of Bad Judgment Around Young Women Journalists," *Vox*, November 20, 2017, https://www.vox.com/policy-and-politics/2017/11/20/16678094/glenn-thrush-new-york-times.
2. Mark DeWolf, "12 Stats About Working Women," U.S. Department of Labor Blog, March 1, 2017, https://blog.dol.gov/2017/03/01/12-stats-about-working-women.
3. Sylvia Ann Hewlett, "How Sex Hurts the Workplace, Especially Women," *Harvard Business Review*, August 24, 2010, https://hbr.org/2010/08/how-sex-hurts-the-workplace-es.
4. Hewlett, "How Sex Hurts the Workplace, Especially Women," 2010.

Chapter 6: Paying the Price

1. A. Theodore Rizzo et al., "The Costs of Sex-Based Harassment to Businesses: An In-Depth Look at the Workplace," International Center for Research on Women, 2018, https://www.icrw.org/wp-content/uploads/2018/08/ICRW_SBHDonor Brief_v5_WebReady.pdf. (Amount from 2007 updated for inflation to 2018 dollars.)
2. Shaw, Hegewisch, and Hess, "Sexual Harassment and Assault at Work," 2018.
3. Rizzo et al., "The Costs of Sex-Based Harassment to Businesses," 2018.

4. Michael Housman and Dylan Minor, "Toxic Workers," Harvard Business School Working Paper 16-057, 2015, https://www.hbs.edu/faculty/Publication%20Files/16-057_d45c0b4f-fa19-49de-8f1b-4b12fe054fea.pdf. (Amount from 2015 updated for inflation to 2018 dollars.)

5. Serena Does, Seval Gundemir, and Margaret Shih, "Research: How Sexual Harassment Affects a Company's Public Image," *Harvard Business Review*, June 11, 2018, https://hbr.org/2018/06/research-how-sexual-harassment-affects-a-com panys-public-image.

6. Shaw, Hegewisch, and Hess, "Sexual Harassment and Assault at Work," 2018.

7. "Even Good Employers Get Sued: The Cost of Not Having EPLI Insurance," Trusted Choice, accessed July 29, 2019, https://www.trustedchoice.com/business -insurance/liability/epli.

8. Feldblum and Lipnic, "Report of the Co-Chairs of the EEOC," 2016.

9. "Even Good Employers Get Sued," Trusted Choice.

10. "Even Good Employers Get Sued," Trusted Choice.

11. "Even Good Employers Get Sued," Trusted Choice.

12. Claire Zillman, "The *Fortune* 500 Has More Female CEOs Than Ever Before," Fortune.com, May 16, 2019, https://fortune.com/2019/05/16/fortune-500-female -ceos.

13. Dionisi and Barling, "It Hurts Me Too," 2018.

14. McLaughlin, Uggen, and Blackstone, "The Economic and Career Effects of Sexual Harassment on Working Women," 2017.

Chapter 7: Keeping Receipts

1. Ben Guarino and Neel V. Patel, "An Academic Reported Sexual Harassment. Her University Allegedly Retaliated," *The Verge*, November 12, 2018, https://www.theverge.com/2018/11/12/18080876/une-university-new-england-sexual -harassment-retaliation-paul-visich; Carlson v. Univ. of New England, No. 17-1792, 899 F.3d 36 (1st Cir. Aug. 10, 2018).

2. McGann, "Exclusive: *NYT* White House Correspondent Glenn Thrush's History of Bad Judgment Around Young Women Journalists," 2017.

Chapter 8: Responses and Reporting

1. Santana v. Marsh & McLennan Cos., et al., 1:17-cv-05755 (S.D.N.Y. filed July 28, 2017).

2. Alford v. Aaron's Rents, Inc., Southern District of Illinois, 3:08-cv-00683.

3. Lauren B. Edelman, "How HR and Judges Made It Almost Impossible for Victims of Sexual Harassment to Win in Court," *Harvard Business Review*, August 22, 2018, https://hbr.org/2018/08/how-hr-and-judges-made-it-almost-impossible-for -victims-of-sexual-harassment-to-win-in-court.

4. Cortina and Berdahl, "Sexual Harassment in Organizations," 2008.

5. Feldblum and Lipnic, "Report of the Co-Chairs of the EEOC," 2016.

6. Jocelyn Gecker, "AP: Women Accuse Opera Legend Domingo of Sexual Harassment," Associated Press, August 13, 2019, https://apnews.com /c2d51d690d004992b8cfba3bad827ae9.

7. Ann Arbor, MI: Inter University Consortium for Political and Social Research, December 18, 2015.

8. Marita P. McCabe and Lisa Hardman, "Attitudes and Perceptions of Workers to Sexual Harassment," *The Journal of Social Psychology* 145, no. 6 (January 2006): 719–40, doi:10.3200/SOCP.145.6.719-740.

9. Russell and Oswald, "When Sexism Cuts Both Ways," 2016.

10. Feldblum and Lipnic, "Report of the Co-Chairs of the EEOC," 2016.

11. Alieza Durana et al., "#NowWhat: The Sexual Harassment Solutions Toolkit," *New America*, September 26, 2018, https://www.newamerica.org/better-life-lab /reports/nowwhat-sexual-harassment-solutions-toolkit.

12. Feldblum and Lipnic, "Report of the Co-Chairs of the EEOC," 2016.

13. Dobbin and Kalev, "Training Programs and Reporting Systems Won't End Sexual Harassment," 2017.

14. Lilia M. Cortina and Vicki J. Magley, "Raising Voice, Risking Retaliation: Events Following Interpersonal Mistreatment in the Workplace," *Journal of Occupational Health Psychology* 8, no. 4 (October 2003): 247–265, https://doi.org/10.1037 /1076-8998.8.4.247.

15. Cortina and Berdahl, "Sexual Harassment in Organizations," 2008.

16. Mike Fleming Jr., "'Beautiful Girls' Scribe Scott Rosenberg on a Complicated Legacy with Harvey Weinstein," October 16, 2017, https://deadline.com/2017/10 /scott-rosenberg-harvey-weinstein-miramax-beautiful-girls-guilt-over-sexual -assault-allegations-1202189525.

17. Candace Bertotti and David Maxfield, "Most People Are Supportive of #MeToo. But Will Workplaces Actually Change?," *Harvard Business Review*, July 10, 2018, https:// hbr.org/2018/07/most-people-are-supportive-of-metoo-but-will-workplaces -actually-change.

18. Adam B. Vary, "Actor Anthony Rapp: Kevin Spacey Made a Sexual Advance Toward Me When I Was 14," *BuzzFeed News*, October 29, 2017, https://www.buzzfeednews .com/article/adambvary/anthony-rapp-kevin-spacey-made-sexual-advance-when- i-was-14.

19. Kim Masters, "John Lasseter's Pattern of Alleged Misconduct Detailed by Disney/ Pixar Insiders," *Hollywood Reporter*, November 21, 2017, https://www .hollywoodreporter.com/news/john-lasseters-pattern-alleged-misconduct-detailed -by-disney-pixar-insiders-1059594.

20. Gene Maddaus, "John Lasseter Will Exit Disney at the End of the Year," *Variety*, June 8, 2018, https://variety.com/2018/film/news/disney-john-lasseter-harassment -bob-iger-1202734060.

21. Irene Plagianos and Kitty Greenwald, "Mario Batali Steps Away from Restaurant Empire Following Sexual Misconduct Allegations," *Eater New York*, December 11, 2017, https://ny.eater.com/platform/amp/2017/12/11/16759540/mario-batali -sexual-misconduct-allegations.

22. Claudia Koerner, "Mario Batali Apologized to His Fans for Sexual Harassment, Then Suggested Pizza Dough Cinnamon Rolls," *BuzzFeed News*, December 15, 2017, https://www.buzzfeednews.com/article/claudiakoerner/mario-batali -apologized-to-his-fans-for-sexual-harassment.

23. Neda Ulaby, "How to Apologize for Sexual Harassment (Hint: It Takes More Than 'Sorry')," NPR, November 22, 2017, https://www.npr.org/2017/11/22

/565913664/how-to-apologize-for-sexual-harassment-hint-it-takes-more-than -sorry.

24. Vanessa K. Bohns and Lauren DeVincent, "To Reduce Sexual Misconduct, Help People Understand How Their Advances Might Be Received," *Harvard Business Review*, April 26, 2018, https://hbr.org/2018/04/to-reduce-sexual-misconduct -help-people-understand-how-their-advances-might-be-received.

25. Schultz, Vicky. Open Statement on Sexual Harassment. 71 Stan. L. Rev. Online 17, 35 (2018).

26. "Google Paid $35 Million to Former Executive Accused of Sexual Harassment," CBS News, March 12, 2019, https://www.cbsnews.com/news/google-paid -35million-former-executive-amit-singhal-accused-sexual-harassment.

27. Ryan Mac and Davey Alba, "These Tech Execs Faced #MeToo Allegations. They All Have New Jobs," *BuzzFeed News*, April 16, 2019, https://www.buzzfeednews.com /article/ryanmac/tech-men-accused-sexual-misconduct-new-jobs-metoo.

28. "2018 Hiscox Workplace Harassment Study," 2018, http://www.hiscox.com /documents/2018-Hiscox-Workplace-Harassment-Study.pdf.

29. Dobbin and Kalev, "Training Programs and Reporting Systems Won't End Sexual Harassment, 2017; Dobbin and Kalev, "Why Diversity Programs Fail," 2016.

30. Dulini Fernando and Ajnesh Prasad, "How Managers, Coworkers, and HR Pressure Women to Stay Silent About Harassment," *Harvard Business Review*, July 13, 2018, https://hbr.org/2018/07/how-managers-coworkers-and-hr-pressure-women-to -stay-silent-about-harassment.

31. Feldblum and Lipnic, "Report of the Co-Chairs of the EEOC," 2016.

Chapter 9: The Stress and the Struggle

1. Cortina and Berdahl, "Sexual Harassment in Organizations," 2008.

2. Monetary values have been updated to 2018 dollars to account for inflation.

3. Buchanan, Settles, Hall, and O'Connor, "A Review of Organizational Strategies for Reducing Sexual Harassment," 2014.

4. Dionisi and Barling, "It Hurts Me Too," 2018.

5. Bryan J. Pesta, Mary W. Hrivnak, and Kenneth J. Dunegan, "Parsing Work Environments Along the Dimensions of Sexual and Non-Sexual Harassment: Drawing Lines in Office Sand," *Employee Responsibilities and Rights Journal* 19, no. 1 (March 2007): 45–55, https://doi.org/10.1007/s10672-006-9031-x.

6. Pesta, Hrivnak, and Dunegan, "Parsing Work Environments," 2007.

7. Dionisi and Barling, "It Hurts Me Too," 2018.

8. Fitzgerald and Cortina, "Sexual Harassment in Work Organizations," 2018.

9. K. S. Douglas Low, Phanikiran Radhakrishnan, Kimberly T. Schneider, and James Rounds, "The Experiences of Bystanders of Workplace Ethnic Harassment," *Journal of Applied Social Psychology* 37, no. 10 (October 2007): 2261–2297, https://doi.org /10.1111/j.1559-1816.2007.00258.x.

Chapter 10: The Head Game Plan

1. Houle et al., "The Impact of Sexual Harassment on Depressive Symptoms During the Early Occupational Career," 2011.

2. Cortina and Berdahl, "Sexual Harassment in Organizations," 2008.
3. Brendan L. Smith, "What It Really Takes to Stop Sexual Harassment: Psychologists Call for a Comprehensive Approach with Real-World Impact," *Monitor on Psychology* 49, no. 2 (February 2018): 36, https://www.apa.org/monitor/2018/02/sexual-harassment.
4. Smith, "What It Really Takes to Stop Sexual Harassment," 2018.
5. Sarah E. Shea et al., "Pathology in the Hundred Acre Wood: A Neurodevelopmental Perspective on A. A. Milne," *Canadian Medical Association Journal* 163, no. 12 (December 2000): 1557–1559.

Chapter 11: Legal Claims and Defenses

1. Ravina v. Columbia University, 1:16-cv-02137 (S.D.N.Y. 2018).
2. 29 C.F.R § 1604.11(a)(1) and (2).
3. 29 C.F.R § 1604.11(a)(3).
4. Tatiana Siegel and Kim Masters, "'I Need to Be Careful': Texts Reveal Warner Bros. CEO Promoted Actress Amid Apparent Sexual Relationship," *Hollywood Reporter,* March 6, 2019, https://www.hollywoodreporter.com/features/i-need-be-careful-texts-reveal-warner-bros-ceo-promoted-actress-apparent-sexual-relationship-1192660.
5. Lipsett v. University of Puerto Rico, 864 F.2d 881, 898 (1st Cir. 1988).
6. Ferris v. Delta Air Lines, Inc., 277 F.3d 128 (2d Cir. 2001).
7. Alagna v. Smithville R-II Sch. Dist., 324 F.3d 975 (8th Cir. 2003).
8. Williams v. GMC, 187 F.3d 553 (6th Cir. 1999).

Chapter 12: Legal Ratchet and Lawyering Up

1. EEOC v. PMT Corporation, No. 0:2014cv00599—Document 28 (D. Minn. 2014).
2. Nitasha Tiku, "Google Walkout Organizers Say They're Facing Retaliation," *Wired,* April 22, 2019, https://www.wired.com/story/google-walkout-organizers-say-theyre-facing-retaliation.
3. Franchina v. City of Providence, 881 F.3d 32, 43-44 (1st Cir. 2018) and Tr. of Jury Trial—Vol. I, at 150–51.
4. Jeff Green, "Sexual Harassment Cases Go Uncounted as Complaint Process Goes Private," *Bloomberg,* April 23, 2018, https://www.bloomberg.com/graphics/2018-eeoc-complaints.
5. Sandra Sperino, "Retaliation and the Reasonable Person," *Florida Law Review* 67, no. 6 (2015), http://scholarship.law.ufl.edu/flr/vol67/iss6/4.
6. David I. Brody, "Punishing Unlawful Employers—Juries Say #MeToo," *The National Law Review,* November 20, 2018, https://www.natlawreview.com/article/punishing-unlawful-employers-juries-say-metoo.
7. Alexia Fernández Campbell and Alvin Chang, "There's a Good Chance You've Waived the Right to Sue Your Boss," *Vox,* September 7, 2018, https://www.vox.com/2018/8/1/16992362/sexual-harassment-mandatory-arbitration.
8. Parramore, "$MeToo," 2018.
9. Sara M. Moniuszko, "Rose McGowan Reacts to Harvey Weinstein Hiring Her Former Lawyers: It's a 'Major Conflict.'" *USA Today,* January 24, 2019, https://

www.usatoday.com/story/life/people/2019/01/24/rose-mcgowan-harvey
-weinstein-hiring-former-lawyers-major-conflict/2666061002.

10. Amy Kaufman, "Harvey Weinstein Is Done. But What About Lisa Bloom?," *Los
    Angeles Times,* October 19, 2017, https://www.latimes.com/entertainment
    /movies/la-et-mn-lisa-bloom-20171019-story.html.

Chapter 13: Keeping Up Appearances

1. Jenn Abelson, "At ESPN, the Problems for Women Run Deep," *Boston Globe,*
   December 14, 2017, https://www.bostonglobe.com/sports/2017/12/14/women
   -who-worked-espn-say-its-problems-far-beyond-barstool-sports
   /L1v9HJIvtnHuBPiMru6yGM/story.html.

2. Ryan Glasspiegel, "ESPN Published a Text Exchange Between John Buccigross and
   Adrienne Lawrence," *The Big Lead,* December 14, 2017, https://thebiglead.com
   /2017/12/15/espn-published-a-text-exchange-between-john-buccigross-and
   -adrienne-lawrence-01dkxxqxcqxh.

3. Alex Putterman, "*Boston Globe* Publishes Full Texts Between John Buccigross,
   Adrienne Lawrence After ESPN Omits Notable Sections," *Awful Announcing,*
   December 15, 2017, https://awfulannouncing.com/espn/boston-globe-publishes
   -full-texts-john-buccigross-adrienne-lawrence-espn-omits-notable-sections.html.

4. Ryan Glasspiegel, "Adrienne Lawrence Responds to ESPN Publication of Text
   Messages with John Buccigross," *The Big Lead,* December 15, 2017, https://
   thebiglead.com/posts/adrienne-lawrence-responds-to-espn-publication-of
   -text-messages-with-john-buccigross01dmmj5757gn.

5. Alex Kuczynski and William Glaberson, "Book Author Says He Lied in His Attacks
   on Anita Hill in Bid to Aid Justice Thomas," *New York Times,* June 27, 2001, https://
   www.nytimes.com/2001/06/27/us/book-author-says-he-lied-his-attacks-anita
   -hill-bid-aid-justice-thomas.html.

6. Kuczynski and Glaberson, "Book Author Says He Lied in His Attacks on Anita Hill
   in Bid to Aid Justice Thomas," 2001.

7. Ronan Farrow, "Harvey Weinstein's Army of Spies," *The New Yorker,* November 6,
   2017, https://www.newyorker.com/news/news-desk/harvey-weinsteins-army-of
   -spies.

8. Yashar Ali and Lydia Polgreen, "How Top NBC Executives Quashed the Bombshell
   Harvey Weinstein Story," *HuffPost,* October 11, 2017, https://www.huffpost
   .com/entry/nbc-harvey-weinstein_n_59de5688e4b0eb18af059685.

9. Jim Mustain, "*National Enquirer* Owner Admits It Buried Stories to Help Trump's
   Presidential Run," *Chicago Tribune,* December 12, 2018, https://www
   .chicagotribune.com/nation-world/ct-national-enquirer-hush-money-20181212
   -story.html.

10. Gene Maddaus, "Toronto Court Rules Against Disney in Weinstein Harassment
    Case," *Variety,* April 12, 2018, https://variety.com/2018/biz/news/disney
    -weinstein-toronto-ruling-1202751530.

11. "Newsroom Employees Are More Likely to Be White and Male Than All U.S.
    Workers," Pew Research Center, November 1, 2018, https://www.pewresearch.org
    /fact-tank/2018/11/02/newsroom-employees-are-less-diverse-than-u-s-workers
    -overall/ft_18-10-30_ageracejournalism-1.

12. "The Status of Women in the U.S. Media 2019," Women's Media Center, 2019, https://tools.womensmediacenter.com/page/-/WMCStatusofWomeninUS Media2019.pdf.

14. "The Status of Women in the U.S. Media 2019," Women's Media Center, 2019.

15. "Writing Rape: Women's Media Center Study Finds Crucial Gap in Coverage by Gender," Women's Media Center, December 16, 2015, http://www.womens mediacenter.com/about/press/press-releases/writing-rape-womens-media-center -study-finds-crucial-gap-in-coverage-gender.

16. Eliza Ennis and Lauren Wolfe, "#MeToo: The Women's Media Center Reort," Women's Media Center, 2018, http://www.womensmediacenter.com/assets/site /reports/media-and-metoo-how-a-movement-affected-press-coverage-of-sexual -assault/Media_and_MeToo_Womens_Media_Center_report.pdf.

17. "Anonymous Sources," AP, 2019, https://www.ap.org/about/news-values-and -principles/telling-the-story/anonymous-sources.

18. "Introduction to the Reporter's Privilege Compendium," Reporters Committee for Freedom of the Press, 2019, https://www.rcfp.org/introduction-to-the-reporters -privilege-compendium.

Chapter 14: Surviving Cyber Scandal

1. Monica Anderson, "Key Takeaways on How Americans View—and Experience— Online Harassment," Pew Research Center, July 11, 2017, http://www.pewresearch .org/fact-tank/2017/07/11/key-takeaways-online-harassment.

2. Anderson, "Key Takeaways on How Americans View—and Experience—Online Harassment," 2017.

3. Ana Kasparian, in-person meeting with the author in Culver City, California, February 7, 2019.

4. Anderson, "Key Takeaways on How Americans View—and Experience—Online Harassment," 2017.

5. Maeve Duggan, "Men, Women Experience and View Online Harassment Differently," Pew Research Center, July 14, 2017, http://www.pewresearch.org /fact-tank/2017/07/14/men-women-experience-and-view-online-harassment -differently.

6. Satnam Singh Narang, conversations with the author in Los Angeles, March 16, 2019; Equality Labs, "Anti-Doxing Guide for Activists Facing Attacks from the Alt-Right," *Medium*, September 2, 2017, https://medium.com/@EqualityLabs /anti-doxing-guide-for-activists-facing-attacks-from-the-alt-right-ec6c290f543c.

7. Hanna Kozlowska, "Paul Manafort Tried to Hide from the Feds Using Encrypted WhatsApp—But Forgot About iCloud," *Quartz*, June 5, 2018, https://qz.com /1297543/paul-manafort-tried-to-hide-from-the-feds-using-encrypted-whatsapp -but-he-forgot-about-icloud.

Chapter 15: Leveling Up

1. Shout-out to Cara Alwill Leyba, master life coach and inspirer.

2. Danielle Commisso, "Job Searching—It's Who You Know," *Civic Science*, January 24, 2019, https://civicscience.com/job-searching-its-who-you-know.

Index

Pages in **bold** indicate charts or tables; those in *italics* indicate figures.

ABOUT THE AUTHOR

Adrienne Lawrence is an attorney and television host who has appeared across TV and digital platforms to discuss legal issues related to current events. She was a litigator for eight years before entering broadcast journalism. A former anchor and legal analyst at ESPN, she became the first on-air personality to sue ESPN for sexual harassment.